More Than
Argentina

The Biography of
Ally MacLeod

More Than
Argentina

The Biography of
Ally MacLeod

Ronnie McDevitt
with contributions from Andy MacLeod

First published by Pitch Publishing, 2014

Pitch Publishing
A2 Yeoman Gate
Yeoman Way
Durrington
BN13 3QZ
www.pitchpublishing.co.uk

ISBN 978 1-90962-631-7

Typesetting and origination by Pitch Publishing
Printed in Gutenberg Press Ltd

Contents

Introduction

THE seed for this biography was sown when the retro football magazine *Backpass* accepted an article of mine reflecting on Ally MacLeod's career and crucially chose to feature the subject on the cover of its spring 2013 edition.

This prompted an e-mail to the editor from Ally's eldest son Andy asking him to pass on his thoughts to me. After the exchange of a few messages I decided to broach the idea of a more in-depth study of what I could already see was a fascinating story.

Andy was enthusiastic although I stressed it had to be an honest account which would likely include some criticism. 'I wouldn't expect anything less than a balanced view, that's why I'm quite happy to get involved,' was the welcome reply and on that we had the basis of a good working relationship.

Following Pitch Publishing's positive response to my proposal, we arranged a meeting in Andy's son Ryan's flat in Glasgow, which was between our homes in Ayrshire and Fife, to check through Ally's own scrapbooks and other memorabilia.

Ryan's flat-mate Ellen is from Ireland and was curious enough to ask, 'Was he a bit of a character then?' The three of us just sat there in silence for a few seconds, looking at each other before laughing.

Over the next few months the project was a pleasure with days spent in the library or at my laptop more of a joy than a chore.

In some respects Ally was ahead of his time in that he was one of the first tracksuit managers who would take training while many of his contemporaries rarely left the office.

One of the things that came out of the dealings with his former players was that he was a master of motivation who knew how to get the best from footballers.

Some of those players concede he was not a great tactician but times were different then. When Ally started out in management most teams had a similar philosophy of concentrating on their strengths and scoring more times than the opposition.

Blackboards and positional strategies were things of the future and the abilities of his own team the main focus for a football manager. In this respect the master Jock Stein and the underrated Eddie Turnbull were ahead of the game as far as Scottish football was concerned with Jim McLean and Alex Ferguson following them in later years.

Eccentric? Sure Ally was eccentric but this did not inhibit his motivation of players. Other successful managers such as Bill Shankly, Tommy Docherty, Brian Clough, Jock Wallace and Martin O'Neill were known to have their eccentricities but they all used this to their advantage. Equally men like Wallace and Willie Ormond were not considered to be master tacticians but they knew how to get the best out of players and enjoyed considerable success.

That Ally played for Blackburn in the FA Cup Final, won the League Cup with Aberdeen then promised he would bring the World Cup home to Scotland pretty much sums up the popular opinion of his time in the game. He is perceived as a court jester who fooled a gullible public and it is commonplace to see mention of his name followed by the obligatory derogatory comment. But as the title of this book suggests his career spanned so much more than that.

As a supporter at the time I had always considered it a myth that he said Scotland would win the 1978 World Cup and other contributors such as Dick Malone and Davie Hay agree on that point. There was an often referred-to but never repeated quote about winning a medal which I was able to track down and have included within the text.

The chain of events which led to Ally's appointment as Scotland manager is fascinating. It commenced with Ayr beating Rangers on the same day Aberdeen lost to Celtic, forcing Jimmy Bonthrone's resignation at a time when Ally had not responded to the offer of a job outside of the game.

Again as a fan the three best Scotland matches I have ever attended came within four months of each other in 1977. When Scotland won in France in 2007 it was undoubtedly one of the best results in their history but as far as the occasion was concerned it could not hold a candle to the events of Wembley 1977 or Anfield.

With only 16 finalists Scotland did have a chance of winning the World Cup in 1978. The Dutch had an identical record of one win, one loss and a draw in the first phase and progressed all the way to the final itself.

I had always been puzzled as to why, having ridden the storm of Argentina, Ally then left to take over at a First Division club…and departed the post after a matter of weeks. It is all much clearer now.

Ally did make mistakes but what manager didn't?

Andy MacLeod deserves full credit for conducting the interviews with Ally's old Blackburn team-mates, former Ayr players, Joe Harper and others detailed in his own preface although I did supply him with some questions. Andy also travelled to Manchester to speak with Sir Alex and arrange the foreword and I would like to extend my sincere gratitude to those contributors also.

I would specifically like to thank Davie Hay, Bobby Clark, Henry Templeton and Ian Clinging for sharing their thoughts with me, and also Chris Gavin of the Aberdeen FC Former Players Association for his help, plus Richard McBrearty at the Scottish Football Museum.

I was always keen to get the supporters' angle on record and for this I am most grateful to the following for their time and contributions: Scott Bremner, Tommy Petrie, Jock Vila, Tommy Collin, John Grigor, Alan Roxburgh, Graham Barnstaple, John Kennedy and Geoff Nicholson. It was a pleasure to deal with you all.

Thanks also to Paul and Jane at Pitch for their faith and support and for accommodating the ever-increasing word count!

When I went to Ayr to meet Faye MacLeod, a lovely woman, she displayed her husband's sense of humour as I sat on the couch armed with 1,001 questions. 'I hope you're not superstitious as you're sitting where he was when he died!' was one of the first things she said! Her contribution to the book, along with Andy's, is invaluable; likewise Faye's daughter Gail Pirie whose input was fascinating. It was a pleasure speaking to you all.

It was interesting to hear both Andy and Gail refer to their father by his christian name which is how they and everyone else knew and remember him, a name which did not appear on his birth certificate as I discovered. Had it not been for his mother's preference of Alistair we may all have been on the march with Sandy's Army in 1978.

People spoke warmly of Ally and although it would be wrong to say he never made any enemies in the game (players he moved on for example) he clearly got on with most people. 'He was revered wherever he went,' says Craig Brown.

It is the family's belief that his playing career has been overlooked and they were also very keen to stress that his sense of humour was one of his most endearing qualities.

I hope I have been able to deliver adequately on both. It is also the MacLeods' wish that one day Ally will be inducted into the Scottish Football Hall of Fame where he surely merits a place.

One other consistent theme throughout his life was Ally's loyalty to those he valued, something which may have cost him during his time in charge of the national side.

This is perhaps best summed up by Davie Hay to whom he gave his first role in management, 'As well as being a loyal person, he was a decent person as well.'

Ronnie McDevitt
May 2014

Preface

OVER the last few months, researching and collaborating on this book with Ronnie on Ally's career and life has, for me, been a labour of love. There was always more to the man to those of us who genuinely knew Ally compared to those who only remember him from those Argentina days and formed an opinion of him based on that time of his life.

Ally breathed, ate, lived and slept football with a passion; a humble, fiercely proud and yet shy person who took on this outgoing personality to overcome his shyness. He was a loving husband, father, grandfather, brother and son; a loyal caring person who possessed a wonderful sense of humour.

Ally was extremely protective of his family and his players. Players became family – he would look after them, protect them and believe in them. He was also a clever, intelligent and inspirational man who had an unending belief and desire to win.

I'd like to take this opportunity to thank Ronnie McDevitt for his foresight, time and patience and for being one of the few people outside of the game to understand Ally's psyche, and Pitch Publishing for believing in us.

To the following for their help, time and stories: Bryan Douglas, Mick McGrath, Dave Whelan, Matt Woods, Sir Alex Ferguson, Dick Malone, Alec McAnespie, Jim McSherry, Davie Wells, Kenny Wilson, Joe Harper, George Peat, George Smith, Craig Brown, Chick Young, my aunt Christine Darling (Ally's sister) and mother Faye MacLeod.

Many thanks as we could have talked for hours and hours more. I enjoyed chatting immensely.

I also thank Andrew Downie and Jim Rust for contact information.

To all the club and Scotland fans, Ally always just wanted to bring the game to you and make it much more entertaining for you. I hope you find after reading this book that you will agree that there was much more to the man than Argentina.

To my wife Jacquie, sons Ryan, Liam and Sean, thanks for putting up with me on this trip down memory lane.

Finally and most of all to my dad Ally. Thanks for the great memories. Football and the world is a duller place without you.

Andy MacLeod

Foreword

HAVING left Falkirk FC in 1973 after being player-coach I knew I still had the energy to play on. I was about to meet with Jim McLean, the manager of Dundee United, when I got a phone call from Ally asking if he could meet me the following day.

I had known Ally from his days as a player but more from his role in the PFA so I was happy to meet him in a restaurant in Glasgow city centre. I went there with a bit of curiosity as I knew that Ayr were a part-time team, and Ally knew I had been full-time at Falkirk, but I was keen to meet him anyway.

He wanted me to come to Ayr as a player but also take on a coaching role with the young players as his reserve-youth coach Jim McFadyin had accepted a teaching post which meant him having to leave his position at Ayr United FC.

It wasn't the coaching position which attracted me. It was Ally's energy, enthusiasm and ambition to, as he put it, 'make Ayr the best team in Scotland'. After an hour or so of the MacLeod brainwashing I was actually starting to believe him!

From the moment I joined Ayr United it was one of the most exciting times I had as a player. Everyone who was part of the Ally MacLeod treatment will testify to his loyalty and belief in his players – two vital ingredients in the art of leadership.

We all knew of his enthusiasm, his boyish behaviour at times, but he was a far more rounded person than that. He was in many ways a father figure to all his players and staff. I look back on his life fondly and only wish I had played under him for longer than I did, but just one year was enough to convince me of his status in Scottish football.

Sir Alex Ferguson

Foreword

1

Young MacLeod

THURSDAY 26 February 1931 was a mild day in the west of Scotland. Items in the news included a report that a British seaplane had crashed in Buenos Aires, Argentina, after catching fire. Closer to home the Corporation of Glasgow voted by a majority of 51 to 26 for a ten per cent reduction of teachers' salaries for the ensuing year.

The main topics discussed by football fans scanning the newspapers were of the previous day's Scottish League management committee meeting where a letter had been read out complaining about the sale of a player to an English club. A commission had been appointed to look into the matter while the books of the anonymous club concerned had apparently been called in for examination. Also announced at the meeting was the intention to restructure the two divisions from the start of the 1931/32 season, reducing the lower league from 20 teams to 16.

Scotland's goalless draw in Belfast the previous Saturday ('very disappointing' was the *Glasgow Herald*'s assessment) was still being digested while Motherwell were three points clear of Rangers at the top of the league with Celtic one point further adrift.

All of this would have been of no interest to a new arrival on the south side of Glasgow that day, born in a bottom tenement flat at 273 Allison Street, Govanhill, just a stone's throw from Cathkin Park where he would later first make his mark in the game of soccer.

Alexander Reid MacLeod was the first child of William and Jane (known as Jean) MacLeod who named him after an uncle who had been killed in the Great War. Another uncle, Robert, had been a goalkeeper with Queen's Park and Raith Rovers and his cousin Jim MacLeod had played for Dumbarton. Continuing this footballing tradition yet another of his uncles, Tommy MacLeod, had turned out for Third Lanark in the days when they were known as the Third Lanarkshire Rifle Volunteers.

Jean's preferred choice of name had been Alistair but it was traditional in those days to name children after relatives. But from his early days both parents called him Alistair which he would be known as until he chose to abbreviate it to Ally.

Even at an early age young Alistair was soon kicking a ball around and it is said that he suffered a 'footballer's knee' at a mere 18 months. Later in life he was to reveal that his father William, who suffered from polio – hence the allocation of the ground floor tenement – had been a major influence. Despite the amputation of a leg William still turned out as goalkeeper for an amateur side, and Ally said, 'My father lost his leg and played in goal for his team. That was my driving force.'

Before long the MacLeods departed Govanhill for Dalmuir where William was employed in the Singers sewing machine factory in nearby Clydebank, one of the largest employers in the west of Scotland at the time. Their home was at 27 French Street and Alistair attended Dalmuir Primary School where his sister Christine, younger by five years, recalls that he was a popular lad who made friends easily.

One of the MacLeods' near neighbours was a professional footballer whom Alistair often called on after school to see if he fancied a kick-about, an invitation which Christine says was rarely declined.

During the Second World War the Clydebank area, with its shipyards and munitions factories, became a prime target for the Luftwaffe and following two nights of sustained bombing over 12–13 March 1941, 528 civilians were killed and a further 617 seriously injured. In the region of 4,000 homes were destroyed as over 1,000 bombs were dropped in what came to be known as the Clydebank Blitz.

In that first night of bombing the house opposite the MacLeods' was flattened and their own windows blown in. This forced the family to retreat to the air raid shelter where Christine remembers they remained until the bombardment finally halted.

In the morning the MacLeods made a decision to uproot to the more peaceful surroundings of Moffat in Dumfriesshire where they had relatives. It was a decision which may even have saved their lives as the Germans returned that night to inflict further devastation on the area just as the locals were coming to terms with the nightmare they had already endured.

It was in Moffat that, at the age of ten, Alistair won his first football trophy in a five-a-side tournament. His team-mates were incidentally all residents of the local borstal.

The horrors of the war seemed to be following the MacLeods when a German aircraft, pursued by an RAF fighter following another raid on Glasgow, jettisoned the last of its bombs on the outskirts of the town. There was a suggestion that the pilot had deliberately dropped his cargo away from any houses. A decision was then taken to return to Glasgow after an 18-month absence and the family settled in Mount Florida, in the shadow of Hampden Park and close to Alistair's Govanhill roots.

Following a brief spell at Lea Primary, Alistair was then enrolled at Queen's Park Secondary School in Grange Road where comedian Stan Laurel had been a former pupil. Many years later when a journalist from the *Scotsman* newspaper pointed out that all three of them had attended the same school (Oliver Hardy was two years younger than Laurel), Alistair's response was, 'But I was a bigger comedian than Stan ever was!'

It was his sense of humour which many of those who knew Alistair would remember him for and his sister says he was a practical joker from an early age.

While at Queen's Park, Christine recalls that Alistair 'took up sport with a vengeance'. Alistair was in the school football, cricket and tennis teams. On occasion if they were short of numbers he had been known to turn out for the rugby side.

Christine recalls that he was already then displaying signs of leadership and had a wide circle of friends. Among those friends were three who went on to play football with Queen's Park FC: Johnny Little, who later signed for Rangers; Bert Cromer; and Junior Ormand. Another close school friend and keen sportsman was John Anderson who would later work as an athletics coach for Commonwealth and Olympic Games athletes with David Moorcroft, Liz McColgan and David Bedford among them.

Anderson is, however, probably best remembered as the judge on the ITV entertainment series *Gladiators* which ran from 1992 until the end of the decade.

Alistair was in those days quite a tennis fanatic and Christine remembers they could often both be found at the Holmlea tennis courts in the summer evenings. Christine often did not have the required two pence for a game but she knew that when her big brother turned up he would see her right.

At home the two of them would play table tennis with a four-penny ice cream cone the prize for the winner. Also in the MacLeod household they made use of their mother's large dresser in the kitchen. The dresser was used as a goal with Christine always ending up as the keeper while her brother practised hitting a football as hard as he could. Christine recalls regularly running to her mother, complaining, 'He's hitting the ball too hard at me!'

Like many lads of his age, Alistair had become a member of the Boys' Brigade whose premises were attached to Mount Florida Church. He was soon turning out for their football team on a Saturday morning and if his beloved Third Lanark were playing at home he could often be found on the slopes of Cathkin Park in the afternoon. His heroes in the Thirds team, also known as the Hi Hi, were Jimmy Mason, a right-back who would later be capped seven times for Scotland, and Bobby Mitchell, a forward who would also represent his country.

As with many club nicknames and songs the origin of the term is unclear with one rumour that the Cathkin crowd chanted 'High! High!' when an opposing defender cleared the ball into the air and soon adopted the phrase as a cry of encouragement.

Living in Glasgow meant there were plenty of opportunities to watch other teams and in the schools commemorative htandbook Alistair recalled skipping afternoon lessons at Queen's Park in November 1945.

Taking a bus to Ibrox where Rangers were entertaining Moscow Dynamo in a 2.15pm kick-off, he had just boarded when he spotted his headmaster Mr Gilmour behind him in the queue. Horrified, he climbed the stairs to the upper deck, looking down through the window at each stop to see where he disembarked. Alistair had to wait until the bus had passed Ibrox meaning an unexpected walk back towards the stadium.

The next day he was called into the headmaster's office to be met with, 'Well MacLeod, what have you to say about missing school yesterday afternoon?' 'I looked him straight in the eye,' he recalled 'and asked, "Did YOU enjoy the match, Sir?" He looked back at me in astonishment until I explained that we'd been on the same bus. I was dismissed – no lines or detention and nothing more was ever said about the incident.'

That same year a scout from Celtic Park had turned up at the MacLeod home keen to sign the promising 14-year-old on schoolboy forms. Father William's response was to tell the scout to come back when Alistair was 17. Two years later an enquiring scout from Ibrox was given similar advice.

His mother was happy to encourage her son's love of football and Christine recalls Jean would be up at 6am to join the queue at nearby Hampden Park when international tickets went on sale. She would keep his place in the queue until he took over at 8am.

Jean MacLeod also played a vital part in him signing for the Hi Hi. She was a regular shopper in the local fishmongers where she passed the time with the other customers, one of whom was the wife of Jimmy McManus, the head scout of Third Lanark. Mrs McManus told her husband how his mother had been raving about Alistair and the scout's curiosity was aroused enough to go and watch the youngster play which led to him signing schoolboy forms with the club in 1947.

Then 16, Alistair left school that summer. Soon he was working as an apprentice draughtsman at Caldwells in Clydebank for a wage of £4 per week. Unhappy there – Christine recalls he 'hated it' – he eventually returned to Queen's Park school for a further year.

During that additional year the school held mock elections and keen to enter into the spirit, Alistair stood for the Communist Party. Without taking it too seriously he promised the voters shorter school hours and longer holidays. Not surprisingly this swayed the students and he won the ballot. This was later picked up by the *Morning Star* newspaper which reported, 'Queen's Park School Goes Communist'.

Alistair's first appearance in a Third Lanark jersey was in a reserve match at Brockville Park on 9 April 1949 but not until after he had turned out for the school team in the morning. The home side Falkirk won 6-3 although most football fans were more interested in events 400 miles away at Wembley Stadium where Thirds' Jimmy Mason scored the first of Scotland's goals in a 3-1 victory over England. The game at Brockville was the last fixture in the Thirds' reserve-team calendar that season but there were still other opportunities for the youngster to showcase his improving skills.

His first real football honour came just three days after the Falkirk game on 12 April when he was chosen for the Glasgow Schools side for a representative match against the Rest of Scotland Schools at Celtic Park which Glasgow won 2-0.

One clipping from his own scrapbook shows that he clearly caught a journalist's eye that day, 'McLeod (Queen's Park) was the danger man among Glasgow's forwards and was directly responsible for Crawford (Govan) opening the score eleven minutes after the interval.'

Another anonymous report contained the following, 'With McLeod serving up some mazy runs on the touchline it was no surprise when they took the lead in eleven minutes, Crawford heading home from McLeod's cross.'

The tendency for these scribes to spell his surname incorrectly, without the 'a', would prove to be consistent with their colleagues well into his senior career.

The youngster did not have to wait long for his first medal. That came when he was selected for the Scottish Schools FA in the National Youth Championship at the end of the season. He got his name on the scoresheet in the semi-final against the Scottish Welfare FA at Brockville Park where his side won 5-2.

Another unidentified entry in his scrapbook records, 'Within a minute of the restart Crawford had a beautiful goal for Schools and McLeod added another with a shot which glanced off a defender's leg.'

In the final at Hampden Park the Schools side triumphed 3-0 against the Scottish Churches team with Alistair supplying the cross for Crawford to score the third. Such fixtures always attracted the attention of the scouts from the senior clubs and there was more than a little interest in the youngster from Queen's Park that day.

2

Alistair the Third

IN June 1949, having recently left Queen's Park Secondary School for the second time, Alistair MacLeod was signed as a professional for Third Lanark, the team he supported, by manager Jimmy Carabine, a former Scottish international. His first weekly wage was £4. There had been another invitation to visit Celtic Park around this time but it is unclear if terms were offered.

In an *Evening Times* article the following year, their scribe offered the following, 'I hardly know whether to describe Alistair McLeod of Third Lanark as "Wonder Boy" or credit Cathkin's Hugh Good as "Wonder Trainer". A year ago Alistair was a star member of the all conquering Scottish Youth Team. Only one thing kept admiring clubs from rushing for his signature. He was only 5' 3" tall and weighed only 9 stone 2. Today he is 5' 11" tall and 11 stone 2 in the short space of twelve months.'

The *Times* article then relates how Good had encouraged Carabine, 'You sign him and I'll build him up.' His mother was now a regular spectator at his matches and had once been mortified to hear someone in the stand utter, 'That MacLeod would be a better footballer if his mother gave him a good feed!'

He was back in the reserve side for the opening Division C fixture of the new season at Cathkin on 13 August when Thirds' A team lined up against Partick Thistle's reserves. During the match he netted his first goal for Thirds albeit in a somewhat unorthodox manner. The *Evening Times* reported, 'In twenty-eight minutes Third Lanark opened the scoring when McLeod placed a corner which Ledgerwood touched but could not stop.'

That game finished 2-2 and Alistair kept his place in the reserves until he got his chance in the first 11 on 5 November 1949. Ironically the opportunity was due to an injury to his idol Jimmy Mason.

Carabine reshuffled the side, bringing in Alistair at outside-left against Stirling Albion at Cathkin Park that Saturday. Watched by a crowd of 9,500 Stirling won the match 4-2 although Thirds' case had not been helped when their goalkeeper John Petrie suffered a leg break in the 66th minute following a collision with Albion's Jones. Despite the score the new boy's debut did not go unnoticed. Writing in the *Evening Citizen*, Archie MacGregor noted, 'Newcomer

McLeod caught the eye when he neatly tricked McKeown to cross accurately'
while Bob Russell offered the following in the *Sunday Empire News*, 'Eighteen
year old Schoolboy Alastair McLeod, brought into the outside left position, was
perhaps their most useful prospect but he will have to put more life into his play
to reach the top grade.'

The debutant created a headline in an unidentified newspaper with 'A Third
Find'. The article reported, 'In his initial try-out youngster McLeod passed the
test despite the lack of service from Cuthbertson. He has veteran coolness and
can cross the ball with accuracy.'

The defeat left Thirds third from bottom in Division A and in danger of
finishing in one of the two relegation places.

Alistair retained his place in the team for the visit to Raith Rovers the
following Saturday where he scored his first senior goal in a 1-1 draw. The *Evening
Times* report described it thus, 'In the forty-fourth minute McLeod opened for
Thirds when he plodded home a Scott cross after McGregor had parried the ball.'

A narrow 2-1 defeat at Celtic Park was followed by Alistair's next home match
on 26 November with Hibernian's feared 'Famous Five' forward line of Gordon
Smith, Bobby Johnstone, Lawrie Reilly, Eddie Turnbull and Willie Ormond
gracing the Cathkin turf. Goals by Johnstone and Reilly (a highly contentious
award with the home players claiming offside) gave Hibs a 2-0 win but the Thirds
youngster still impressed. John McShane, in the *Evening Citizen*, recorded, 'Third
Lanark's school winger Ally McLeod had a dazzling run, beating man after man,
only to see his shot at goal rise over the bar.'

As the crowd were leaving the ground an oil stove knocked over in the
recently-vacated press box set the area alight with the flames soon spreading
to the stand. Or as the *Evening Times* put it, 'The blaze spread with astonishing
rapidity and in no time flames were leaping out.'

Units of the Glasgow Fire Brigade promptly arrived on the scene and soon
had the blaze under control but the press box was completely destroyed as was
part of the centre of the stand. 'Thousands who had been present at the match
watched this extra thrill,' was how the *Edinburgh Evening News* reported the
spectacle.

This incident is sometimes wrongly linked to Ally's first match against
Stirling Albion although given his debut took place on Guy Fawkes Day it would
perhaps have been more appropriate.

The Hi Hi finished the season in 12th place, five from the bottom and nine
points clear of relegation. Alistair made a total of 11 appearances that term,
scoring twice. His other goal came in a 5-1 defeat at the home of Glasgow rivals
Partick Thistle against the same goalkeeper he had outwitted in the reserve
match.

It is worthy of mention if only because of the rather eloquent description
given by 'Olympic' (many sports writers of the time used a pseudonym) in the
Evening Times, 'In the eighteenth minute Friel centred to the far post. McLeod
was there and for quite a time he stood fiddling with the ball at his feet. It was

surprising that Ledgerwood did not act before McLeod wakened up and shot through.'

Thirds manager Jimmy Carabine retired from football at the end of the season with Alec Ritchie succeeding him.

Unlike Carabine, Ritchie chose to nurture the young Alistair (he was still only 19) and he failed to turn out for the first team at all during the following season, 1950/51. Undeterred, Alistair still managed a few games (and goals) for the reserve team.

Although his mother had always encouraged his football Jean stressed on him the need to gain further qualifications should he need a career outside of the game. In 1950 Alistair enrolled at Paisley Technical College for a course in applied science. Alistair opted for a part-time course with evening classes which allowed him to train with Thirds during the day.

Third Lanark finished that campaign in 13th position, one down on the previous season, but come the new term the determined youngster was banging on the first-team door. At the end of August 1951 Alistair scored four times for the reserves in a 6-1 victory against Dumbarton which led to his recall to the senior team on 1 September. The opponents at Cathkin were Airdrie in a League Cup match and again Alistair found his name on the scoresheet with a header in a 5-0 victory. Records give the crowd as 16,000 that Saturday.

Ritchie now had no doubts that Alistair was ready for a run in the first team and he went on to play in 22 of the club's 30 league matches that season. He managed just one league goal in a 3-2 victory over Aberdeen at Pittodrie in January. Other highlights in a campaign which saw the team finish in the familiar territory of 12th place included a 3-3 thriller with Celtic at Cathkin and a 2-2 result in the return at Celtic Park. Two 1-1 draws with Rangers showed they could raise their game against the best sides although twice they lost five goals to eventual champions Hibernian.

But it was in the cup competitions that the Thirds produced some of their best football in 1951/52. Despite failing to progress from their League Cup section, finishing third to Celtic and Morton, the Hi Hi went all the way to the semi-final of the Scottish Cup.

Following a goalless draw at Celtic Park in round one, Thirds won the replay in extra time by the odd goal in three. Alistair later recalled the first match was played on an icy pitch which caused him to slip and miss 'a cert' close to the end. All was forgiven when Thirds won the replay and the directors saw the match takings his miss had generated.

Hamilton Academical were then overcome in the next round following another replay. Victories over Albion Rovers and Falkirk set up a semi-final with Dundee at Hibernian's Easter Road ground and Thirds went into the game on the back of an 11-match unbeaten run. But the Dark Blues ran out 2-0 winners only to lose heavily to Motherwell in the final.

Along with the Glasgow Cup, the Glasgow Charity Cup was popular at that time with those tournaments' importance only diminished with the arrival of

European competition a few years later. A crowd of 75,000 turned up at Ibrox to watch Rangers play Third Lanark for a place in the final. Just one goal separated the sides – and it was scored by none other than Alistair MacLeod, best summed up by the *Evening Times*, 'It was in the eighteenth minute of the first half that Thirds got the solitary goal of the match – a short cross from the right, headed on by Dick, came right across goal to the completely unattended McLeod, who had ample time to place his header into the corner of the net.'

Previewing the final with Clyde on 10 May, Alan Breck of the *Evening Times* was of the opinion, 'Thirds have very likeable forwards …McLeod is always full of zest.'

In what the *Herald*'s scribe described as 'an exhilarating final' the match at Hampden finished 2-2 after extra time with the attendance given as 25,000. There was no replay and the two clubs shared the trophy for six months each.

Alistair had now succeeded in establishing himself as a first-team regular and earned a reputation as an entertainer who having beaten an opposing player, often could not resist the temptation to repeat the exercise. He was easily recognisable too with a mop of fair hair, considered long for the time if not by today's standards, and his prominent nose.

In the first *The Scottish Football Book* published a couple of years later the editor Hugh Taylor said of Alistair, 'He follows in the distinguished footsteps of Bobby Mitchell, the Third Lanark outside left who went to Newcastle United.'

Looking back at his Cathkin days in the eighth volume of the same publication the player himself confirmed this to Taylor, 'I tried to emulate Bobby's ball-playing style, for he was a truly great player. I never considered passing a ball until I had beaten at least one player.'

The following season, 1952/53, was not a good one for the Hi Hi although it started well, winning their League Cup section and finishing above East Fife, Falkirk and Queen of the South. They then had the misfortune to draw Rangers in the quarter-finals, losing 2-0 on aggregate.

Alistair played in 19 of the first 20 league matches and scored once, a sequence which saw the club acquire just 13 points. During that first half of the season they lost 4-3 at Aberdeen and 5-4 at Celtic Park to a last-minute Charlie Tully goal, defeated Hibs 2-0 at Cathkin but were heavily beaten 5-1 at Falkirk. A home loss to Aberdeen on 17 January saw Thirds slip to the bottom of the table.

When injury kept Alistair out of the side to face Hamilton in the Scottish Cup the following week, his place was taken by Willie Barclay, an outside-left who had recently been signed from Clyde. Due to his committed style of play Alistair found himself ruled out through a number of injuries in his days with the Thirds including torn ligaments and a broken collarbone.

Fit enough to play for the reserve team three weeks later at Ayr United, Alistair was unable to fight his way back into the senior team with Barclay performing well. He played just two more league matches that season, against East Fife and Clyde, and made no contribution to Thirds' march to the semi-finals of the Scottish Cup. On the day the senior side played Aberdeen at Ibrox for a place in the Scottish Cup Final MacLeod turned out at Cathkin against Kilmarnock reserves. There was no place for him in the semi final replay either (the first match ended 1-1) as the Dons won 2-1.

League results did not reflect the club's cup form and a 5-2 defeat to Clyde at Shawfield on Wednesday 22 April confirmed Thirds' relegation to Division B. Alistair had been recalled to the side but was unable to inspire his team-mates. Eighteen defeats throughout the campaign (including seven at home) and just eight victories saw them finish bottom of the table with 20 points from 30 league matches.

But Alistair had more than football on his mind at this time. Having achieved an 'A' pass in an applied science course with a score of 72 per cent he had begun working as a chemical analyst for a company called Tatlock and Thompson in Bath Street in the centre of Glasgow.

The determined youngster was back in the first team for the opening game of the 1953/54 season. Recreation Park was the venue where he scored twice as Thirds romped to a 10-0 win over Alloa Athletic in the League Cup. 'THIRDS MAKE MINCEMEAT OF ALLOA' was the *Evening Times* headline.

Again Thirds topped their League Cup section after scoring no less than 25 times against Alloa, Cowdenbeath and St Johnstone. Cowdenbeath had also found themselves on the wrong end of a heavy 7-0 drubbing when they visited Cathkin on the last Saturday in August. The Hi Hi however got a taste of their own medicine in the quarter-finals, losing home and away to Hibs by a 4-0 score on both occasions.

At the end of September 1953 Thirds were at Hampden to face Rangers in the final of the Glasgow Cup but were always second best, losing 3-0 with the *Herald*'s football correspondent considering, 'Rangers can rarely have had an easier task.' He did however single out Alistair as 'Thirds' best forward', advising he had been unlucky with one effort which hit the underside of the crossbar with the deficit then 2-0.

That year Alistair met Faye Dunwoodie, his future wife, at a dance in the Kingsbridge Halls in Croftfoot. Today Faye recalls that Alistair, who turned up with some friends, ought not to have been there as he was not from the area but the group had managed to get someone to sign them in.

'All the local kids went dancing there,' Faye recalls of the Kingsbridge, noting that boys and girls sat on separate sides of the hall. 'We just started dancing and that's it,' she says of their first meeting.

Faye knew nothing about football and laughs, 'When he said he played football I thought he played for the former pupils. So he wasn't very chuffed, I don't think. So I can't say I went with him because he was a footballer.' But before too long Faye became a spectator at Cathkin Park where she watched his matches alongside his mother Jean.

The winger found himself the subject of transfer speculation throughout the season. 'ARSENAL MAY BID FOR MCLEOD' ran one headline after the London club were said to have been represented at the Thirds v Motherwell match that November. In another piece 'Sauchie Hall' valued the player at £15,000. Four years into his professional career the press were still unable to spell his surname correctly although I suspect the initial cause of this was Third Lanark whose matchday programmes continued to list him as McLeod, just as they had done from his earliest appearances.

Playing in the lower division did not seem to be a handicap and as well as the transfer speculation there was the possibility of international recognition. That 1953/54 season would be the closest Alistair MacLeod ever came to representing his country.

Selected for a B international team to play England at Sunderland's Roker Park on 3 March, he would have the opportunity to impress the selectors ahead of the Home International against the English in April. In those days there was no such luxury as an international squad for the manager to select 11 players from. The Scottish FA selectors would announce a team of 11 with one player listed as a 'travelling reserve' (there were no substitutions allowed) generally about ten days ahead of the match. So if your name was on the list, barring withdrawal, you knew you would be playing.

The selectors on this occasion listed all of six new players with no international experience at any level which drew praise from Alan Breck in the *Evening Times*, 'The selectors will not be criticised for not being adventurous. It is a team very much selected on current form.'

Thirds were at home to Rangers in the third round of the Scottish Cup four days before the Sunderland match. The match drew Cathkin Park's all-time record attendance with the official crowd given as 45,591 although the *Glasgow Herald* noted that this figure 'excluded several hundred who managed to "break in"'. Indeed the kick-off was delayed as hundreds of spectators rushed the main gates, resulting in some people being trampled on and many treated for injuries.

With the game goalless and entering its final stages Alistair had the chance to win the tie as an anonymous report in his scrapbook records, 'Just before the final whistle MacLeod after a lovely solo run struck the post with Niven nowhere.' This was apparently one of the game's few bright spots as the same report summarised the match thus, 'What a disappointment this game was… almost devoid of any thrills.'

With the Ibrox replay set for the Wednesday, Alistair had to withdraw from the Scotland squad along with Hearts' Willie Bauld who had picked up an injury. The two replacements for the trip to Sunderland were Jackie Henderson of Portsmouth and Celtic's Neil Mochan.

The *Scottish Daily Mail*'s Andrew Clunie paid the MacLeod household a visit and the player confessed to being disappointed. 'But it's not so bad. Maybe I'll get a cup medal instead,' he reasoned, displaying the optimism which would be so prominent throughout his career.

If the first match had been a bit of a let-down the same could not be said of the two replays. On the Wednesday afternoon the sides were level at 3-3 after 90 minutes with Thirds having fought back from a 2-0 deficit. Eventually the tie finished 4-4 after extra time. Although such scorelines were perhaps not the norm high-scoring matches were frequent in those days with little thought given to negativity and stifling the opponents' game, but instead an emphasis on trying to score more times than they could find the net. A spectator that afternoon was 12-year-old local lad Alex Ferguson.

Today Sir Alex still recalls Alistair's performance, 'I remember the first time I saw Ally play. I went to the football with my staff sergeant in the Boys' Brigade Alistair Miller who was inside-left at Thirds and went on to play for St Mirren. In the first game at Ibrox Ally gave George Young a really hard time of it. Big Corky was a great Rangers player and Ally really gave him a hard time. It was freezing cold and I was in the Celtic end as it was the nearest to where we lived in Govan. Normally I would go to the Rangers end where the atmosphere was fantastic.'

Later that night (with floodlights permitting an evening kick-off) the B international finished level at 1-1 and was summed up by the *Glasgow Herald* headline, 'SCOTLAND LUCKY TO DRAW AT SUNDERLAND'.

Alistair soon made the headlines again with 'MCLEOD'S "CAP" CLAIM STRONGER THAN EVER' in an unidentified publication.

The report read, 'Alastair McLeod of Third Lanark surely deserves the most serious consideration for a cap against England following his magnificent exhibition against Rangers. It is difficult to recall a wingman enjoying such spectacular success against a Light Blues defence at Ibrox. On three occasions he dribbled through the centre almost from mid field to lay on two goals and one near miss. If gamble it is we say it is a worthwhile gamble because in addition to his solid merit, McLeod is in the tradition of Patsy Gallacher and Tommy McInally – an entertainer, something out of the common rut.'

The writer was by no means a lone voice as Morris Peden echoed the sentiments in the *Daily Herald* with 'LET'S BE ADVENTUROUS IN SELECTING', calling for the selectors to include not only MacLeod but also Celtic's Willie Fernie and Jock Aird of Burnley.

None of Peden's recommendations were included although one irony was the selection of Jackie Henderson for the England game after he had been Alistair's replacement in the B squad. Alistair may not have realised it at the time but there would be no further approaches for him to play for his country. It would be another 23 years before Scotland came calling on him again.

The second Scottish Cup replay the following Monday, also at Ibrox following the toss of a coin, was another thriller. Thirds scored first through Bobby Kerr but exited the tournament on the wrong end of a 3-2 scoreline. Sir Alex also attended this match and his memory is, 'Thirds really should have won in the third game. There was nothing in it and Rangers just pipped it.'

The three cup ties had produced an average of over four goals per game which is not a bad statistic considering the first match had ended scoreless.

Third Lanark did end the season on a high when they gained some revenge on Rangers for the Glasgow and Scottish Cup defeats in the final of the Glasgow Charity Cup at Hampden on 7 May, a Friday evening.

More convincing than the one-goal victory may suggest, the press were unanimous as to who had been the better side. The *Glasgow Herald* report contained the following, 'There can be no diversity of opinion as to the correctness of Third Lanark's victory.'

Singling out two players the scribe continued, 'Dick and McLeod in particular tantalised Rangers' defence with immaculate ball control and precise passing.' Indeed the match's only goal came as a result of a series of passes between the two allowing Bobby Kerr to finish off the move. Writing in the *Daily Record*, 'Waverley' (real name William Gallagher) was in agreement, 'Third Lanark were good winners. For most of the game they played super football."

The Hi Hi finished third in Division B that season and missed out on promotion by six points. There had been some bizarre league results by today's standards – notably a 9-1 home win over Dundee United, a 9-2 victory against St Johnstone at Cathkin and a 6-0 win at Ayr United. These results however were counter-balanced by a 6-1 reverse at St Johnstone and a 7-3 home defeat to Morton.

Towards the end of the season both Newcastle and Rangers, who had an offer turned down, were said to be interested in signing Alistair but he was to remain a Division B player for the following term.

The winger had now established himself in the first team and had been an ever-present that season, playing in all 45 of Third Lanark's competitive matches. The statistics are 30 Division B matches, eight League Cup ties and seven in the Scottish Cup. He amassed a total of ten goals – seven in the league and three in the League Cup.

No sooner had the new season started than Alistair was called up for National Service at the age of 23. Most fit youngsters of the time were enlisted when 18 but because of his studies his date had been deferred by five years.

He and two other footballers, Davie Mathers and Willie Crawford, both from Partick Thistle, reported to Glencorse Barracks in Midlothian on Thursday 19 August to begin their two-year conscription, or as the *Daily Record* put it, 730 days.

Writing in the *Evening Times* 'Jaymak' informed readers that the trio had 'a depressing introduction. The barracks were grim in the rain and to welcome them were lined up two press photographers and Sergeant Major John Craig of the Headquarters Company, who is by the way of being slightly"Rangers daft".'

Alistair referred to the type of posting as BHFF – Be Home For Friday. This meant he was off duty at weekends which was ideal for seeing Faye and turning out for the Hi Hi. Indeed he played for Thirds at Broomfield just two days later where Airdrie defeated them 2-0 in a League Cup tie in which, again quoting 'Jaymak' in the *Evening Times*, 'Soldier McLeod had a lean game.'

The following Monday all three of the new recruits were included in a Scottish Command side to play Hibs at Easter Road. Hibs fielded pretty much a reserve team but did include two of the Famous Five in Ormond and Turnbull.

They won comfortably 5-0 although in his match report Jim Rodger considered the goal margin 'unfortunate' and absolved Celtic keeper Andy Bell (also serving with the Royal Scots) of any blame for the goals.

'The crowd were entertained by the delightful play of the Partick and Third Lanark players,' he added, singling out MacLeod and Joe McInnes (also with Partick and serving with the Glasgow Highlanders) as 'stars' while 'Crawford and Mathers were heroes in the Army defence'.

Just two days later Alistair was given an early pass from Glencorse to catch the 4pm train from Edinburgh Waverley to Glasgow from which he made a quick dash to Cathkin Park for a Glasgow Cup first round tie. This was hardly ideal preparation for a game against Rangers but he was there in time to start the match which finished 2-0 in favour of the visitors. Since joining up at the barracks just six days earlier Alistair had already managed to play three 90-minute games of football as part of his hectic new lifestyle.

Ally was made ration corporal at Glencorse which meant he was never short of food and he made sure he kept on the right side of his sergeant by giving him extra helpings. As a corporal he was often in charge of the Guard House and on one occasion there he 'accidentally' spilled an ink bottle on the leave book. When he went to apply for some time off he was advised he had exhausted his entitlement. Alistair disagreed and asked to see the ledger after which he was granted his day off!

That season he made 20 league appearances out of a 30-game fixture list, played in six League Cup matches and both Thirds' Scottish Cup ties where they went out to Motherwell after disposing of Queen's Park. He did manage to get his name on the scoresheet during the 3-1 reverse to the Steelmen.

He also found the net once in the League Cup which had been a disappointment with failure to progress from the qualifying section, Thirds finishing second to Airdrie and above Cowdenbeath and Queentts Park. Four league goals took his scoring total to six for the season.

Thirds finished in fifth place in the Division B table having won 13, drawn seven and lost ten of the 30-game schedule. The highlight in the league had been a 9-0 mauling of Ayr United in December and a thrilling 4-3 home defeat to champions Airdrie who were promoted with Dunfermline.

Interest in Third Lanark's prized asset had continued throughout that season with both Sunderland and Stoke City having offers rejected. Now writing as a journalist for the *Scottish Daily Express*, the manager who had first signed MacLeod, Jimmy Carabine, ran a story with the headline 'NEWCASTLE AFTER MACLEOD' which included, 'Recent improvements in the play of Third Lanark's soldier outside left Ally MacLeod has again attracted the attention of Newcastle United.'

Before the end of the campaign Rangers had another offer rejected by Thirds manager Jimmy Blair who had succeeded Alec Ritchie earlier in the year. It was said they were believed to be holding out for £5,000 before sanctioning Alistair's departure.

3

Briefly a Buddy

THINGS did not start well for Third Lanark in the 1955/56 season. They finished third in a League Cup section containing three other Second Division (as Division B was under a restructure) teams, Morton, Brechin and Stenhousemuir, and sat 14th in the table with just nine points from 14 matches at the end of October.

With Alistair unable to practise with his team-mates Thirds had arranged for their player to train at Heart of Midlothian some evenings but a loss of form accompanied by criticism from the terraces was documented in the *Sunday Empire News* after a home defeat by Brechin. Reader John Walker was awarded the £3 prize for the best letter which claimed that the barracking of both George Dobbie, another conscript, and Alistair at Cathkin was justified. Pointing the finger at Alistair's army career, Walker said, 'The services have taken the edge off his football...not so long ago he was a blonde bombshell and now the explosives have gone damp.'

Towards the end of his service the player corroborated the reader's view when he told Alex Cameron of the *Scottish Daily Mail*, 'I get hardly any chance to train in the Army, which must have its effect on me.'

Faced with dwindling gates, Thirds had to look at ways of cutting costs – and that meant cashing in on their most valuable asset. News of the transfer on 3 November was a shock which generated headlines in the sports pages and came without warning. The transfer even made the front page of the *Evening Times* with the headline 'THIRD LANARK CRISIS'.

The lead story by Alan Breck began, 'A crisis in the affairs of Third Lanark is pinpointed today by the transfer of their outside left Ally McLeod to St Mirren. In addition to selling their star player Thirds have been forced to take other measures to ease the financial strain. I learned today that trainer Bobby Reid is leaving the club within the next few weeks and that manager Jimmy Blair may also give up his position.' On the back page of the same newspaper Gair Henderson reported on a secret rendezvous during the players' lunch hour when he had slipped out of the barracks to attend a meeting at the nearby golf club with Jimmy Blair and St Mirren manager Willie Reid.

The financial situation was explained and after half an hour Corporal MacLeod returned to the barracks a St Mirren player. Informing Breck he had had six happy years at Third Lanark, Alistair said he was 'very sorry to leave' and was quoted, 'But I would rather go to St Mirren than sign for an English club.'

He had played in eight league matches for Thirds that season, scoring both goals in a 2-1 win over St Johnstone, and appeared in five League Cup games, netting once against Stenhousemuir. He was now joining a club sitting third from bottom of the First Division who clearly needed his services to get them out of the relegation zone.

It does appear that no ultimatum had been issued and Alistair did have a choice of staying with Thirds. He was however conscious that the transfer fee – undisclosed but believed to be around £4,000 – would greatly aid the club's desperate situation. But he had been reluctant to leave the club he had supported as a boy.

Tottenham Hotspur had also shown interest at the time but delayed an approach, allowing St Mirren to step in.

With little time to adjust to his new surroundings, Alistair was in the Saints' side to face Partick Thistle little more than 48 hours after signing. The *Evening Times* predicted his appearance would add as much as 1,000 to the Firhill attendance.

Only a superior goal average kept St Mirren ahead of Partick in the league table with both clubs on four points. Thistle were second from bottom and in the relegation zone along with Stirling Albion who had just two points. Clearly the Buddies were looking to Alistair to help drag them away from the threat of the Second Division.

By an odd coincidence the match was taking place on 5 November, exactly six years to the day since Alistair's Third Lanark debut. At least he did not have to face either of his army colleagues that afternoon with neither Crawford nor Mathers listed. Mathers in fact played at Love Street in the reserve fixture between the two teams.

Just as at Third Lanark, Alistair's St Mirren career began with a defeat as the Jags won 2-0. With the result Partick leapfrogged the Saints who now occupied the second relegation slot. All eyes seemed to be on the new boy and writing in the *Evening Citizen*, Malcolm Munro offered, 'The crowd was roaring for St Mirren new boy Alistair McLeod. Ally made a gallant effort to respond…McLeod was really in the thick of it now and though harried he was sending high swirling crosses to the far post which carried loads of danger.'

Another sports writer present, Tommy Allan, assessed Alistair's performance as over-anxious, adding in an unknown publication, 'He tried to justify his transfer fee. He just didn't get the service.'

That same afternoon his former team, who had already dispensed with manager Blair's services, went down 6-1 to Morton in Greenock. William and Jean MacLeod did not see their son's Paisley debut as they were at the Thirds match where their loyalties remained throughout the season. A Third Lanark match programme later in the campaign highlighted the fact MacLeod senior was yet to watch his son play for his new club five months after signing as he preferred the slopes of Cathkin.

Alistair's first goal for St Mirren arrived on the very last day of the year and was the second the Buddies netted in a 7-2 home win over Airdrie. With Partick's drawn match that day Saints climbed to fourth from bottom, two points clear of relegation. The name of MacLeod appeared twice more on the scoresheet during the 22 league appearances Alistair made that season, in a 4-1 defeat at Aberdeen in February and during a 4-0 home win over East Fife in the last home match.

At the end of 1955 the first edition of Hugh Taylor's *The Scottish Football Book* was published which contained a feature highlighting eight 'up and coming' players. Alistair – still listed as being with Third Lanark and in the army – was given the following write-up, 'Now and then Scotland produces a player who becomes a "character" – a player with that little bit extra, a flair for the unorthodox. There is certainly a touch of eccentric genius about young Alistair McLeod, the Third Lanark left-winger.

'Tall, lanky, with a mop of fair hair, Alistair is a great favourite at Cathkin, where his unusual touches make the crowd grin – and opposing defenders blush. Alistair is always a problem to defenders. They never know what his long legs are going to do next. Sometimes Alistair confesses he doesn't really know himself! But Ally has a flair for doing the unexpected at the right time. He is not nearly as awkward as he looks and he has superb ball control. Now in the army, he will be knocking at the international door when he returns soon to Cathkin.'

As fate would have it Saints drew Third Lanark in the Scottish Cup that season with the teams meeting on a rain-sodden pitch at Love Street in the first round proper on 4 February.

It was goalless at half-time but Saints went ahead seven minutes after the restart through Bobby Holmes who went on to score a hat-trick as they eventually ran out 6-0 victors. MacLeod was not on the scoresheet nor did he have a hand in any of the goals. The gate was given as 10,252 with receipts totalling £739.

A thrilling 4-4 draw at Broomfield in the next round, enjoyed by a crowd of 20,620, was followed by a disappointing 3-1 home defeat in the replay, allowing Airdrie some revenge for that Hogmanay hammering.

During two weeks' leave from the barracks that March Alistair spent each day training at Love Street and announced he felt 100 per cent fitter as a result.

One of the many myths of Alistair's career is that his time at Love Street lasted around six weeks (even his own autobiography claims he was at the club for eight weeks) when he was actually a St Mirren player until the end of the season, a period of six months.

St Mirren completed the league campaign fourth from bottom on 27 points, but more importantly they were five clear of relegation. Alistair turned out for the Buddies for the last time in a Paisley Charity Cup match at Love Street on 12 May 1956 where the visitors Leicester City won 3-1.

His old club Third Lanark did finish the season on a high note by lifting the Glasgow Charity Cup after beating Partick in the final.

4

Ally the Anglo

IN his autobiography Alistair's recollections of signing for Blackburn Rovers amount to little more than agreeing once he had been approached by manager Johnny Carey. Alistair recounts he had been so impressed by Carey's skills in the Coronation Cup semi-final at Hampden when Celtic defeated his Manchester United side in 1953 that he needed little persuading. Newspaper reports of the time however reveal that the deal was rather less straightforward and that the player did have some doubts.

Carey, a former Northern Ireland international and captain at Old Trafford, had been on holiday in Scotland during the close season. Aware of Alistair's abilities, he had called in at Love Street to enquire about the player with Willie Reid.

Alistair was then introduced to Carey, who invited him and Faye down to Blackburn on 21 June, to look at the set-up for themselves. Prior to the trip Alistair discussed his thoughts on the possible move to a journalist (source of article unknown), 'I know it's a great offer. But you could have blown me over when Mr Carey arrived on the scene. I hadn't the slightest inkling there was any such move afoot. I've never had the slightest desire to leave Scotland.

'Moreover this is just about the most difficult time they could have picked to ask me. I get demobbed on 9 August and it has been a big enough problem working out all my plans on the assumption I was going to be at home. Mr Carey has invited me down to Blackburn and I'm going. After all, I've nothing to lose.'

During this period Scots who signed for English clubs were referred to as 'Anglos' by the press and often vilified as greedy deserters or 'Big Time Charlies'. There were repeated calls for an 'All Tartan Team' of home-based Scots when it came to internationals and the selectors were urged to ignore the Anglos who, it was said, had forfeited the right to represent their country. Many Scottish supporters agreed with this viewpoint as they watched promising players leave their own clubs, lured south with the promise of higher wages and lost to the Scottish game.

Whether this played on Alistair's mind is unclear but he had stated at the start of his St Mirren career that he would rather join them than 'an English team'.

At any rate he was still undecided on the couple's return from Lancashire on the Friday but he had promised to let Carey know by the following Wednesday. Blackburn and St Mirren agreed on a transfer fee believed to be £8,000 – a 100 per cent profit in less than a year for the Saints – but were kept waiting for the player's decision.

On the Monday his former boss Jimmy Carabine told *Scottish Daily Express* readers, 'Ally McLeod will sign today.' Blackburn had despatched the necessary paperwork and the player had told Carabine, 'I am going to Love Street this morning and if the forms have arrived I will sign.'

He did leave Paisley with some regrets and felt that the Saints' supporters had not seen the best of him due to his army posting which ruled out training with his team-mates. One St Mirren fan gave Alistair a parting gift – a 'lucky' silver American dollar which Faye still has to this day. Faye remembers that their friends were all surprised he had made the decision to uproot to England.

The last few weeks of Alistair's army service were spent in Carlisle on a civil defence course before he returned to Glencorse Barracks where he was demobbed on 9 August. Alistair and Faye were soon on their way south to live in a semi-detached villa in Blackburn's Livesey Branch Road which they rented from the club for one pound a week plus ten shillings for rates as part of the transfer deal.

Not far from the football club in the Feniscowles area, Faye recalls there were fields both to the front and rear of the house. There had been an opportunity to remain in the forces as Faye recalls 'they wanted him to go on an officer's course' but Alistair was eager to devote his time to a career in football. Blackburn had also agreed that the 25-year-old would be allowed to complete his analytical chemist studies once he had first endured three months of full-time training at the club.

Although a Second Division club, Blackburn Rovers were ambitious. They had last played in the First Division in 1948 and had only just missed out on promotion the previous season. With an average home attendance of 23,000 they had finished fourth in the table, level on points with third-placed Liverpool and behind the two promoted clubs.

Carey was determined to reach the top division and had assembled a decent team which included England international Ronnie Clayton and future England player Bryan Douglas, both of whom were 22 years of age and local lads. Douglas would go on to be capped 36 times. Also on the payroll at Ewood Park was 19-year-old Roy Vernon, who would be honoured 38 times for Wales and play in the World Cup in Sweden two years later.

But just as it had done at both Third Lanark and St Mirren, Alistair's debut ended in defeat – and how. The final score at the Vetch Field on the opening Saturday of the season, 18 August 1956, was Swansea 5 Blackburn 1. With Blackburn trailing to a goal from Mel Charles, the younger brother of Leeds and Wales star John, one English journal adequately described the equaliser, 'In the twenty-ninth minute McLeod again made the running with a quick shuffle, a body swerve, and the ball was curling to the waiting head of winger Douglas who made no mistake.'

Just a matter of minutes later came the game's turning point when Clayton was carried off with a shin injury which left Blackburn with ten men for the remaining 55 minutes. Almost immediately Charles scored again and he helped himself to another two goals before the end. The same anonymous reporter offered 'McLeod hardly did a thing wrong' while another headline gave no mention of Swansea or the margin of their victory. 'McLeod's Great Game for Rovers' it read.

'In all the misfortune there is one definite credit item – the real promise of McLeod,' wrote 'Centurion', before continuing, 'Fast and skilful, quick to take position and ever-ready to have a shot, he pleased enormously; even the Swansea crowd applauded some of his moves.'

'Centurion' was the pseudonym of Alf Thornton who was assigned to cover Blackburn's matches for the *Northern Daily Telegraph* which would soon change its name to the *Northern Evening Telegraph*.

Clearly, and in spite of the heavy defeat, after just one game the new boy had already made an impression. Faye remembers it was shortly after his arrival at Blackburn that he started to call himself Ally, partly because he found it easier when signing autographs.

Bryan Douglas, who became good friends with Ally, today remembers that he was 'quite a character', if 'a bit eccentric', who brought balance to the side. Douglas soon found out the Scotsman had a 'terrific imagination' and he recalls one Friday at training when Ally told him he had dreamt that they would win 23-0 on the Saturday with Ally scoring all but one of the goals!

Just two days after the Swansea match Ally scored his first Blackburn goal as Carey's team won 3-1 at West Ham United. With Blackburn already leading by two Douglas goals, Jack Wood's match report read, 'Gregory only partially cleared from an inswinging centre from Douglas. He diverted the ball on to right back Wright's head, and it went to Blackburn left winger McLeod who slammed it straight back for the third goal.'

A run of inconsistent results followed which included victories over Rotherham, Sheffield United and Liverpool at Anfield as well as defeats at the hands of Lincoln City, Nottingham Forest and revenge for West Ham at Ewood Park.

The two points won at Liverpool on 6 October left Blackburn firmly in the bottom half of the division, 16th out of 22 having amassed just nine points from 11 matches.

Ally and Faye headed north after the Anfield match for an important fixture of their own in Glasgow two days later when they were due to be married. The ceremony took place at Croftfoot Parish Church with the evening reception held at the Marlborough Hotel in Shawlands. Best man at the wedding was Ally's old schoolfriend John Anderson who, with the couple in Blackburn, had been responsible for arranging their short honeymoon in London.

Ally and Faye were seen off by their guests in a taxi from the Marlborough with the groom dressed in his football strip and bedecked with balloons. He changed into his suit during the journey to Glasgow Central Station where they were due to catch the overnight sleeper.

As John had made the booking and knew the departure time, a number of guests had followed and surprised the couple. Ally was carried shoulder-high to the platform with Faye wheeled along on a porter's trolley. They then spent the first night of their married life on the train before enjoying three days in the capital.

During their stay they attended a trial at the Old Bailey and even bumped into a referee who wondered what Ally was doing in London during the football season. When they arrived back in Blackburn on the Friday they left their suitcases in the railway station's left luggage office while Ally headed straight off to train with his team-mates and Faye went to get the shopping in.

Ally was back in Scotland again just three days later, this time with his team-mates for a challenge match at Broomfield on Monday 15 October to celebrate the switching-on of Airdrie's newly-installed floodlights. In the days when friendlies were played with a competitive edge rather than the extended training sessions they later came to resemble, the 12,000 supporters witnessed an exciting match. The teams were level at 2-2 as the contest moved into the final minute.

John MacKenzie of the *Scottish Daily Express* takes up the story, 'Running into the inside right position, he collected the ball, wheeled quickly and sent a raking left-foot shot high into the net.'

Ally had snatched the winning goal in a match most reports suggest the home side were unlucky to lose. But it was Ally who made the headlines. 'Paisley's Ally McLeod Was Never Like This' was Bobby Bogan's header in an unknown publication. In his summary Brogan observed, 'This is a McLeod whom Paisley has never seen. Here was confidence and zip where once there was hesitancy and lethargy.'

Clearly benefitting from the full-time training at Blackburn, Ally told Bogan, 'I'm much fitter since my demob...and I think that I'm playing better.'

In his *Express* report MacKenzie again called for international recognition, 'The selectors can stop worrying about their outside left position after last night's game.' The main focus of Peter Hendry's report for the *Evening Times* was that Ally was now sporting a much shorter hairstyle.

Rovers' irreverent league form continued when they lost 6-0 at Leicester then in their next match defeated Bury 6-2 at home with Ally among the goalscorers.

But a good run towards the end of the year saw Blackburn climb ten places during a five-week period from 24 November. Starting with a home victory against Middlesbrough they won seven of their next eight games, a run which included payback, 5-3, against Swansea. Bizarrely the only defeat in that run was a heavy one, 7-2 at Fulham.

Ally was soon a favourite among the Blackburn fans who christened him 'Noddy'. This was more due to the way his head bobbed from side to side when he ran with the ball than any physical resemblance to the popular Enid Blyton children's book character from which the name derived.

Blackburn supporter John Kennedy offers this explanation, 'Back in the late 1980s I worked with a lovely old chap called Bill. I remember that he was born in 1926. He stood on The Riverside [a large terrace at Ewood Park that almost ran alongside the banks of the River Darwen] for 50 or more years and claimed to have coined the nickname due to Ally's peculiar head movement with "Come on Noddy get that head bobbin". Bill said it took off straight away and became his nickname.'

A ripple of excitement would spread across the Ewood Park terraces when 'Noddy' embarked on one of his runs.

Soon most of his team-mates referred to him as such and on occasion the local newspapers did too. Ally himself would claim, 'It was because I nodded all the goals in!' to which Faye remembers his team-mates were quick to correct him that it was to do with his running.

With Rovers still very much in the promotion race a crucial point dropped at home to Notts County on Easter Friday meant nothing less than victory at Bristol Rovers the following day, 20 April, would be acceptable.

Before the match Johnny Carey took a telephone call from Ally's mother. Jean broke the news that Ally's father William had just passed away aged 67. She insisted the manager did not tell her son the news until after the match lest it affect his performance in the vital fixture.

Blackburn won the match with the only goal of the game and Ally was reported as having played well. Walking from the pitch he saw Carey coming towards him not looking like a manager whose team had just won. Instinctively Ally knew that his father had died that day. Later he related to his sister Christine that he had felt his father had been with him as he ran up the wing that afternoon.

Blackburn's last game at Notts County was due on the Tuesday but this would be the only match Ally would miss in that first season south of the border as he was attending his father's funeral.

County won 2-0 to put an end to Blackburn's dreams of playing in the top flight for another season and they finished fourth in the table. The three points County took from Blackburn in the last four days of the season cost the club dearly. But they too had been desperate for results and only just avoided demotion to the Third Division, finishing third from bottom.

Leicester were champions and promoted along with runners-up Nottingham Forest with Liverpool again third, one point ahead of Blackburn. Had Rovers won their last match they would have equalled Forest's points total of 54 but were way behind on goal average.

Between January and the last game of the season Rovers had lost only twice, at Middlesbrough, and at County in the last fixture. Blackburn's record in the last 24 league games was 15 wins, seven draws and two defeats. Early in January they had lost at Everton in the first round of the FA Cup.

On the same Tuesday evening as the Notts County game, in one of those strange coincidences that football often throws up, Ally's first club had cause to celebrate. As Blackburn's bid failed Third Lanark secured promotion to the Scottish First Division with a 4-0 home win over Albion Rovers. It is unclear if Ally attended the match although his family think it likely he would have been required to head back down to Blackburn after the funeral.

Ally had been a success during his first season in English football, turning out in 41 of 42 league matches during which he scored seven times. He had also become good friends with many of his team-mates. 'Everybody got on with him,' says Bryan Douglas, remembering 'he used to tell some tall stories' which the others took 'with a pinch of salt'.

Left-half Mick McGrath, a Dubliner, remembers 'a great team man who worked so damn hard for the team and was always there to help out if you were in trouble', adding that he was 'always talking, encouraging people'.

Full-back Dave Whelan came into the side around the same time and got to know Ally well as they always shared a room together if they had to stay overnight for an away game. Dave was not a big eater and recalls Ally used to eat both of their breakfasts! 'To be in the dressing room before a match with him was something special,' the Yorkshireman says. 'He had an attitude that we were going to win. There was never any talk of losing when he was about, not one iota. He was so confident we could beat anybody and he was like that at training.' This confidence and encouragement would later continue into Ally's managerial career.

Defender Matt Woods has fond memories of a lively team-mate who was always joking at training in the morning and can still barely tell his favourite Ally story without bursting into fits of laughter.

Ally, Bryan, Dave and Matt played golf together most Wednesdays at Pleasington Golf Club not far from the MacLeods' home. On one occasion Bryan and Matt decided to wind Ally up in the clubhouse. Seeing him arrive they faked a conversation just as he walked in. 'You can't do it!' said Matt. 'Of course you can,' replied Bryan to which Matt insisted, 'No you can't!'

Ally rose to the bait. 'What can't you do?' he interrupted. Ally had recently passed his driving test and now claimed to be the best driver in the golf club in his first car which had a faulty door. His team-mates explained they were debating whether it would be possible to turn a nearby hairpin bend at the bottom of a slope while in top gear. 'I can do it!' he insisted, relishing the challenge to showcase his driving skills.

Ally then got into his car and set off downhill as the others stood on a wall overlooking the bend. As he went into top gear the car door flew open and Ally started to fall out. With his legs trailing he succeeded in holding on to the steering wheel with one hand while operating the foot brake with the other and the vehicle came to a halt. By this time the others were in hysterics.

'He could have killed himself and we were killing ourselves laughing!' Matt remembers.

Ally then fell out of the car and calmly said to the others, 'That just shows what a good driver I am!'

They could often be seen at the local dog track as well. Ally had come by a greyhound which he jointly owned with Bryan called Royal Flush and, unbeknown to her, had registered the dog in Faye's mother's name.

Dave Whelan has never forgotten their first visit to the dogs when five of them put a pound on the greyhound to win at odds of 3-1. 'It came out of the traps like a rocket and was leading by about eight yards when it came to the first bend. We thought "this is magnificent!" but it didn't go round the bend, it went straight over the fence and we never saw it for two days!' he laughs.

One day Ally told Matt that he was sure the window cleaner he was paying was not providing the service and he was determined to catch him out. Leaving early, Ally returned to Livesey Branch Road where he pulled a table up next to the window and crouched underneath it. After some time he was disturbed by a knock at the window. Ally looked up to see the window cleaner polishing away, looking down at him and shouting through the glass, 'What are you doing under the table Ally?'

With the club's training facilities close by a number of the players were regular afternoon visitors to the MacLeods' house where they would pop in to watch the horse racing on television. Faye remembers she used to spend a fortune on biscuits for her guests.

If Ally's introduction to English football had been exciting it was nothing but a warm-up for the 1957/58 season. Unbeaten after their first four league games (albeit with three draws), Blackburn then won eight of their next 13 matches, drawing three with only two losses.

When they went to Anfield on 23 November they were sitting on top of the Second Division, two points clear of Liverpool. In what was already developing into a tight race for those two promotion places only five points separated ten clubs at the top. A 2-0 defeat allowed Liverpool to leapfrog Carey's men to claim top spot by virtue of a superior goal average.

Middlesbrough came to Ewood Park the following Saturday and led 3-2 with just seven minutes to play. Ally then grabbed an equaliser – his second goal of the match – and almost a hat-trick when another effort was cleared off the Boro line one minute later. That 3-3 draw sparked a poor run where Rovers lost three of their next five matches including a 5-1 thumping at the hands of Leyton Orient.

The last game of the year, on 28 December, saw Notts County as the visitors. In a match described as 'so one-sided as to be farcical' by Jack Parker (who in an unknown publication referred to 'Alex McLeod'), the County defence held out until the 70th minute when Peter Dobing set up Ally to open the scoring. Four minutes later the same two combined for a second goal and in the last minute Bryan Douglas 'waltzed through the defence in a cheeky chappy dribble' before allowing Ally to complete the hat-trick denied him against Middlesbrough, when Douglas might have scored himself.

It finished 3-0 with Ally the first Blackburn player to score three goals in a match in the same number of years since Frank Mooney had done so in a 9-0 win over Middlesbrough. Some doubters did claim that Mooney's achievement did not qualify as a true 'hat-trick' as his goals had not been scored successively, that is to say other team-mates found the net in between his strikes. A few weeks later the Blackburn programme editor – having had time to do his research – stated that Ally's hat-trick was the first scored by a Blackburn winger since 1936.

Along with Roy Vernon, Ally was now the club's joint top scorer with eight goals. Douglas remembers being surprised that Ally took the match ball with him although the tradition of a hat-trick scorer keeping the ball may have been more common north of the border at the time.

Faye, still a keen spectator at her husband's games, missed his big moment as she was packing for their trip home to Scotland for Hogmanay with Rovers not due to play again until 4 January. At the turn of the year Blackburn had dropped to sixth place but were still only two points behind Fulham and Liverpool who shared the coveted top two slots with 32 points each.

The first game of 1958 was in the third round of the FA Cup and Rovers progressed with a 4-1 win at Rotherham United. They then gained revenge for the previous season by beating First Division side Everton 2-1 at Goodison Park. Cardiff soon fell after a replay and suddenly Blackburn were in the quarter-finals, just two games from Wembley.

They were unbeaten in the league from the start of 1958 and took six points from four games ahead of a crucial double date with Liverpool. The clubs met at Ewood Park on successive Saturdays in the league and FA Cup on 22nd February and the first day of March respectively.

Both sides were level on 36 points, three behind Charlton Athletic at the top, when they met for the league match. And what an encounter it turned out to be. Even a *Liverpool Echo* report confirms that the Reds were fortunate to go in level at 0-0 at half-time, 'The Liverpool goal had another amazing escape when Younger saved brilliantly from McLeod at almost point blank range.'

Five minutes after the break the score was incredibly 2-2. Billy Liddell drew first blood for the visitors in the 47th minute before Douglas and Ray Stephenson turned things around only for Liddell to score again. Dobing then made it 3-2 before Liddell headed home from a corner to complete his hat-trick and the points were shared.

Describing the match as 'one of the best seen at Ewood Park for years', 'Centurion' had some simple advice for the cup tie concerning Liddell, 'Curb his menace and Rovers are through to the semi-finals.'

The following week's quarter-final was equally competitive. Liverpool led at the break through a Bobby Murdoch (not the Celtic player of the same name) goal and held out until the 78th minute when Clayton levelled. Encouraged by the equaliser, Ally hit the winner three minutes later and Blackburn were in the semi-final.

The draw paired Rovers against First Division side Bolton Wanderers at Manchester City's Maine Road on 22 March. Almost 75,000 supporters watched the contest and it was Blackburn who took the lead when Dobing headed a corner from Ally past Alan Hodgkinson on 19 minutes. But two goals in quick succession by Ralph Gubbins sent the Rovers players in at half-time scarcely able to believe their lead had been wiped out so quickly.

Both teams created chances during the second period but there were no further goals and it was Bolton who went to Wembley for the final. The irony for the losers was that Gubbins had only played due to an injury to Nat Lofthouse.

Blackburn had enjoyed their cup run and taste of the big time but promotion was still achievable and they concentrated everything on their nine remaining league games.

Their form came good, winning six of the next eight with one defeat (at Cardiff) and a draw in the penultimate match of the campaign at Fulham when a late, controversial, but ultimately vital Ally equaliser kept his side in the promotion race. That meant one match was left and everything was to play for.

West Ham were uncatchable at the top with Charlton second on 55 points, one ahead of Carey's men.

In an end-of-season finale no one could have scripted the two were due to meet on the very last day. A point would be enough for Charlton who had home advantage so Blackburn were only too aware that even a draw would see their season end in failure. The BBC sent its outside broadcast unit to film the match with highlights shown later that evening.

Looking back for the *Edinburgh Evening News* three years later, Ally chose the promotion clash as the highlight of his time in England, greater even than the occasion of a Wembley FA Cup Final he was later to experience.

A crowd of 56,345 saw Charlton lead after four minutes but Blackburn turned it around to go in 3-1 up at the break. This is Ally's recollection of the second period, 'Hardly had the second half started when we scored again to make it 4-1. I thought to myself, "We're in easy street." Then Charlton got a goal to make it 4-2 and the fat really was in the fire when John Hewie converted a penalty kick in the last seven minutes to make it 4-3. Charlton simply threw everything at our defence in the closing stages, a spell that had the crowd in a ferment with so much at stake, but we managed to hold out. It was easily the most fantastic football match I have ever played in.'

So Blackburn had snatched the second promotion slot on the very last day of the season and the disappointment of the semi-final defeat was forgotten. After a gap of ten years Carey's Rovers were back in the big time.

The Blackburn team were given a civic reception on their return from a tour in Holland. Thousands lined the streets as the coach brought the team from Ewood Park to the Town Hall accompanied by the sound of car horns as drivers showed their appreciation.

The last few minutes of the commentary from the Charlton game was relayed over the loudspeaker system to encourage the crowds whose appreciation was evident by the clacking of wooden rattles. Each player then received a standing ovation as he climbed the stairs to the balcony overlooking the supporters as the band of the Fourth Battalion East Lancashire Regiment TA played 'See The Conquering Heroes Home'. The tune changed to 'When Johnny Comes

Marching Home' when Carey appeared with the chairman and directors. The only sad note that evening was that Bryan Douglas was unable to attend as he had been refused permission to take leave from the England party.

For Ally the season had been another success as he played in 38 out of 42 league matches, scoring 17 goals, plus one in the FA Cup against Liverpool.

And now the First Division beckoned with the promise of 14 derby matches as Blackburn joined seven other Lancashire clubs in the top flight including their main and closest rivals Burnley.

No one could have dreamt of the start Blackburn would have to life in the First Division as they scored five goals in each of their first three matches. Rarely can a promoted team have made such an impact in the top division. First up on the fixture list was a trip to Newcastle on 23 August 1958 where they came away with a 5-1 victory in front of a crowd of almost 53,000. 'Centurion' reported that hundreds of travelling fans had mobbed the Blackburn players as they left the field, summarising, 'They made Newcastle look a very poor team indeed.'

Two days later on the Bank Holiday Monday Leicester left Ewood Park having been on the wrong end of a 5-0 drubbing with all the goals coming in the last 25 minutes. 'The Rovers have arrived again as a power in football,' raved 'Centurion'. 'They are going to be crowd-pullers and pleasers with their own particular blend of science, power and punch.'

Tottenham Hotspur were the visitors the following Saturday when a crowd of 41,830 saw another 5-0 slaughter. 'I have never seen a team so wholeheartedly together,' praised Frank McGhee in the *Sunday Mirror*. 'Blackburn played as a team, the stars not trying to steal the show, the older players encouraging the youngsters.'

Antony Butcher in an unknown publication sounded a note of caution in his report, 'Blackburn obviously realise that this cannot last indefinitely and that eventually they will come up against far stronger opposition than they have so far.'

After three matches the newly promoted side sat proudly at the top of the First Division with six points. Fifteen goals had been scored with just one conceded, and they even scored that with Dave Whelan putting the ball into his own net at Newcastle.

But, as Butcher had predicted, the run was too good to last and they drew with Leicester before losing 6-1 to a Manchester United team which had been decimated by the events of the Munich air disaster just seven months earlier.

A sequence of draws and defeats was the story of September, the month in which they lost the manager who had built the team and taken them to the First Division. After nine matches Everton were sitting at the very bottom of the league with just four points. The Everton board had been following Johnny Carey's progress for some time and after a meeting between the two parties at Goodison Park on the evening of 23 September Carey agreed to take over.

Three years later Carey was dismissed from his position by Everton chairman John Moores during a taxi journey between the FA headquarters and their

London hotel. This gave birth to the supporters' cry of 'Taxi for...' which can still be heard if a manager's position is under threat.

'We had a very close-knit team,' recalls Whelan, remembering seven-a-side training matches where each competitor contributed two shillings with the bounty going to the winning team. Whelan would generally mark Ally with both matching each other's desire to win.

'We had some fantastic clashes!' he remembers. Once during training Ally set fire to a material which created a lot of smoke inside a toilet cubicle. The trainer got into a bit of a panic and thought someone was in trouble after smoking a cigarette. When he got no response the door was forced only for him to be engulfed by smoke to the amusement of the players. 'You could never predict what Ally was going to do next,' laughs Whelan. 'There was never ever a dull moment when he was about.'

Following their explosive start Blackburn failed to win another game until the middle of October when they beat local rivals Preston North End 4-1. Now with Aberdonian Dally Duncan in charge, a former Scotland international, things picked up again with away wins at West Bromwich Albion and Manchester City.

A 3-0 home defeat by Chelsea on Christmas Day was partly avenged with a 2-0 win at Stamford Bridge two days later. It was not at the time unusual for clubs in the Football League to meet twice within a matter of days.

Going into 1959, Blackburn sat in a healthy tenth position in the table. January saw defeats at Tottenham and Wolverhampton Wanderers and an early exit from the FA Cup. A 4-2 home win over Leyton Orient in round three (where the First Division clubs entered the contest) was rewarded with a home tie against their fiercest rivals Burnley. The whole of East Lancashire looked forward to the match on 24 January which was only the third time the rivals had been drawn together in the competition.

Blackburn forced three early corners but the game soon descended into a farce with players slipping on a pitch covered in not only ice but packed snow. During the half-time interval both managers came out with the referee to inspect the conditions and a decision was taken to abandon the match. The hard ice with jagged edges was considered a danger to the players although one suspects had the scores not been level the two managers may have been rather less in agreement!

With the game rescheduled for the following Wednesday, Blackburn were boosted by the return to fitness of Bryan Douglas following a two-month absence. While far from perfect, the pitch was less treacherous and the game went ahead. Blackburn struck first but Burnley fought back to level and went through courtesy of a late headed goal from Jimmy Robson.

Revenge came in March with a 4-1 league win over Burnley at Ewood Park which was part of an 11-game run during which Blackburn lost only once – to Leeds United.

Rovers did however lose their last two matches, away to Birmingham and Bolton, but finished in a respectable tenth place in the 22-team division with 44 points from 42 matches. They had also added to their attacking options with

Dally Duncan signing Northern Ireland striker Derek Dougan from Portsmouth that March and attendances at Ewood Park had increased by a third to an average of 30,544.

Ally, like his team-mates, had acquitted himself well in the First Division. He had turned out in 40 of the 42 league matches, scoring four times in addition to an FA Cup goal against Orient. Given the upheaval the team had faced in losing their manager Blackburn had every right to be satisfied after their first season back in the big time.

5
Noddy Goes to Wembley

AGAIN Blackburn started the 1959/60 season in top form with four wins and a draw in their first five matches. This sequence included Rovers' first double in 50 years over local rivals Bolton Wanderers.

Just as 12 months previously, Blackburn were at the top of the First Division on 5 September with nine points, one ahead of Wolverhampton Wanderers with the two due to meet at Molineux the following week.

Wolves' 3-1 triumph sent them to the summit and Blackburn then hit a run of indifferent form which included wins over Everton (with Ally scoring), Leicester City and Leeds United interwoven with losses at Tottenham Hotspur, Newcastle United and Chelsea. There were two drawn matches, both 1-1, at home to Arsenal and Manchester United with Ally equalising against United with five minutes left. Come the end of 1959 Dally Duncan's team were sitting in a healthy fourth in the table and the club and their fans looked forward with optimism to the new decade.

The MacLeods held a Hogmanay party at Livesey Branch Road with a number of the Blackburn players and their partners attending. Bryan Douglas was somewhat curious as to why the Scots seemed to celebrate New Year more than Christmas. Faye remembers Derek Dougan arriving at the door with his girlfriend and a vanload of alcohol as the party got going.

Just after midnight Dougan's girlfriend heard Ally wishing his mother a happy New Year over the telephone and told him how sweet she thought that was. She then asked if he minded if she telephoned her mother which Ally was all for until he discovered she lived in Sydney!

Considered to fit the bill as tall and dark, if not so much a stranger, Matt Woods was ushered outside shortly after midnight before crossing the doorstep with a piece of coal as the traditional first foot of the year. The socialising continued into the early hours of 1960 and eventually two of the guests were put to bed upstairs while Mick McGrath fell asleep with his head in the fireplace.

Perhaps not surprisingly Blackburn then went down 2-1 at home to Nottingham Forest on 2 January and Ally later remarked to Faye that he knew they were in trouble when Dougan kicked off with a back-heel.

The following Saturday Rovers drew 1-1 at Sunderland in the third round of the FA Cup. Although they had no way of telling, it was the start of a run which would eventually lead to the twin towers of Wembley.

Blackburn won the replay with goals to spare – 4-1 it finished with Ally among the scorers. A fourth-round 1-1 draw at home to Blackpool on the last Saturday of January was not too encouraging although the Monday draw for the next stage was incentive enough with the winners of the replay travelling to either Tottenham or Crewe Alexandra.

The Seasiders started well in the midweek replay. 'BLACKPOOL MUFF THEIR CHANCES' was the *Daily Mirror* headline. 'Blackpool missed countless chances while Blackburn snapped up everything,' was the opening paragraph of the report. Two Dobing strikes either side of a headed goal by Dougan saw Rovers safely through with a 3-0 win. But the margin of victory paled into insignificance when the result of the other replay came through – Tottenham 13 Crewe 2. The half-time score had been 10-1!

Before the Spurs game Blackburn lost Roy Vernon, who followed his old manager Johnny Carey to Everton. But Dally Duncan snapped up Louis Simpson from Liverpool for £5,000, a player who was to make a significant contribution to the side's progress in the cup.

The bookmakers now made league leaders Tottenham favourites to win the trophy. The 55,000 crowd inside White Hart Lane were shocked when Spurs appeared for the 20 February clash without the injured Dave Mackay. The *Evening Times* report described Matt Woods's opening goal as a 'freak' as his free kick from the halfway line 'soared high into the air, struck the sawdust in front of Bill Brown, bounced up on to his chest, and twisted off him into the net'.

Cliff Jones levelled but Simpson gave Blackburn an interval lead on 41 minutes and he later sealed a 3-1 result with his second on 70 minutes to send Blackburn safely through to the quarter-finals. The draw paired them away to the winners of the Bradford City v Burnley replay which Burnley won easily, 5-0. Having only previously met twice in the FA Cup prior to the previous year the two local rivals had now been drawn together in successive seasons.

In one of football's not uncommon coincidences the two sides met at Turf Moor on league business seven days before the FA Cup tie. Caution was the order of the day with neither side wishing to show their hand ahead of the cup game. The *Blackburn Times* described that afternoon's events as 'one of the most concentrated efforts in concealment since Hitler masked his real intentions when he met Chamberlain at Munich'. Burnley won the match with the only goal and cup fever intensified in the area over the next week.

A crowd given as 51,501 (all 54,000 three-shilling tickets had been snapped up) were packed into Turf Moor for the 12 March cup tie.

Blackburn came looking for revenge for their previous cup exit as well as the league defeat although the day's events bore no resemblance whatsoever to the week before. What a game of football the crowd were treated to, a match still talked about in that part of the world by those old enough to remember.

An eventful but goalless first half was summed up by the *Telegraph*'s 'Centurion' as 'HONOURS WENT TO THE ROVERS IN THE FIRST HALF BY A VERY WIDE MARGIN'.

But the old cliché, 'It's goals that count', proved accurate as Burnley shocked the visitors by scoring three times in a 13-minute period. It looked over but a Douglas penalty on 73 minutes followed 60 seconds later by a Dobing 20-yarder reduced the deficit to one.

'This was stuff only for the strongest of nerves – several spectators in the stand in front of me left the ground saying they couldn't stand the tension any longer,' Centurion informed. Those early departees missed Mick McGrath earning his side a replay four minutes from time.

A crowd of 53,889 saw the replay four days later but with neither side able to find the net after 90 minutes the game entered extra time. Dobing gave Blackburn a deserved lead after 103 minutes and victory was secured when Ally got behind the Burnley defence to head home after a long Clayton throw-in had been knocked on by Simpson. There were just two minutes left and hundreds of jubilant home fans who ran on to the park to celebrate Ally's goal had to be cleared before the match could be completed. So Blackburn had their derby revenge and were drawn to meet Sheffield Wednesday in their second semi-final in three years.

To say that Blackburn's league form had suffered during the cup run would be an understatement. Rovers had won only one league match since the turn of the year – against Manchester City – and now sat 14th in the table. The additional fixtures were not the only reason for the loss of league form as Matt Woods revealed in an interview with the *Lancashire Telegraph* on 6 January 2012, 'I should not really say it but we were not really interested in the league because the cup was everything back then. None of us wanted to get injured as we progressed to the latter stages.' He justified this by pointing out the club's league position was quite secure at the time.

Ally was enjoying his time in England and in his autobiography would later reflect, 'My five years at Blackburn were far and away the happiest of my playing career.'

In an interview with 1960's February edition of *Soccer Star* magazine he revealed he owned a car and was teaching his wife to drive. 'She'll be my chauffeur once she's passed the test,' said an apparently grinning Ally. The article was accompanied by pictures of a smiling Ally, Faye and a poodle which Ally had named Simon.

The dog had been Ally's 21st birthday present to Faye and was named after Simon Templar, the lead character in Leslie Charteris's *Saint* novels. Ally was an avid reader of the series of books before they spawned the popular television series starring Roger Moore a couple of years later. Ally also chose the name for their next poodle – Noddy.

He appeared to have no managerial ambitions at this stage when he revealed to *Soccer Star* that he would like to own his own business once his playing days were over, 'I haven't given it serious thought just yet awhile, of course; but that's what I'd like to do most of all.'

Mick McGrath recalls that, like many footballers even today, Ally had some pre-match superstitions. Around 2.30pm before a Saturday game the trainer would ask the players if they wanted a rub-down from a container of olive oil kept warm by the fire. McGrath recalls that 'Do you want a rub-down Noddy?' invariably generated the response, 'Who had the oil last?'

If McGrath had been the last to use it the answer was always 'No bloody way!' and Ally would only partake if one of the other players had gone first. This was because when once before he had followed McGrath with the treatment the team had lost the game.

The date of the semi-final was 26 March with 74,135 spectators inside Maine Road, the same venue as Blackburn's cup exit to Bolton two years earlier.

Derek Dougan was the hero with a goal in each half, his first after 13 minutes and the second after a pass from Ally put him through on goal. The match's controversial moment came when Alan Finney netted for Wednesday in the second half with the score at 1-0. But the linesman had already flagged team-mate Wilkinson, whose saved shot fell to Finney, offside.

Dougan – taken off injured near the end and who left the field in tears of happiness – inevitably grabbed the headlines but goalkeeper Leyland was also singled out for keeping Wednesday at bay after John Fantham had pulled them back into the contest at 2-1 on 76 minutes.

Although a virtual spectator in the first period, Leyland denied Wednesday the equaliser with saves from Finney (twice), Craig and Kave while McGrath played his part with a clearance off the line during the Yorkshiremen's late pressure against the ten men. Today McGrath sums up the semi-final with, 'We came through it 2-1 after a struggle.'

Now in the final they had a Wembley date with Wolverhampton Wanderers on 7 May. Rovers won their next league match against Chelsea but managed only one other victory that season against Leeds in their last home fixture. Since the start of 1959 Blackburn's league record read as played 18, won three, drawn two and with 13 matches lost. They finished the season in 17th place on 37 points, 17 behind runners-up and FA Cup Final opponents Wolves, who were just one behind champions Burnley. The loss in league form had seen Blackburn finish just three points ahead of relegated Leeds courtesy of that crucial home win on the season's penultimate day.

Ally had taken part in 39 out of the club's 42 league matches during which he had found the net eight times. He also played in all nine games of the FA Cup run, scoring twice.

The build-up to Blackburn's big day was soured to a degree when many season ticket holders were unable to purchase one of the 30,000 cup final tickets allocated to the club. There were rumours that club employees, players among them, were reselling tickets at a profit and in doing so depriving regular fans who had been saving hard for the trip to London.

Having won both league meetings between the sides Wolves were firm favourites for the FA Cup. In his match preview on the eve of the game, Gair Henderson told *Evening Times* readers, 'It will be the surprise of the year if they [Blackburn] follow up their victory over Tottenham by winning the Cup.'

But the Blackburn players were confident they could take the scalp of the league runners-up having disposed of the first- and third-placed sides earlier in the tournament in Burnley and Spurs. They were also aware that they were a better side than their league form suggested having chosen to concentrate on the FA Cup.

The Blackburn party were in London for the whole weekend with the players meeting up with their wives for the post-match banquet. The women had travelled down by train on the Friday and were due to attend a concert by Liberace that evening before retiring to the Flamingo Hotel on London's Half Moon Street. At 11.30pm on the Friday Bryan Douglas received word that his expectant wife had been forced to depart the train before reaching London having gone into labour. Douglas had to seek permission from the club on the morning of the final to visit her and their newly-born son, travelling by bus and Tube. He was instructed to report back to their Hendon Hall hotel before noon, when the team were setting off for Wembley.

Just as the team were boarding their coach the club chairman Norman Forbes received a written request from Derek Dougan for a transfer. Dougan, who was apparently having difficulty settling in the north-west, had sent the letter by registered mail the previous evening ensuring Forbes received it on the morning of the match. Dougan's team-mates, even Peter Dobing whom he lodged with, knew nothing of the letter until after the game.

With receipts of £49,815, the FA Cup Final crowd of 98,954 (just short of the 100,000 tickets sold) populated Wembley Stadium in sweltering heat. The match was live exclusively on the BBC where commentator Kenneth Wolstenholme dubbed it the 'white shirt final' in recognition of the crowd's attire. At the time supporters dressed up in their best clothes for the showpiece match of the season but the temperature was too great that day for many to don any form of jacket.

The heat affected the players too, sparking discussions inside the Blackburn dressing room. Mick McGrath remembers that there was some debate over the thick new tracksuits the team had been presented with which did little to boost team spirit. 'Some did and some didn't want to wear the tracksuits and some just wanted to wear the top,' he recalls. 'In the event we wore the whole lot.'

The destination of the cup was decided in a fateful four-minute period just after the half-hour point. Put through by Clayton, Dobing for once beat a well-organised Wolves offside trap and looked likely to score but panicked when shooting, allowing Malcolm Finlayson to gather the ball. The Wolves goalkeeper then cleared upfield and Barry Stobart swept the ball across the six-yard line where McGrath, attempting to clear for a corner, only succeeded in knocking the ball into his own net.

As if that was not bad enough Blackburn were reduced to ten men within 90 seconds when Dave Whelan went into a tackle with Norman Deeley only for the two of them to collapse on the pitch. Deeley got up but his opponent remained on the turf for some minutes before being stretchered off, leaving his side a man short. It was later revealed that Whelan's leg was broken in two places. Ally had looked promising up until then with a number of attacks but was switched to left-half after the interval to compensate for Whelan's absence.

During that interlude the Wolves supporters gave their rivals a rendition of 'Bye, bye Blackbird' with Blackburn substituting in the chorus.

Although Duncan's players dug in the loss of Whelan inevitably took its toll as the ten men toiled in the heat. Deeley scored a second on 68 minutes and netted again at the death to seal a 3-0 win for the Midlands side.

Some of the Blackburn supporters were heavily criticised for booing as the Wolves players collected the trophy – this was an unusual occurrence at an occasion when those attending were not only expected to dress up for the day but also behave in a sporting manner.

The FA Cup Final post-mortem called for a substitute to be allowed in the case of injury, referring to the Wembley jinx which had also seen the 1959 final marred in similar circumstances. Nottingham Forest goalscorer Ray Dwight had been carried from the play with a leg break at a similar stage in the game as Whelan, although Forest did go on to win the cup.

Ally won praise for his performance and was named as Blackburn's man of the match in some newspapers. In a piece headed 'A Very Dull Cup Final', Gair Henderson told *Evening Times* readers, 'McLeod…did the job of two men as a half-back and as an auxiliary in attack.' Rex Kingsley in the *Sunday Mail* offered the following, 'Ally McLeod was at his best in the first half when repeatedly he swept round Showell with that deceiving coltish style and laid on many chances. But in the second half, when playing at left-half, he was more defensive though always game for a sudden break through.'

Although hardly a classic it was looked upon as one of the poorest Wembley FA Cup occasions and towards the end of his commentary Wolstenholme advised viewers there were 'three minutes left of the most disappointing of cup finals'. The existing BBC recording of the match is not as bad as these reports suggest. The late third goal did flatter the winners a little although it is only fair to point out Wolves also had two disallowed efforts. From a Wolverhampton point of view their players never believed they got any credit for winning the cup due to the imbalance in numbers.

Dougan was anonymous in the match although this was more due to an injury, having pulled a thigh muscle against Birmingham the previous week, than any lack of commitment. Once his transfer request became known this led to a lot of bad feeling from the supporters, most of whom saw his actions as an act of betrayal.

Speaking to the *Daily Telegraph* years later, Wolves' Bill Slater commented of Dougan, 'I never expected to play in the cup final against someone who didn't seem to be trying.' Whatever the truth of the matter it is still difficult to imagine that a player would not want to give their best for the chance of a winner's medal. Certainly Bryan Douglas confirms Dougan's lack of fitness, 'He had a bit of a fitness test but it was left to him to decide how he was.'

Dougan said he was fit and wanted to play. Early in the match Douglas became aware of just how unfit he was. He recalls an attacking move when he came up against Slater and had to make a decision whether to take it round him or pass the ball, 'I pulled him over and slipped it through the gap to Dougan who could normally catch pigeons but it nearly went out for a goal kick. I knew then he wasn't fit.' Not only handicapped by Whelan's early departure, Douglas considers that due to Dougan's lack of fitness Blackburn were really up against nine men that day.

In his autobiography *Doog*, published in 1980, Dougan claims that he knew he was in trouble as soon as he set foot on the Wembley turf while also admitting to a 'pang of conscience'. Having had time to reflect on the timing of his transfer request he admitted it was an 'insensitive and indiscreet decision. The one action for which I reproach myself.'

In the player's defence it is hard to see how the transfer request could have affected the side's morale given that his team-mates were – and probably deliberately so – completely in the dark over it. A greater crime was probably Dougan's decision to play.

Douglas remembers the FA Cup Final as 'the biggest disappointment I had in football', and still believes Dougan should not have played. Whelan believes the manager should have left the player out rather than leaving the decision to Dougan himself. McGrath has a recording of the match which he has watched on one occasion but says that he, 'Wouldn't watch it again. As a team we were crap.'

A post-match meal and cabaret was arranged for the Ballroom in Park Lane where the team were joined by their partners. In the morning some of the players, including Ally, visited Whelan in hospital while the women surprised new mother Joyce Douglas. They then all met up and visited the famous Petticoat Lane market before getting ready for an evening at the theatre.

The Blackburn party had tickets for the audience of the hugely popular *Sunday Night at the London Palladium* variety show which was broadcast live on the ITV network each week. Compered by a young Bruce Forsyth, the format of the hour-long evening show was a mix of entertainment acts and games. On the bill that evening were singer Connie Francis, comedy band Sid Millward and his Nitwits plus a performance by the resident London Palladium Girls and Boys.

A regular feature on the show was 'Beat the Clock' in which couples tried to perform tricks or games within an allocated period (sometimes as little as 30 seconds, depending on the task) which the audience could monitor as a large second hand counted down on a huge clock face. A hooter sounded to signal the end of the allowed time. The final test was for a jackpot prize which rose by an increment of £100 each week until claimed.

With Ally considered the joker in the pack, he and Faye were nominated to represent the FA Cup finalists. Faye recollects the host prodding them around the stage to make sure they followed instructions and stood in the correct places. In one game Ally was supposed to help his wife collect four pound notes concealed within balloons inside a makeshift telephone booth. 'Ally nearly knocked it over shoving me into it,' Faye remembers. He was then caught in the act of trying to substitute a missing note with one of his own.

Unclaimed for a number of weeks, the jackpot prize had risen to £500 for which the couple were required to tilt the top of a table they were holding until a number of balls were pocketed in a special order. 'It had four tennis balls with pockets,' recalls Faye. The pressure was mounting and the clock was ticking. 'Ally got more and more impatient,' she laughs.

He eventually dropped the table, sending the balls bouncing all over the stage, and they left to a round of applause from the audience with Ally having made an appearance on both television channels during the course of the weekend. 'It was quite an experience,' Faye says, reminiscing that although they failed to collect the jackpot, which now rose to £600, Bruce had presented the couple with a trolley and a silver tea service which she still has.

Faye's mother later informed her that her neighbours had all been knocking on the door to advise of her daughter's television appearance.

On the Monday they all travelled back to Blackburn for a civic reception which Dougan attended even though his transfer request was by then public knowledge. 'We may not have the best team in the world, but we have the best supporters in the world,' Ally said as he addressed the crowd from the balcony of the Town Hall. Following a meal at the town's White Bull Hotel they all finally headed for home.

Dougan withdrew his transfer request soon afterwards and remained with the club for a further season before signing for Aston Villa. But his actions, along with the scandal over Wembley tickets, disgusted a large number of supporters who vowed never to watch the side again. This appears to have been reflected in attendances the following season when the team still had a decent cup run and performed much better in the First Division. In the FA Cup Final season the average home gate was 27,299 which was down by almost 8,000 to a figure of 19,343 by the end of the 1960/61 term.

Although the FA Cup Final was not shown live in Scotland, BBC viewers north of the border were able to watch a re-run of the full match on the Sunday afternoon. This prompted Margaret McAinsh of Glasgow to write to the *Evening Citizen*, again raising the question of international recognition for Ally, 'Why does Scotland seem to overlook ex-Third Lanark wingers? Bobby Mitchell was positively neglected by the selectors when at his best. Ally is at the right age for an honour.'

There was an amusing postscript to the disappointment of the FA Cup Final when some weeks later Ally received a letter from a Canadian millionaire who had been watching the television broadcast of the match. The woman had helped launch American Bob Hope's comedy career and having studied the player's motions and appearance was of the belief Ally had all the required characteristics for a future in comedy.

In the letter she offered to take him to the States for two years and pay him a couple of thousand dollars to train to become a comedian. When a flattered Ally wrote back explaining he was hopeless at telling jokes she still persisted but Ally always saw his future in football. With hindsight it is perhaps not beyond the realms of possibility that the Canadian had actually tuned into Ally's appearance on *Sunday Night at the London Palladium* rather than the FA Cup Final!

Following some less than flattering comments by the club chairman regarding the manager at the post-final dinner, reports of ill discipline among the players on a close-season tour of Germany increased the pressure which had been building on Duncan. But the Scot refused to resign and was eventually dismissed by the board. Duncan took the club to court and almost two years later was awarded £3,000 for unfair dismissal.

Although the players liked Duncan they rarely saw him except on a Friday morning or prior to a game, unless they had cause to go to his office. Of Duncan, McGrath remembers, 'A very nice gentleman who couldn't handle the players. We had one or two in the dressing room who would push it to the limit and he couldn't handle it. He was too nice for that.'

Whelan is less diplomatic on the subject, 'The manager was not really up for it. He had no control on us and we used to do really what we wanted. When we got to the final we stopped playing and were not really up for it.' Although he likely took advantage of it, Ally never forgot the lack of discipline in the side which at the very least contributed to the Wembley defeat.

There would eventually to be a happy ending for Whelan when, now a successful businessman and chairman of Wigan Athletic, he led his side out at Wembley in the 2013 FA Cup Final as massive underdogs against Manchester City. Wigan won 1-0 and a grinning Whelan was pictured on the pitch clutching the trophy some 53 years after his unfortunate accident on what ought to have been the highlight of his playing career.

Whelan and Ally had actually considered going into business together at one point and had their eye on a property which was for sale between Livesey Branch Road and Ewood Park. Whelan recalls the building housed a post office and a pub, 'I thought it was a good site and we could have developed it.'

But Whelan soon left the club for Crewe and their paths went in separate directions. After working on a market stall Dave opened a supermarket which led to a chain of Whelan's Discount Stores throughout England which he later sold for £1.5m. He then formed Britain's second-biggest sports goods retailer, JJB Sports, before buying Wigan Athletic in 1995.

Duncan's successor was Jack Marshall who had been in charge at Rochdale and was to earn the nickname 'Lucky Jack' during his time at Ewood Park. Blackburn got off to their usual good start in the league the following season.

Leading Manchester United 2-1 at Old Trafford in the last minute, Dougan, trying to appease the fans, completed a hat-trick and secured the points.

They went one better in the first home game by winning 4-1 against Nottingham Forest with Ally among the goals. This was followed by a defeat of the same scoreline at home to Tottenham who led 3-0 after just 17 minutes in front of a crowd of 26,819. Spurs would go on to win the league and cup double that season.

A mixed bag of league results, which seemed to be a pattern whoever the manager was, followed for Blackburn. Heavy losses including a 4-1 defeat at home to derby rivals Burnley and a 4-0 reverse at Manchester City were offset with wins over Fulham (5-1) and Chelsea (3-1) and another high-scoring match saw them go down 5-4 at Sheffield Wednesday.

On the very last day of 1960 Blackburn lost to Tottenham again – 5-2 – despite Douglas grabbing the first goal. They now sat right in the middle of the table with 23 points from 25 matches.

Blackburn had also taken part in the inaugural Football League Cup tournament that season, eliminating York City and Swansea Town, both away from home, and Rochdale at Ewood before exiting the tournament to Wrexham in a replay just ahead of Christmas.

Early in 1961 Ally had a part in the abolition of the £20 a week maximum wage restriction for professional footballers. At the time football was commanding huge attendances and it rankled with the players that they were unable to further benefit from the income they were generating.

A skilled workman in the early 1960s was earning around £12 a week with a labourer taking home seven pounds and ten shillings. But opportunities for players once their playing careers were over were limited in those days and there were many cases of ex-professionals falling on hard times after hanging up their boots. With the Football League's offer of an increase to £30, but staged over a five-year period, not likely to be improved upon, there were calls for strike action and three meetings were held between the players and the Professional Footballers' Association throughout the country during the second week of January.

Following overwhelming votes in favour of a withdrawal of the players' services for matches scheduled for 21 January at meetings in London and Birmingham, Manchester was the last venue where 344 players were addressed by the PFA chairman and Fulham player Jimmy Hill. Members of the press were excluded from the proceedings but were eagerly awaiting the outcome outside.

Before the show of hands was taken one of the players on the floor spoke up. His name was Ally MacLeod. Ally suggested that if the impending vote resulted in a majority in favour of strike action that the vote should be staged again with the waiting press reporters present so that they could gauge the players' mood.

Hill agreed and with only one objector to the motion, and after two and a half hours of waiting, the reporters were invited into the room. 'You are about to see history being made,' Hill told them before addressing the players.

A resounding 'no' was the response to 'Do you accept the offer of the Football League?' while a unanimous 'yes' was heard when the players were asked to back the PFA to continue negotiations on their behalf. It was the third question which made the headlines. 'Is there anybody in this room who would not strike on Saturday week if the Football League refuses to negotiate?' Hill asked. A unanimous 'NO!' echoed around the hall as the pressmen looked at each other knowing they had a real story on their hands.

Combined with the results of the southern and Midlands meetings, the northern players' vote ensured a majority of 712 in favour of a strike with only 18 against.

Protracted negotiations took place and on 18 January, just three days ahead of the proposed action, the Football League caved in and agreed to abolish the maximum wage.

Although it is possible to exaggerate Ally's contribution to the saga there is no doubt the decision to allow the press to see the depth of feeling the players had was an act of genius. Hill remembered this and always credited Ally's contribution, something Ally himself respected.

Back on the park Blackburn required a replay to dispose of Third Division side Chesterfield in the third round of the FA Cup and they needed another after they shared six goals with Bolton, with Ally contributing two. Rovers won the replay comfortably 4-0 only to go down 2-1 at Sheffield United of the Second Division in round five.

In the league Blackburn lost only twice between the defeat at Spurs in December and the end of the season although there were only five victories with ten draws. The club finished in a respectable eighth place with 43 points from 42 games played.

Ally continued to score goals, grabbing the winner in a 2-1 home victory over Wolves and the equaliser in the 1-1 derby draw at Burnley. He also netted twice in a 4-1 win over West Ham and scored Rovers' final goal of the campaign as his side went down 4-2 at home to Newcastle on 29 April, the last day of the season.

He finished with 11 league goals from 38 appearances having missed only four league games. He had also added those two FA Cup goals against Bolton to his account.

Although Ally did not realise it at the time not only was his goal against Newcastle his last for the club, it would also be his last game for Blackburn Rovers.

With the lifting of the £20 maximum wage restriction most players looked forward to the prospect of a greater lifestyle in the new season. A keen archivist of his career, Ally had kept a newspaper article in which Jack Marshall was quoted as saying that should the wage restriction ever be lifted then MacLeod would be worth double his wage.

When he was only offered an increase to £25, while Clayton and Douglas were given £40 and two others £30 per week, Ally stormed into Marshall's office wielding the likely forgotten-about press report. Marshall directed the blame at the club's board and advised Ally that he had 24 hours to accept the offer or he would be made available for transfer.

Bryan Douglas remembers that Ally had already felt the writing was on the wall for him prior to confronting Marshall, and he had urged his team-mate not to make a hasty decision. But Ally would not listen to his friend's advice. Always a man of principle, there would be no going back and he walked out of Ewood Park for the last time as a Blackburn player on 4 May 1961 although he remained on the club's books into the close season.

Now 30 and seeking a new club, he had become a casualty of the new wage conditions he had played a part in establishing. What now did the future hold for Ally MacLeod?

6

A Capital Captain

B Y the summer of 1961 Faye was expecting their first child which was a factor in the couple's desire to move back north of the border once things had turned sour at Blackburn.

With permission from the club Ally travelled back to Scotland in the middle of July for talks with Airdrie and Hibernian. St Johnstone had also expressed an interest in signing the 30-year-old at this point. The Broomfield club appeared to be winning the race for his signature, but the Edinburgh side, with Willie Ormond the last of the Famous Five yet to re-sign and looking likely to be moving on, took up the initiative.

With board meetings at both Easter Road and Ewood Park due on the afternoon of Monday 24 July there was a quick turn of events. A telephone conversation between Hibernian manager Hugh Shaw and Blackburn boss Jack Marshall resulted in agreement between the two parties for a £6,000 transfer deal.

Ally was then summoned through from Glasgow to hear the details before agreeing to join Hibs late that night. Things had moved so quickly that there had been no time to type up a contract and it was another few days before Ally signed the agreement which stated his weekly salary would be £27. During this impasse there were a couple of attempts to hijack the deal.

A telegram arrived from Blackburn with the words, 'Do nothing until you telephone the manager.' A curious Ally called Marshall to be told that the board had reconsidered and wanted to offer him £35 a week. Always a man of principle, Ally explained that he had made a gentleman's agreement to go to Hibs which he felt he could not go back on. 'If I'm worth it now I was worth it then,' he told Faye. 'Once he had made up his mind about something that was it,' she says of Ally, revealing a stubborn side to the joker.

There was then a telephone call from Stoke City manager Tony Waddington asking him to join, hinting that he would be playing with a very big name who he was on the brink of signing. Again Ally, not having yet put pen to paper, insisted that he had committed himself to the Edinburgh side and turned down the chance to go to the Victoria Ground. It would be another three months before

Waddington's perseverance paid off and Stoke's new signing was revealed as none other than Stanley Mathews.

Willie Ormond left Easter Road for Falkirk on 8 August for what was reported as 'a moderate fee'. It would not be the last time that Ally succeeded Ormond in their footballing careers.

Although the glory days of the Famous Five were now confined to history, Hibs were nonetheless still a decent side who had finished eighth in the First Division the previous season. Ally was joining a team which included former Newcastle goalkeeper Ronnie Simpson (who had been at Third Lanark with Ally and who would go on to win a European Cup medal with Celtic) and ex-Ranger Sammy Baird. They would be joined by Gerry Baker, the brother of Joe, in November.

Scottish football was in a much more healthy, competitive state at this time. While the Old Firm of Rangers and Celtic commanded the largest attendances by far, they were a long way from dominating the league before it transcended into a two-horse race from the mid-1960s onwards.

Rangers had been champions the previous season – but only by one point over Kilmarnock in a race that went to the last match of the campaign. Dunfermline Athletic (under an up-and-coming manager by the name of Jock Stein) were Scottish Cup holders having defeated Celtic in the final following a replay. Kilmarnock were runners-up to Rangers again in the League Cup while Hearts had won the First Division in 1959/60. And that very season of 1961/62 would see Dundee win the league and subsequently go all the way to the semi-finals of the European Cup.

Just before his debut Ally became a father when Faye gave birth to a son, Andrew, in Glasgow on 6 August. The MacLeods were now resident in Struma Drive in the Clarkston district of the city from where Ally travelled through to Edinburgh and back every day by train. His first game in green and white was at Perth six days after the birth in the opening League Cup game of the season.

The game with St Johnstone finished 1-1 which at least broke the pattern of defeat in Ally's three previous debut matches. It appears to have been a quiet start with *Edinburgh Evening News* reporter 'Outlook' observing, 'Ally MacLeod making his debut for Hibs hardly had a sight of the ball. The men behind were far too busy trying to check St Johnstone's eager attack.'

The *Evening Times* anonymous reporter was a little kinder, crediting him for his part in his new side's goal. Under the headline 'ALLY PAVES THE WAY' he wrote, 'New boy Ally McLeod shook off McFadyen for once, raced up the wing and sent over a perfect cross for Baxter to head home.'

With Partick Thistle due in Edinburgh in the League Cup the following Wednesday, 'Outlook', previewing the game, penned a more encouraging piece on the new boy, 'This will be Ally MacLeod's home debut. Badly supported at Perth, the former Blackburn winger did enough to suggest that he can play a valuable role in keeping the attack flowing when younger players are apt to hesitate.'

Hibs won by the odd goal in three and 'Tron Kirk' in the following day's *Edinburgh Evening News* had been keeping a close watch, 'Sammy Baird and Ally McLeod struck up a good understanding and the former Blackburn player impressed in his first home appearance. He and Baird on several occasions worked a fast one at a throw-in. McLeod would hold the ball as if he was ready to take it, then at the last second give it to Baird before dashing into the centre of the field for a quick throw. McLeod is going to upset defences with his long throw. Twice last night he caught the Partick defenders on the wrong foot.'

His first Hibs goal came in the return with St Johnstone at Easter Road on 26 August, the last in a 4-1 victory just as some of the supporters were beginning to voice their doubts. 'Our Own Reporter' in *The Scotsman* advised readers, 'McLeod placated those who had told him to "Go away back to Blackburn" with a neat score in the dying seconds.'

St Johnstone went on to win the group by twice beating Celtic (who amassed three points from Hibs) with only one team progressing from the group stage that season in a tournament that was forever tinkering with its format. Hibs finished third on six points, one behind Celtic with Partick bottom.

Hibernian were to give Ally a taste of European football when, almost immediately after he had signed, both Hibs and Hearts' applications to compete in the Inter-Cities Fairs Cup had been approved by the tournament's committee at a meeting in Basle on 29 July. All 28 applicants had actually been accepted as the organisers decided to enlarge the tournament.

Two days after the final League Cup match Portuguese side Belenenses visited Edinburgh for the first leg of the opening round on a Monday evening, 4 September. In a thrilling match the Scots found themselves three down at the interval but pulled it back to earn a 3-3 draw with Sammy Baird equalising from the penalty spot.

Ally won further praise for his performance from 'Outlook' in the *Edinburgh Evening News* with, 'This was Ally McLeod's best game since joining Hibs. He worked very hard in helping his defenders when the pressure was on.'

Shearer Borthwick, writing in the *Evening Times*, concurred, 'Ally MacLeod had his best ever game since joining the Easter Road team.'

Surviving Scottish Television footage of the match shows Ally not only helping out in defence but driving forward past the Portuguese defenders to mount a number of attacks.

Hibs went one better in Lisbon three weeks later and completed the comeback with a 3-1 victory.

The league season started with a 3-0 loss at Rangers followed by a 3-2 home win against Raith Rovers on 9 September. Hibs then lost 4-2 to Hearts at Tynecastle the following week where Ally opened his league and derby account with a headed goal. Another 3-2 home victory over Kilmarnock saw Ally grab his first home league goal for the Hibees on 23 September.

He seemed to be winning over the Edinburgh fans as 'Outlook' recorded in the *Evening News* where the reporter was clearly of the opinion he had surpassed his performance in the Belenenses game, 'Ally McLeod had the best game I have seen him play since moving to Easter Road from England, making a lot of the terracing critics change their tune.'

A poor run in the league saw heavy defeats at Dundee United and Partick as well as a home loss to Third Lanark. Following a draw with Aberdeen, Hibs sat third from bottom of the league with just seven points from ten matches at the start of November. The poor form prompted manager Hugh Shaw's resignation and after a failed bid to lure Jock Stein to Easter Road, Tranmere Rovers boss Walter Galbraith was appointed as Shaw's replacement.

That month the team went out of the Fairs Cup in the second round, losing 5-0 on aggregate to Red Star Belgrade, and at the start of 1962 Hibs were fourth-bottom in the First Division table having amassed 13 points from 17 matches.

Two Scottish Cup ties against Partick (with Thistle winning the replay) were punctuated by a scoreless draw when Rangers came to the capital on league business. During the match there was a debate between Ally and Rangers' Davie Wilson as to whose side had been awarded a throw-in. Ally told a *Scottish Daily Express* reporter that while they were both hanging on to the ball a whisky bottle thrown from the crowd had hit him on the back of the head. 'Next time I hope they'll leave something in the bottle before they chuck it at me,' he joked while apparently still rubbing the back of his head.

The cup exit was followed by a run of up and down league form. Hearts completed a derby double with a 4-1 Easter Road win while Hibs won at Falkirk by the same result.

After playing Ally in a different position during a friendly with Morton in February (arranged with both teams out of the Scottish Cup), Galbraith then switched him to wing-half in place of the injured John Baxter for the match at Dundee on 24 March. Speaking to the *Evening Times* in April, Galbraith said, 'Ally was not at all taken with the idea when I put it to him, but he's enjoying it now.' Galbraith made Ally captain shortly afterwards.

With Hearts also out of the Scottish Cup the East of Scotland Shield match was arranged for the day of the semi-finals, Saturday 31 March at Tynecastle. A disappointing crowd of only 8,000 saw Hearts continue their recent good derby form by winning 3-1, but Hibs had been handicapped and reduced to ten men from the 19th minute.

It was then that Ally MacLeod had collapsed in his own penalty area before being carried to the pavilion on a stretcher. The incident proved to be less serious than it looked and it was later revealed he had suffered from concussion. Ally was back training on the Monday and started against St Mirren in the league two days later.

Jimmy Wardaugh certainly approved of Ally's new role, telling *Evening News* (which now referred to him as Ally M'Leod) readers that he 'looks like being the find of the season in his new position. Since coming to Edinburgh Ally M'Leod has had a mixed reception...but in the last few weeks an old familiar cry has been heard – "Gie the ball to Ally!"'

The last match of the season, a 3-1 home win against already relegated Stirling, was watched by just 2,942 spectators. The two points secured that afternoon meant that under Galbraith Hibs had climbed to eighth place in the table, finishing with 33 points from 34 matches.

There had been renewed calls for international recognition for Ally with one anonymous article from his scrapbook appearing in a January newspaper along with the headline 'Scotland can use this "new" McLeod'. The writer of the piece considered, 'McLeod is at this moment the best left-winger in Scotland...if the Hibs player continues to dazzle as he has done recently against Celtic, Rangers and Partick Thistle, then he must be seriously considered as Scotland's No. 1 choice against England on April 14.'

The article concluded that his form merited at least an inclusion in the Scottish League v Scotland trial match on 5 February. The journal referred to his age as 'the ripe old age of 29' when in fact he was approaching his 31st birthday – a piece of misinformation by the subject perhaps? At any rate there was no call-up for either the selectors' trial or the England match and it finally looked as though international football had passed Ally by.

At the end of a five-match post-season Czechoslovakian tour in May, chairman Harry Swann told Ken Robertson of the *Scottish Daily Express*, 'He [Ally] has been a great captain on this tour, both on and off the field.' Another report on the tour also praised the new skipper and summarised 'not since the days of the "Famous Five" has there been such harmony in the camp'.

In truth the camp was far from harmonious. As the team were gathering in Edinburgh to set off for Czechoslovakia trainer Eddie Turnbull took a telephone call from Mrs Galbraith advising that her husband was ill and that he was to take charge of the team for the trip. There was already tension between Galbraith and Turnbull with the latter feeling he had been a better candidate for the manager's position after Shaw's departure.

In his autobiography Ally looks back on his time at Easter Road as 'not a happy episode in my career'. Elaborating, he felt that there was an element of politics between the trio of Swann, Galbraith and Turnbull who 'were often pulling in different directions'.

His family feel that Ally may have come to regret not taking up the 11th-hour change of heart by the Blackburn board. But then to go back on his word would just not have been Ally.

The team returned from Czechoslovakia unbeaten with three victories and two drawn matches. Some of the events in Czechoslovakia had descended into farce. For the opening match, one of three meetings with Spartak Pilsen, the Hibs team had to endure a long and bumpy coach journey from their hotel. They led 3-2 (two goals from Ally with one apparently a rocket shot, the other a tap-in) with six and a half minutes remaining when there was an unscheduled interruption.

The players, the 16,000 crowd and thousands of television viewers were stunned when play was stopped as a parachutist landed in the middle of the park. The stunt had been planned but scheduled to take place just as the match concluded as part of the national May Day celebrations. But there had been a delay with the game and with no communication to the parachutist possible the jump went ahead at the agreed time. The young intruder then apparently saluted the cheering crowd before walking off the pitch past the astonished players. The game was not restarted therefore depriving the home side of the opportunity to draw level.

More farcical scenes followed in the match with Vitkovic Ostrava. The start was delayed by some 20 minutes to allow a cycle race to pass through the stadium. After 67 minutes, and as a Czech player was being treated for an injury, a team of Swiss mechanics rushed on to the park and began to assemble a steel platform which supported a clock to welcome the racers. The end of the race had been synchronised to coincide with the match's final whistle but the delayed kick-off had upset the schedule. The protests of the players were dismissed and they were actually told to play around the structure! The game was soon abandoned with the Scots side 2-0 ahead, allowing the cyclists to take centre stage.

Ally played in every single one of Hibs' competitive matches that season – 34 league games, six in the League Cup, two Scottish Cup, and four Fairs Cup ties. He also turned out in the East of Scotland Shield match and took part in all nine of the club's friendly matches that term – including all five tour games in Czechoslovakia. The other friendly opponents were quality opposition such as Torino, Bolton, and Everton. That is a total of 56 matches at the age of 31 at a time when substitutions were not permitted in competitive matches.

The responsibilities of being a father did little to curb Ally's sense of humour and during those days in Struma Drive he got a colleague to telephone the mother of his old schoolfriend Junior Ormand. Margaret Ormand was told the call was from the electricity board informing she had to shut down all her appliances which she did before informing a grateful neighbour who was just about to cook dinner. Margaret did later find out Ally had been behind the ruse but was too embarrassed to tell the neighbour the truth.

Hibernian's qualifying group for the League Cup in 1962/63 was a tough one, placing them with favourites Rangers and two of Ally's former clubs, St Mirren and Third Lanark. Only one team progressed to the quarter-final stages of the tournament and a vital point dropped to St Mirren in a 3-3 draw proved costly as the Edinburgh side finished one behind Rangers in the table. Hibs had only lost one game – crucially at home to Rangers, despite grinding out a goalless draw at Ibrox.

Ally injured a knee in training the day before the Ibrox game and was ordered to take a complete rest during which he was unavailable for a month. By the time he was fit Hibs had started poorly in the league, having gone down at Clyde in their first match then lost 4-0 in the derby at Easter Road. Hibs had approached the new league season with optimism but that had all but evaporated after the derby as Hearts maintained their record of not having lost to their city rivals at Easter Road since September 1952 – a period of ten years during which Hibs had achieved one solitary draw and suffered a number of heavy defeats.

A point at Motherwell was followed by Ally's return for the next home match on 22 September. Tommy Preston retained the captaincy for the visit of Rangers with Ally playing in his old forward position due to other absentees. He did little to lift the gloom as his side ended up losing 5-1, leaving Hibs with one point after four games. The following week Ally regained the captaincy for another hammering as they conceded five without reply at Dundee United. During a miserable afternoon Hibs even missed from the penalty spot although they were already in arrears of three goals before Jim Scott's miss.

With Hibs bottom of the table John Ayres wrote in the *Edinburgh Evening News*, 'Hibs had hopes that McLeod would prove an inspiration to the team when he moved to left half last season, but his own and other injuries interfered with this plan at the start of the present term.'

A welcome break in the form of the Fairs Cup provided some cheer as Hibs put four goals past Danish side Staevnet without conceding in the first leg of the opening round.

The European result boosted Hibs and they beat fellow strugglers Raith Rovers at home the following Saturday before drawing their next two matches ahead of the return leg in Copenhagen which they won 3-2.

Wins over Queen of the South and Third Lanark saw Hibs claw themselves off the bottom but they then lost three consecutive matches. Following the third of these – a 2-1 reverse at Airdrie notable only from a Hibs point of view for a goal on his debut for youngster Peter Cormack – they had at least climbed to fifth from bottom and sat on nine points at the end of the third week in November.

The draw for the second round of the Fairs Cup had paired Hibs against Dutch side Utrecht and again their European form was at odds with their domestic performances. They came back to Edinburgh with a one-goal advantage from the first leg which left John Ayres exuding praise for the captain, 'Skipper McLeod set a splendid example from the start. For my money this was the finest game he has ever played in Hibs colours. Resourceful, strong and constructive, this lanky and sometimes almost ungainly player got right on top of his job and exercised complete dominance over a remarkably wide area in midfield.'

The job was completed with a 2-1 win in Edinburgh on a night which saw Ronnie Simpson saving a penalty kick and Hibs found themselves in the quarter-finals.

The club's last match of 1962 was a home game against fellow strugglers Clyde who were just a point behind them. Just a few days earlier many young boys' Christmas stockings would have contained a copy of *The Scottish Football Book* – now in its eighth year. Inside the annual Ally explained to editor Hugh Taylor how his playing style had adapted over the years, 'At Blackburn I just had to come back and help out the defence – otherwise I heard all about it. So it's no bother for me to play that role now that I'm back in Scotland. In my Cathkin days I would never resist the temptation of trying to beat a man. Now I only attempt a dribble if there is no-one to pass to.'

But it would not be his qualities of passing or defending which defined Ally's afternoon during the Clyde game. When Hibs were awarded a first-half penalty, following Scott's earlier miss at Tannadice, the captain elected to take it himself and scored easily.

Aided by an own goal, the Glasgow side then turned things around to lead 2-1 before Hibs were given a lifeline on 78 minutes. Following a goalmouth melee the referee awarded Hibs another penalty for handball, a decision which was met with vigorous protests from the Clyde players.

The *Sunday Post* report described what happened next, 'This time McLeod aimed for McCulloch's other side but the keeper dived and clutched brilliantly.' The match concluded with no further scoring, allowing Clyde to climb above Hibs who were jeered by their supporters as they left the field. A group of the unhappy fans stood outside the stadium's main entrance to vent their anger at the chairman with a chant of 'we hate Swann!' before being moved on by police. After attempting to deflect the blame on to the manager, Harry Swann, in language which would be most unwise for a club chairman today, was of the opinion, 'We can do without them. No club can afford to let the supporters dictate to them.'

Hibs now sat uncomfortably, third from bottom in the table and just a point better off than Airdrie who occupied one of the relegation positions.

The treacherous winter of 1962/63 played havoc with football fixtures meaning Hibs were unable to do anything about their league position until as late as 9 March when the elements allowed their home game with Third Lanark to go ahead. But even with MacLeod playing up front they could only manage a draw.

Airdrieonians pulled off a shock by beating champions Dundee who had just returned from Brussels where they had triumphed 4-1 over Anderlecht in the quarter-final of the European Cup. This allowed Airdrie to force Hibs into the second-bottom slot although the Edinburgh side now had three games in hand over the Diamonds due to the postponements. Hibs' only other action in 1963 had been a 2-0 victory in the Scottish Cup at Brechin City at the end of January on a pitch apparently covered by one hundred tons of sand, according to the *Evening Times*.

Hibernian then made the long journey to Spain for their Fairs Cup quarter-final meeting with Valencia. But their European adventure was all but over with the second leg a mere formality after they found themselves on the wrong end of a 5-0 result.

After a Scottish Cup exit at Dundee, Hibs travelled to Rugby Park to face Kilmarnock on 23 March. Ally was back in the left-half position but with Kilmarnock a goal ahead at the break Galbraith switched Ally and Baxter round in search of an equaliser. The change was to no avail and the game finished 2-0, leaving Hibs four points adrift of Clyde with Airdrie above them both. The Edinburgh men did have the advantage of four postponed matches in hand over Clyde but it was difficult to see where any points would come from.

Ally's name did not appear on the teamsheet for the midweek trip to Falkirk. Although he would not have been aware of it he had played his last match for Hibs at Rugby Park. He wore the green and white of Hibs on one more occasion – a reserve league match against Hearts at Easter Road on 9 April which finished 1-1. On that occasion Jim Scott did convert from the penalty spot. A team photograph appeared in the following day's *Evening News* in which Ally looks slightly out of place and possibly a little unhappy among the reserves.

In his absence Hibs closed the gap on Clyde to four points with one game in hand following a 3-3 draw in the derby match at Tynecastle at the start of May. They had led Hearts 3-2 after being two down at half-time. When Clyde lost at Celtic Park two days later Hibs' destiny was in their own hands. If they could win their last three matches they would finish above Clyde due to a superior goal average. But it was still possible that Ally's missed penalty in the drawn match between the teams in December could yet prove costly.

The players rose to the challenge and collected the required six points, bringing the season's total to 25. A 4-0 win at already doomed Raith Rovers in Hibs' last match on 18 May (the season had been extended to cope with the fixture backlog) virtually assured their First Division status. Now it was Clyde who had the game advantage but their last match was against champions Rangers whom they had to beat 9-0 to survive. Although Clyde did take the lead Rangers finished the game 3-1 winners.

A shock statement from Easter Road the following Friday advised that team captain Ally was one of three players being released on a free transfer after 22 months at the club. Following his ever-present record in 1961/62, Ally had played just 18 league matches in his second season at Hibs and scored just once – the penalty against Clyde. He had also appeared in five of the club's six Fairs Cup matches, two League Cup games and a friendly against Barcelona as well as coming on as a substitute in another challenge match with Dunfermline Athletic. This added up to 27 appearances for the season, just below half of his 1961/62 total.

Ally himself was on a short holiday in London with his old Blackburn teammate Bryan Douglas and found out the news by chance when he telephoned Faye in Glasgow that Friday just as he and Bryan were setting off to watch the England v English League match at Highbury.

He told the *Edinburgh Evening News*, 'I would like it put on record that Hibs have given me a very fair deal in not putting a fee against my name. I shall be sorry to leave Easter Road but I shall do so with happy memories.' He added that he hoped to remain in football for another season or two, possibly in a part-time capacity as he had recently resumed working as an analytical chemist.

Ally's recollections in his autobiography of the events surrounding his Easter Road departure are difficult to reconcile with much of the above. In the book Ally states that he was not happy with the way the club was going which led to him relinquishing the captaincy. He then claims to have been dropped for the next match against Raith Rovers before being reinstated just ahead of the kick-off and insinuates that the Rovers game was his last in Hibs colours. There is no indication of a date although he clearly did not feature in the last match of the season at Starks Park.

The home fixture against Rovers was on 6 October and he was certainly listed in the previous day's *Evening Times* as playing (Friday papers often published team line-ups in those days) and he took part in over a dozen matches thereafter. Ally also states that he had made a decision to retire once leaving Hibs which again contradicts his comments to the *Evening News* that he hoped for another year or two elsewhere in the game.

About the only detail the two versions agree on are that Ally had taken up a position as a sales representative with Bert Chemicals in Glasgow by the end of the season which would be consistent with his desire to finish his playing days in a part-time capacity.

7

Back to Cathkin

ALLY did not have long to ponder whether he had a future in the game. Almost as soon as his availability became public Third Lanark manager Willie Steel was in touch to see if he was interested in a return to Cathkin Park. Other offers came from Airdrie – who he had previously turned down in favour of Hibs – Queen's Park, who Faye remembers were rejected due to their amateur status and not paying wages, and Partick Thistle, who were also keen to win the player's signature. Having taken time to weigh up the options Ally signed for Third Lanark for the second time on 5 June.

Thirds had finished the previous season in a respectable 14th position, two places and one point ahead of Hibs. None of the squad Steel had assembled had been with the club in Ally's day and no less than 18 of the playing staff of 25, including Ally, had been signed that year of 1963. This influx of players saw references to 'new look Third Lanark' in the sports pages. Steel chose the experienced Ally to be captain of the side.

Fielding six recent signings and with new metal goalposts gracing Cathkin Park, Thirds kicked off the season on 10 August at home to Dundee in the League Cup with 4,783 watching. The new season did not dominate everyone's thoughts that day with the subject on most people's lips the robbery of the Glasgow to London overnight mail train two days earlier.

Jimmy Dunbar's match report for the *Evening Times* was headed 'McLeod Shines for New Thirds' and included the following, 'Old Third Lanark favourite Ally McLeod, the team's new skipper, immediately earned a welcome back cheer for a fine touchline run.' There was further praise with, 'McLeod who began his career as a schoolboy at Cathkin was a revelation on Thirds' left wing. With ten minutes gone he was the personality that shone.'

Ally's return was going well and it got even better after half an hour as the *Sunday Post* reported, 'New skipper Ally McLeod back on his old territory started off like an express. Slipping the ball to McMorran he raced downfield, collected the return pass, and gave Slater no chance with a fierce right foot which went in off a post.' The strike gave Third Lanark the lead but almost immediately Dundee levelled and went on to win the match through an Alan Gilzean goal.

The team began to gel and came away with a 3-2 win at East End Park, Dunfermline, in their next match although it was Dundee who qualified from the League Cup section. Thirds finished joint second with Dunfermline on six points, but with a poorer goal average having defeated bottom side Airdrie home and away.

The opening league fixture saw a quick return to Easter Road for Ally but it was not a happy one as his side went down 3-0. To complete the misery his old team-mate Ronnie Simpson saved a Jimmy McMorran penalty right at the end. Success followed in the next match with a home win over Partick where McMorran made amends by scoring twice including one from the spot.

In a high-scoring game, which was not uncommon at the time, Thirds shared eight goals at Celtic Park in an astonishing match watched by a crowd of only 18,528. Celtic led 4-0 after 14 minutes but Thirds rallied and the half-time score was 4-3. A Johnny Graham equaliser five minutes into the second period completed the scoring, leaving Thirds with three points from three games played.

After Ally had started the opening six matches at outside-left Willie Steel switched him to the left-half position he had filled at Hibs once the league campaign progressed. Steel's men then hit a bad run with just one point in their next six matches. Consecutive victories against Motherwell and St Johnstone plus a draw with Queen of the South saw the Hi Hi fourth from bottom of the division in mid-November.

A 2-1 home defeat at the hands of East Stirling on the last day of November saw Steel ring the changes for the trip to Falkirk on 7 December. Ally was dropped in place of youngster Jim Geddes, a recent signing from junior side Kilwinning Rangers. Geddes retained his place in the team for a period during which Ally broke a toe playing in a reserve game which meant he was unable to train.

Having fought back to fitness Ally made his first-team comeback at outside-left against St Mirren on 25 February 1964 after an absence of three months. Without him Thirds had slipped to third-bottom of the league and departed the Scottish Cup to Second Division side Stranraer, but a 4-2 win over Saints, with McMorran scoring all four, lifted spirits.

Aided by the transfer of Pat Buckley to Wolves, Ally and Geddes both retained their places in the side right through to the end of the season.

A visit to Motherwell on 29 February saw Ally's first and last league goal of the campaign. With Thirds trailing to the home side the *Sunday Post*'s anonymous reporter eloquently described the action, 'Thirds' late equaliser was a stunner. The move started when 'keeper Mitchell threw a long ball to Ally McLeod out on the left. With a swift scissors-like advance the four man attack was on 'keeper Wyllie's doorstep in a flash. There was McLeod in the middle. With a supreme effort he shook off a herd of defenders and piloted the ball into the net.' The game finished 1-1 with the *Sunday Post* headline highlighting the importance of the strike, 'This Goal Could Mean Safety'.

Two consecutive 4-2 victories over St Johnstone and Queen of the South kept the Hi Hi out of the bottom two although they lost their last three matches, one of them a 7-3 home defeat at the hands of Falkirk.

Third Lanark finished the season third from bottom having accumulated 25 points from 34 matches but with a nine-point cushion on second-bottom Queen of the South who went down along with East Stirling. But the spectre of relegation still hung over the club with the threat of the imminent reduction of the Scottish League by five clubs favoured by some.

The implications of the plan were that five teams in the lower division would drop out of league football with the bottom four of the First Division joining the lower tier to form two leagues of 16.

The proposal by Rangers was backed by 26 other clubs (one more than the minimum figure required to carry the motion) and vigorously contested by the five teams likely to be expelled plus Third Lanark. Four clubs expressed no preference.

There was still some football to be played as 1964 saw the revival of the old Summer Cup tournament which had not been played since 1945. Similar in format to the League Cup, it contained four groups of four First Division teams with the winners of each going through to the two-legged semi-finals with the final itself also contested over two matches. The Old Firm clubs both declined to take part while Second Division champions Morton replaced relegated East Stirling.

Third Lanark were drawn in Group Two along with Morton, Partick and St Mirren. Unbeaten in their first two matches, they then lost the remaining four to finish bottom of their section with three points. Ally missed the last two matches due to a broken thumb sustained 50 minutes into the home game against Morton on 13 May. The injury saw him walk off the pitch for the last time in a Third Lanark jersey before heading to the Glasgow Royal Infirmary where he was detained overnight. Faye remembers being astonished that a thumb injury could require a stay in hospital.

Ally had played a total of 34 matches for Third Lanark that season, 24 in the league, six in the League Cup and four in the Summer Cup with a goals total of two – one league and one in the League Cup.

Still threatened with the possibility of relegation, Third Lanark did not have their problems to seek during the close season. On 5 June it was revealed they owed £2,000 to the Inland Revenue after the club chairman and one of the directors had resigned following a meeting the previous evening. It was also announced that the club's development fund, which had contributed £8,500 towards ground improvements during the season, would be winding up.

On 10 June 1964 Johnny Graham was sold to Dundee United and the next day Ally and Bobby Dickson were offered free transfers by the club. Quoted in the *Evening Times*, Ally, apparently still suffering from the injury to his thumb, was said to be in 'slight shock' at the development, adding that he felt he still had some football left in him.

Thirds did receive some good news that summer when they and the other clubs opposed to the planned league reconstruction took their fight to court. Although the court did find in favour of Rangers the group then appealed to the Inner House of the Court of Session and the proposal was eventually dropped.

8

An Honest Man

FOLLOWING a meeting with Bobby Flavell on Monday 21 June, it was at Somerset Park in the seaside town of Ayr that Ally found himself playing football at the start of the 1964/65 season.

Again the newspaper reports contradict Ally's autobiography where he claims to have retired before being persuaded by Ayr United manager and former Scottish international Flavell to sign. Although he could have had no idea at the time, it was to be the beginning of an 11-year spell of employment at the club nicknamed the Honest Men after a line in Robert Burns's *Tam o' Shanter*.

'He was only going temporarily to Ayr when he first joined them,' says Faye.

Ayr were a part-time team with a part-time manager and had just finished 14th in the Second Division, or sixth from bottom, and often played to home attendances of under 500. Their previous season's average had been 1,187 – a figure inflated by a crowd of over 6,000 for one match against Morton. As at Thirds the club's part-time status allowed Ally to continue his sales rep job during the day although it meant a hectic schedule on training nights, not to mention trying to fit in his family life with Andrew now three.

Andrew never at any time felt neglected and has fond memories of a 'kind, loving, generous dad'. He remembers Ally reading him the 'most outlandish bedtime stories, totally made up as he went on'.

Ally's debut in the black and white of Ayr took place at Berwick and, predictably, ended in defeat just as all his first-team debuts had, including both with Third Lanark, with the exception of Hibernian where the match was drawn.

The 3-1 League Cup defeat at Shielfield Park was avenged two weeks later when Ayr hammered Berwick Rangers 6-0. Not surprisingly it was First Division Morton who progressed from the group with Ayr finishing third on five points, behind runners-up Dumbarton with Berwick rooted at the bottom.

Ally's league debut, playing at left-half, also ended in defeat in Coatbridge with Albion Rovers scoring both of the match's goals. Ayr went on to lose all five of their opening league fixtures before a 3-0 win against Dumbarton allowed them to get off the mark.

Three further defeats and a drawn match with Arbroath left the club joint bottom with Dumbarton on three points at the beginning of October.

After injury ruled him out for four weeks Ally came back into the side in the outside-left position for a home match with East Fife at the end of November where Ayr let a three-goal advantage slip and ended up sharing the points.

In December, Flavell unexpectedly quit the club. Although his parting gift was a 3-0 win against Stenhousemuir, the team were now anchored at the very foot of the table. His replacement was Tom McCreath who had been running the Ayr reserve team.

Early in 1965 Ayr disposed of Highland League side Keith in the Scottish Cup after a replay then gained a creditable 1-1 draw with First Division club Partick in the next round when Ally played his only match in the competition for his new side. It is difficult to think his presence in the replay would have made much of a difference to the scoreline of Partick Thistle 7 Ayr 1.

Ally's first-team outings continued to be limited after the turn of the year and the last of his 17 league appearances was in a home match where Berwick scored the only goal on 27 February. He had taken part in all six of Ayr's League Cup games and one Scottish Cup match that season, a total of 24 games without scoring.

Ayr finished second from bottom in the Second Division, a position they had occupied throughout much of the campaign. They finished five points clear of Brechin City having accumulated 24 points from 36 matches.

Still registered as a player and now 34 years of age, Ally remained at Somerset Park without kicking a single ball for the club in the 1965/66 season. The Berwick match in February proved to be his last first-team appearance although he would make an unlikely playing comeback more than 25 years later.

With McCreath in charge of the team Ally started to take a keen interest in the coaching side of the game. As one of the older and more experienced players he helped with the training in what would probably be best described as an unofficial coaching role.

The draw for the League Cup groups was seeded, guaranteeing that the Honest Men would be placed among other Second Division sides. Ayr ended up in the only five-team section meaning they played the other sides, Brechin, Forfar, Montrose and Stenhousemuir, just once.

They could hardly have performed better and won each of their matches to top the group before beating Third Lanark home and away for the right to face local rivals and First Division champions Kilmarnock in the quarter-finals.

Killie were at home in the first leg on 15 September with 10,798 crammed into Rugby Park. Ayr competed well for an hour before succumbing to a McIlroy shot and losing a second on 73 minutes, leaving the home side with a comfortable if not irreversible lead.

The loss of an early goal in the home leg seven days later meant Ayr had a mountain to climb but they fought back with goals from Murray and McMillan to give them a half-time lead on the night. A McIlroy header ten minutes from time sealed a 4-2 aggregate win for Kilmarnock but Ayr had far from disappointed the 8,495 spectators.

Things went well in the league. Following a home win over Dumbarton on 6 November, Ayr were sitting third in the division on 16 points having won seven matches, drawn two and lost two.

A narrow loss at Airdrie the following week was followed by a ten-match unbeaten run until Ayr fell at East Fife on 9 March. Still sitting third in the table behind Airdrie and Queen of the South, they knew promotion was a real possibility.

In the Scottish Cup, Highland League side Fraserburgh had been beaten in January before Ayr lost to St Johnstone after a replay.

McCreath's men lost just once more in the run-in, to Alloa, and clinched promotion with a point in a 1-1 draw at Arbroath on 23 April. Two days later the championship trophy was won after a 4-0 win at Stenhousemuir. 'Sporting smiles as wide as Somerset Park eleven happy Ayr United players left Ochilview Park on Monday knowing that they had clinched the Second Division Championship,' was how the *Ayrshire Post* match report began. It continued, 'The team slipped away from Larbert for a celebration champagne supper in Glasgow.'

They concluded the season having earned 53 points from the 36 matches. In the space of 12 months Ayr had risen from the bottom of the Second Division to a place in the top flight. Throughout that close-season of 1966 there was a definite feel-good factor around Somerset Park.

A civic dinner was held in the town's Station Hotel on Monday 16 May to honour the club's achievement. Shortly before and feeling that his job was done, McCreath had resigned and chairman Tom McGawn had offered the manager's position to Ally.

According to Ally's autobiography he was reluctant at first but accepted the post in which he would be limited by a squad of just 17 players, all of whom were under the age of 22. In a speech at the reception he told the audience, 'I would like to think of myself not as manager of Ayr United but of United Ayr.' Continuing, he acknowledged the goodwill expressed to the team from the town and its surrounding villages.

Ally told a reporter from the *Ayrshire Post* that he did not anticipate they would be champions of the First Division but he felt that Ayr could be considered a team of the future. The new manager's first activity in the transfer market saw forward Alex Ingram join from Queen's Park, closely followed by centre-half Stan Quinn whom he brought in from Shettleston Juniors at the beginning of July.

In an *Evening Times* interview several weeks later Ally gave Gair Henderson an insight into his management approach, 'One of the first things I did when I took over at Somerset Park was to tell the playing staff that no one who did not give me all he had in every game could expect to find a place in the team.'

On the eve of the new season an article appeared in the *Ayrshire Post* under the heading 'Ayr United's Track Suit Manager Sets the Pace'. It wrote, 'Ayr United may not be the most fashionable club in Scottish football but those who have been around Somerset Park in the last few weeks agree that there is no more energetic a manager in the business than Ally McLeod. He seems to thrive on hard work and determination. Every training night manager McLeod comes bustling into the ground from his job in Glasgow and changes into training gear – proof that United have a track suit manager who knows full well how to put his vast experience of the game into practice when it comes to getting his players ready for the months ahead.'

Faye looks back on those days in Clarkston when her husband had two jobs, 'I used to say this was halfway house. He'd come in the front door, have a cup of tea, then out the back door and away to training.'

In a good piece of business Ally arranged for his former club Blackburn to take part in a pre-season friendly at Somerset on 6 August. His old team-mates Ronnie Clayton and Bryan Douglas played that afternoon in front of a crowd estimated as 5,000. Blackburn won the match 3-1 with all the goals scored before half-time.

As a newly-promoted side Ayr again had the luxury of being drawn among the lower division clubs for the League Cup group. Berwick, Cowdenbeath and Raith Rovers were their opponents and as expected Ayr topped the group with seven points but only due to a better goal average than Cowdenbeath.

With the town buzzing the opening First Division fixture was a home match against Dunfermline on 10 September which attracted 5,401 supporters. A newly-recorded disc titled 'The Ayr United Song', by local musicians The Tommy Trousdale Set, was played over the public address system. Although there were no goals in the match the crowd went home happy according to the *Ayrshire Post*, 'Apprehension about what might happen against a team of Dunfermline's undoubted ability turned to scenes of joy as the fans gave United a standing ovation at the end of ninety all-action minutes.'

Like many of its contemporary journals the local newspaper was unsure of the spelling of the manager's name and on one occasion referred to him as Allie McLeod.

Rangers were Ayr's quarter-final opponents in the League Cup and were due at Somerset Park for the first leg on the Wednesday after the league opener.

When Ally heard that the visitors had returned a substantial number of their 10,000 ticket allocation he took it upon himself to contact the local police who agreed to allow cash payments at the turnstiles for the 6.15pm kick-off. This impulsive action helped swell the attendance on the night to 14,071.

Alex Ingram gave Ayr a sensational lead after just 15 minutes, an advantage that lasted until the hour-mark when Willie Johnston levelled. There were no further goals and Ayr were praised by the *Glasgow Herald*, 'The real surprise of the game was Ayr's ability, as a part-time side, to last the fast pace. Even when forced back into defence for most of the second half they still found sufficient energy and boundless enthusiasm to stage a number of troublesome attacks.'

Before the second leg Ayr narrowly lost the derby date at Kilmarnock which attracted a crowd of 9,094. They went down to a first-half Matt Watson header but were considered unlucky not to go home with a point.

Key to Ayr's gameplan for the second leg of the Rangers tie was the fitness of forward Ian Hawkshaw, who had been suffering from bruised ribs in the first encounter. If Hawkshaw was fit Ally planned to, 'Definitely have a go at Rangers. We have everything to win and nothing to lose.' More cautious tactics would be considered if Hawkshaw was not available.

The forward did play but Ayr's attacking approach was in vain when George McLean put Rangers in front after 16 minutes. Ayr players were accused of unsporting behaviour following the award of a penalty which delayed John Greig from scoring before McLean sealed a 3-0 win with his second.

The *Herald* considered the match 'a ragged ill-tempered contest...a game which left a bad taste in the mouth because of its roughness and reflected no credit on many players from whom better was expected'. Murphy and Monan of Ayr had their names taken by the referee along with Rangers' Henderson. Although no one from Rangers complained about Ayr's robust tactics it was highlighted that five injured players had reported to the Ibrox treatment room the next day.

Defending his players, Ally told Gair Henderson of the *Evening Times*, 'We did not play it rough at Ibrox. It was a hard game and tackles were tough and we had injured men in Quinn, McAnespie, Hawkshaw and Grant. It could be that some of the Ibrox fans mistook 100 per cent effort for rough-house stuff. I could not fault a single player for lack of effort. If enthusiasm makes them tackle hard you must remember football is a man's game.'

The following Saturday, Dundee United called at Somerset and were lucky to go in with the score 0-0 at the break. Hawkshaw had a goal ruled out for offside while the *Evening Times* report said, 'In a lightning blitz on the forty minute mark Ayr could have been three up.'

There was no hint of what was to follow as the visitors scored two goals within 30 seconds on 52 minutes before further scoring at will ended up with them 7-0 winners.

Further defeats to Falkirk, Hearts, Aberdeen and Celtic left Ayr bottom of the table on 25 October with just the one point gained from seven matches. Ayr were still getting praised for their attacking brand of football but were already in relegation trouble with the optimism of the close-season gone.

There was an improvement with three consecutive draws against Motherwell, Stirling and Dundee but they still sought that elusive first victory. 'What do we have to do to get our first win?' asked a frustrated Ally following the 1-1 draw with Dundee when visiting goalkeeper John Arrol had produced a heroic second-half display.

The breaks continued to desert the side with the *Ayrshire Post* headline 'A Clear Case of Daylight Robbery' summarising a 1-0 home loss to Airdrie at the end of November during which Ayr had no fewer than three goals ruled out.

One of these decisions provoked a supporter to jump the wall to remonstrate with Mr Syme, the referee.

A home loss to Hibernian in mid-December was the first of ten straight league defeats which saw Ayr marooned at the foot of the table with just five points from 23 games played by the middle of February. There was further embarrassment that month when the club lost to Highland League side Elgin City in the first round of the Scottish Cup.

Ally's side did manage one win in the league, but required a penalty kick to defeat St Johnstone 1-0 at home on 8 April.

Ayr supporters must have experienced contrasting emotions the following Saturday as the loss of four goals at Easter Road confirmed their club would be back playing in the Second Division the following season.

The Hibs v Ayr match was one of only two First Division games taking place that Saturday with the Home International between England and Scotland taking centre stage at Wembley. Scotland recorded a famous 3-2 victory over the world champions to ensure celebrations in most parts of the country.

Ayr's final home match was contested with the other relegated side, St Mirren, and perhaps not surprisingly ended with neither being able to find the net. The crowd was under 1,000 – 946 to be exact – some 4,500 down on the opening day of the season, although the match was competing with the Scottish Grand National at Ayr Racecourse the same afternoon. The draw boosted the points total for the season to just nine collected from a possible 68.

The latter half of 1966/67 is perceived to be something of a golden age in Scottish football. Not only did Scotland end England's 19-match unbeaten run, becoming the first team to defeat them since they won the World Cup, but club football also enjoyed good times.

In May, Celtic became the first British side to win the European Cup with Rangers almost making it a Glasgow double only to lose in extra time to Bayern Munich in the European Cup Winners' Cup Final the following week. Kilmarnock also performed well on the continental stage, going all the way to the semi-final of the Fairs Cup where they lost to Leeds United.

But if the season had been unkind to Ally's Ayr their experience was nothing compared to the fate of his former club Third Lanark. Following an enquiry by the Board of Trade into financial irregularities amid mounting debts, the club was declared bankrupt in June 1967 and vanished from Scottish football forever.

Ally took the news badly. 'He was heartbroken,' Faye remembers. 'That was his team, and his father's, and he was very sorry.'

9

Bouncing Back

TO suggest that Ally's first season in management was anything less than poor could be interpreted as rather kind to say the least. With relegation, one solitary league victory and Scottish Cup defeat to a non-league side, disastrous would perhaps be a more appropriate adjective.

But there had been some good signs early in the season and there was no doubting the enthusiasm, optimism and commitment shown by the inexperienced manager. With the club not in a particularly healthy state at the time finances may have played a part in the decision, but the chairman made a choice to stick with his part-time boss for another season.

Again Ayr topped their all-Second Division League Cup group above St Mirren, Stranraer and Berwick by winning five of their six matches, losing only at Berwick.

They won their opening league match 3-1 against Clydebank at Somerset Park with 3,573 in attendance, then drew 3-3 in an exciting game at St Mirren where all six goals came in the first period.

Their opponents in the quarter-finals of the League Cup were Celtic, who had recently added the European Cup to the three available domestic trophies. Ally was realistic when chatting to the *Evening Times*'s Gair Henderson ahead of the first leg. Presumably thinking of Second Division Berwick Rangers' shock Scottish Cup defeat of their bigger Glasgow namesakes earlier that year, Ally reasoned that upsets were possible in one-off cup ties but not over two matches. 'We will give Celtic a darn good run for their money,' he began before acknowledging, 'Few teams could possibly expect to beat Celtic over 180 minutes – and we are certainly not one of them. What we hope to do is give the crowds who will watch us two nights of entertainment.'

Jock Stein's men led 3-0 at Celtic Park before two Bertie Black goals pulled Ayr back into the tie at 3-2 on 67 minutes, but the final score of 6-2 ensured the second leg would be a formality.

Celtic suffered three setbacks before the game at Somerset, losing an Old Firm league match, drawing at home with St Johnstone and going down in the first leg of a European Cup tie to Dynamo Kiev in Glasgow while Ayr had picked up three points in the Second Division. This form gave Ayr a glimmer of hope of at least salvaging some pride and Ally's men held out for 67 minutes in a match they eventually lost 2-0.

Concentrating on the league programme Ayr lost only three of their next 12 matches and sat third in the table at the end of 1967, but defeats by St Mirren (3-0) and Queen of the South (4-0) on the first two days of the New Year saw them slip to fifth place. At the end of January they exited the Scottish Cup to second-placed Arbroath and a bad run from March into April saw the Honest Men pick up just one point from five matches. Those defeats to Queen's Park, Forfar, Stranraer and Brechin all but ended the club's promotion hopes.

The fifth-placed finish was nonetheless a reasonable achievement in Ally's second season although St Mirren, who had come down with Ayr, did achieve an immediate return with Arbroath also promoted.

After two seasons in management Ally was gaining in experience and was not short of ambition. Having had a taste of the First Division he was desperate to get Ayr back among the big boys again. If any of the players had doubts over their boss's ability or judgement they were kept to themselves following one incident during Ally's early days of management.

After pinning the team sheet for a match on the wall at training one evening Ally left the dressing room but overheard one of the players complain that he couldn't believe one of his team-mates was not on the list. Ally promptly strolled back in and scored out the name of the complainer before adding in the name of the player who had previously been left out.

In spite of having two jobs no one could ever accuse Ally of neglecting his family. In 1964 Faye had given birth prematurely to their daughter, a sister for son Andrew. Initial fears that the child may not survive proved needless but led to her being christened Gail. The reasoning behind this is down to the father's sense of humour when during the worrying period Ally had said that their daughter had put the wind up both of her parents. I am sure if he thought he could have got away with spelling her name Gale he would have done just that! Two years later the family was complete when another son, David, arrived.

Andy has fond childhood memories of his father who was a practical joker in the household. He remembers the rest of the family checking every door they passed through should it be slightly ajar as one of Ally's favourite tricks was to balance a small beaker full of water ready to soak them if disturbed.

Gail recalls, 'Even all our friends who came to the house knew to look above the door if it was opened that tiny wee bit, as there would be a lid off a hairspray or something on the top of the door. That and an apple pie bed. He used to do that quite a lot as well.'

The trick with the bed was to fold the inner sheet back on itself halfway down so that the unsuspecting victim was unable to get into it.

Having worked hard himself Ally always made sure that his family enjoyed a good summer holiday but always in June to allow him to be back in time for pre-season training. Andrew recalls one such holiday during the late 1960s when the MacLeods and near neighbours the MacDonalds travelled to Spain together.

No one who had lived through the bombings of the Second World War, as Ally had done, was likely to forget the horrific experience and he was apparently not too pleased to learn a number of German tourists were resident in their hotel. By the end of the vacation that had all been forgotten as Jurgen, Peter and their partners became great friends with the families from Glasgow. They kept in touch for many years and Andrew remembers them telephoning every Hogmanay to wish each other a happy New Year.

Andy also recalls his father shared a characteristic which many football managers carried in to the home – he absolutely hated losing at anything. Be it tiddlywinks, Monopoly or one of the more sporty pastimes such as tennis or football, Ally did not like even his own family members to get the better of him. At Christmas any new game destined for one of the children would be tried and tested by Ally first of all to ensure none of his offspring gained the upper hand.

The changing of rules was not beyond Ally either if things were not going his way. 'If we played him at anything you had to earn your victory,' Andy remembers. 'You could be beating him at tennis and he'd get into your head and I'd end up losing focus, throwing my racket around and losing. It didn't matter if it was Gail, David or I. We would play rock, paper, scissors best of five then if he was losing it would be best of seven or nine until he won!' Even when his grandchildren came along Ally still continued in this vein.

This shifting of the goalposts was consistent with his football training as well. It was not unusual for participants in training matches to suddenly be ordered to switch to the opposing team and Ally was the only person who seemed to know the correct score. Sometimes three goals would be awarded if a header was scored, so a degree in mathematics was required to keep track. This confusion was deliberate and, so Ally claimed, a lesson in psychology to help players accept disputed refereeing decisions.

Defender Dick Malone reflects on the training sessions as, 'Fantastic fun, but tough. Everything was done with the ball.' He recalls Ally's advice that you had to be able to control the ball when tired. Malone also remembers how each of the players would be required to practise shooting as Ally was of the belief that due to his attacking philosophy any one of them may get an opportunity during the game. 'If you don't attack you don't win!' he continually drummed into the players.

Malone says his own accuracy improved due to one training innovation. Two boards were placed inside one of the goalmouths with a gap of two feet between the posts and the boards. It was these gaps that the players had to aim for during shooting practice.

The new campaign of 1968/69 could not have started better for Ayr, who won their League Cup section containing Stirling, Arbroath and Cowdenbeath by dropping only one point. They came out of the traps fast in the league by winning their first two matches before facing Clyde in the quarter-finals of the

League Cup. Clyde were a decent side who had finished mid-table in the First Division the previous term and were obvious favourites to beat the part-timers and progress to the semis.

Playing at home first a bumper crowd of 7,942, Ayr's biggest of the season, watched as Clyde took the lead on 27 minutes. Just that Ian Stewart goal separated the sides as the contest entered its closing stages which signalled a period of sustained pressure on the visitors' goal but 1-0 it finished.

Ayr were given credit for their performance in the second leg with Clyde not scoring until six minutes from time through Harry Hood. A second goal at the death from Stewart 'rather over-emphasised Clyde's superiority' according to the *Glasgow Herald* and the 3-0 aggregate score, while convincing in itself, did not tell the full story.

Ayr's league form had stuttered between the two Clyde matches and they went down 4-1 at Motherwell, followed by a 5-1 reverse at home to amateurs Queen's Park. They then suffered only two more defeats that year and finished 1968 with five straight wins which left them sitting fourth in the table and ready for a promotion push.

A 7-1 home victory over Stenhousemuir in October proved to be the biggest win of the season during which both Ingram and Malone – benefiting from that shooting practice – helped themselves to hat-tricks.

But there were doubts within the local community as to the ambitions of the club which stemmed from a comment the manager had made earlier in the season to the effect that he would be happy to see Ayr finish near the top of the table before making a sustained challenge for promotion the following year with a team more likely to survive in the First Division.

Commenting on what it referred to as 'the persistent and annoying "whisper" that goes round the town that Ayr United just do not want promotion', the *Ayrshire Post* challenged the club's directors to respond to the matter in their first edition of 1969.

It was not the directors but the club's clearly angry manager who replied using phrases including 'completely untrue', 'quite fantastic' and 'utter nonsense' to dismiss the speculation. 'I would not be the manager of any club – including Ayr – that took such a line of policy,' he told the newspaper.

A home win over Queen of the South saw Ayr into the second round of the Scottish Cup where they lost 6-2 at Dundee United. The good spell of league form continued and the winning run extended to a remarkable 11 matches before they were held to a goalless draw at Stirling Albion on 8 March. This was championship form but unfortunately for the Honest Men, Motherwell and Stirling Albion occupied the promotion places and looked in no mood to surrender.

On the last Saturday of March, Motherwell, on 51 points, looked uncatchable and Ayr, having dropped a point at Hamilton, were now five adrift of Stirling Albion who were on 46. East Fife were very much in the equation on 40 points, one less than Ayr who crucially had three games in hand over Stirling with eight left to play.

The good form continued while Stirling squandered valuable points. A point at home to promoted Motherwell on 23 April saw Ayr finally climb to second in the table. They now required just two more points to ensure promotion as they faced Queen of the South in Dumfries. Their promotion rivals were playing their last matches that day but Ayr still had the advantage of two rearranged fixtures to follow.

Leading Queens 2-0 early in the second half, it looked as though they would get their rewards that day until Ayr's world fell apart as a Jimmy Welsh hat-trick turned the game around and despite an all-out assault on the home goal in the final minutes Queens held on for the win.

But fortune smiled on the Honest Men when, having come off the park, news came through that both Stirling and East Fife had also lost on the day. That left Ayr a point clear of both clubs and promoted with the luxury of two meaningless matches remaining.

Both outstanding fixtures were won 1-0, leaving Ayr on 53 points from 36 games. Just for good measure the club had also won the Ayrshire Cup in April by winning 3-1 at First Division Kilmarnock.

Ally took his family on their annual June holiday before planning for the new season, desperate to learn from the mistakes of two years earlier and avoid relegation.

Still managing in a part-time capacity Ally was now employed in a sales position during the day with a different chemical firm, Hardman and Holdman.

When called on by the company to entertain an American businessman, one of their biggest clients, Ally duly wined and dined him at the Buttery, one of Glasgow's top restaurants. Having been well catered for the visitor was in fine form by the small hours and had a favour to ask of his generous host. The American had always harboured an ambition to stand in the waters of Loch Lomond singing 'The Bonnie Banks' and this could be his one chance. Although it was by then very late and far from Loch Lomond, Ally offered to take him there, conscious of the importance of the client.

The two grown men took off their shoes and socks and rolled up their trouser legs before wading into the water. There they stood in the middle of the night with arms around each other belting out 'The Bonnie Banks of Loch Lomond' into the dark. Ambition achieved, the client retired to his room at the MacDonald Hotel in Newton Mearns and returned to the States a happy man where he would surely boast that he had sung in Scotland's famous Loch Lomond. He never did find out that he had been no further than Rouken Glen Boating Park in Newton Mearns!

Ally had a squad of 23 part-time players to choose from at the start of the 1969/70 season. If all were fit there was just enough personnel for the first and reserve teams with the luxury of one substitute.

Before the glamour of First Division football returned to Somerset Park the usual formalities of the League Cup qualifiers took priority. For the fifth consecutive season Ayr won their group, containing Queen of the South, Queen's

Park and East Stirling – losing only at Queen of the South in the last game. This gave Queens nine points, equalling Ayr whose superior goal average saw them edge through to the quarter-finals where Dumbarton lay in wait.

Ayr were at home for their First Division opener with Hibernian the visitors on the last Saturday of August 1969, seen by 6,955 fans. The Edinburgh side had finished third in the First Division behind the Old Firm clubs the previous season and were again expected to do well.

But it was the part-timers who attacked from the start and they held a two-goal advantage at the break. An Ingram goal in the second half completed a 3-0 win, and Ayr had the perfect start to life in the First Division. It was a fantastic result and boosted the players' confidence no end.

A draw at Dunfermline followed by a narrow loss at Dundee led to the first leg of their quarter-final at Dumbarton. The League Cup tie was Ayr's tenth match of the season and the same 11 players took to the field that had started every game. A Davie McCulloch goal set Ayr on their way after just five minutes and the team finished comfortable 4-1 winners, already looking good for a semi-final place.

Interviewed by Peter Hendry in the next day's *Evening Times*, Ally told the journalist it would be business as usual for the forthcoming visit of Rangers, 'The team are playing well and with no injuries I have no intention of making even one change for Saturday. Why should I?'

But he did sound a warning should complacency start to creep into any of his players, 'If any player in the reserve team shows consistently good form and his opposite number in the first team shows a falling off in form I then have no hesitation in making a change for the good of the team.'

Speaking to Alex Cameron of the *Daily Record* on the eve of the game Ally was in a confident mood, 'We have a good enough side to do the job. They will take the field with attack in mind.'

The match, on Saturday 13 September, was not an all-ticket occasion which helped boost the attendance with the gates closed at ten minutes to three. The crowd figure was given as 25,225 which was slightly above the ground's capacity and is still to this day Somerset Park's record home gate.

With the emergence of the teams hundreds of youngsters climbed over the boundary wall and were allowed to sit near the touchline just a couple of yards from the play. There were clearly safety concerns as Ally and the referee were seen to be having a deep discussion with a police inspector just ahead of the kick-off. The match started five minutes late but the home side were still a goal up through Quinton Young before 3.15pm. The Ayr fans were delirious when Jackie Ferguson doubled the lead after just 13 minutes.

Still Ayr adhered to the manager's attacking policy and might have added to their tally before Colin Stein scored in the last minute to make the final score 2-1.

Dick Malone remembers that much of Ally's pre-match talk had centred around Jim Baxter. Baxter had just returned from Nottingham Forest for a second spell at Ibrox and Ally stressed the importance of minimising his influence.

Malone remembers Ally as a 'brilliant strategist' who 'always had a plan to beat the opposition'.

Ken Gallagher's assessment in the *Daily Record* was, 'Ayr had an appetite for the game which their mighty rivals did not.' Speaking to the *Evening Citizen*, Ally perhaps surprisingly was not getting too carried away, 'I'm very happy with the team's performance – naturally. But we have a long season ahead yet.'

Ayr now sat sixth in the league table after four matches, above both Rangers and Celtic who had lost at home to Hibs that same day. The top six were Motherwell, Morton, Dunfermline, Hibs, Aberdeen and Ayr.

Ally's men were brought down to earth seven days later by losing the derby match at Kilmarnock before completing the job against Dumbarton with a 1-0 victory to ensure that they were through to their first ever semi-final. Despite the formality of the match there were still no changes to the personnel with the same 11 of Stewart, Malone, Murphy, Fleming, Quinn, Mitchell, Young, Ferguson, Ingram, McCulloch and Rough taking the field. The benefits of playing a settled team was something Ally claimed to have learned from Johnny Carey at Blackburn. Two points were collected against Morton followed by a defeat at the hands of Aberdeen in which Ally had now fielded the same 11 players for all 15 matches since the start of the season.

Ayr confidently approached their League Cup semi-final at Hampden Park on 8 October. Their opponents were Celtic who were giving a promising 18-year-old his third first-team appearance. His name was Kenny Dalglish.

The manager exuded confidence when speaking with Gair Henderson in the *Evening Times*, 'I can tell you this – we have no fear of Celtic. The fact that they scored seven goals against Raith Rovers on Saturday does not worry us. We hope they have the idea that this will be another easy game.'

Quoted in the same article, Celtic manager Jock Stein praised Ayr's achievements so far, 'Ayr are entitled to feel confident. They have beaten Rangers, Hibs and Morton so they must be treated with respect.'

Inside the Hampden dressing room shortly before the teams were due to take to the field, Ally locked the door and slipped the key into his pocket. 'Whatever happens we are not going out first,' he instructed his players, keen to exploit any slight psychological advantage such as keeping the opposition waiting.

A crowd of 35,037 witnessed a classic cup tie in which David Potter in his book *Celtic in the League Cup* concedes of Ayr United, 'They almost made the soccer sensation of the decade.'

Bobby Rough headed the underdogs into the lead just after the half-hour only for John Hughes to level for Celtic four minutes from the interval. Stan Quinn felt Willie Wallace's boot connect with his face two minutes later and once inside the dressing room discovered he had lost 11 teeth. The manager forbade any medication in case it affected the centre-half's timing but Quinn was determined to play on regardless.

It was a tragedy for Ayr when they went behind to a penalty early in the second half which Gemmell blasted home but a McCulloch goal squared it, taking the tie into extra time. Sensationally Ayr took the lead again after just five minutes with Rough once more the scorer. Ally was to later recount that he turned to coach Sam McMillan in the dugout and said, 'It's okay. Even Celtic can't score two goals against our defence now.'

Just three minutes later it was all square again courtesy of a Bertie Auld strike, prompting McMillan to assure the manager, 'It's all right, they can't score any more against us!' Indeed neither side did score again and Ayr lived to fight another day.

Eight years old by this point, Andy MacLeod remembers being allowed to stay up late that night to watch the match highlights on television in the family home in Clarkston. Sitting in his pyjamas he was surprised when his father came in with the entire Ayr United team keen to share in the viewing, having parked the coach at the end of the street. 'That's when I realised he didn't do the ordinary,' Andy reflects.

In his *Daily Record* report Alex Cameron described the match as, 'The most dramatic soccer Hampden Park has seen for a long time.' Stein was quick to praise his opponents and was quoted in the *Record*, 'It would have been unfair had they lost.'

Quinn made a visit to the dentist on the Thursday but was told his dentures would not be ready until the Saturday morning. He arranged for them to be delivered to Queen Street station in Glasgow and collected them before boarding the Dundee train with the rest of the team for the game at Tannadice that afternoon.

For the replay the following Monday the same 11 were named although Rough had missed the Dundee United match on the Saturday due to a foot injury sustained in the 3-3 draw. This was the first change to Ayr's line-up since the start of the season.

There was no let-up in Ally's pre-match mood as Gair Henderson found out, with the manager telling the reporter, 'We'll go one better this time. We'll win – and there will be no need for extra time…Celtic will be out.'

He was a little more conservative with George Aitken of the *Evening Citizen* and expressed concern as to how the crowd may affect his players, 'It'll be the biggest we've ever played in front of and I hope it inspires my fellows, though you can never tell.' Contemplatively he added, 'I don't think we'll give them as much room as the Italians,' referring to Celtic's recent European Cup match against AC Milan.

Indeed the attendance had increased to 47,821 which in itself was a tribute to Ayr's performance in the first game. Incredibly the part-timers took the lead again through Ingram on 14 minutes. Eight minutes later Harry Hood, the former Clyde player, scored for Celtic and, following poor defending by Quinn, Steve Chalmers made it 2-1 after the interval. Ayr refused to give up and only a breathtaking save from Simpson denied them extra time.

The *Ayrshire Post* described the incident, 'Cutty Young set up the move on the right with a pass to Jackie Ferguson who pushed the ball to Ingram. The centre flicked the ball for the corner of the net for Simpson to bring off an amazing save with a leap to his left. Landing on the point of his shoulder the 'keeper rolled over in agony.'

The save came at a cost as Simpson – a former team-mate of Ally MacLeod at Third Lanark and Hibernian – was carried off with a dislocated shoulder which effectively ended his career. Just two days earlier he had kept a clean sheet at Airdrie on his 39th birthday. Gemmell took over in goal but try as they might Ayr were unable to exploit this weakness and there was no further scoring and no fairytale ending. 'We knew we had to bomb Gemmell. The lads panicked in trying to do so,' Ally later told the *Daily Record*.

'Ayr Go Out in a Blaze of Glory' was the headline in Hugh Taylor's *Record* summary where he praised the part-timers' style of play. 'Once again United's reliance on neat triangular on-the-ground football and their willingness to have a go turned this semi-final into a blazing advert for Scottish football.'

The Ayr players were told not to report for training until the Thursday evening (Tuesday was the other training night) to allow them some recovery time. Ever the optimist, Ally turned his attention to the next match and told the *Record*, 'I don't just want to finish in the First Division. I want to finish well up the table.'

Ally travelled down to Lancashire the following Monday to take part in his old friend Bryan Douglas's testimonial match at Ewood Park. Ally turned out for Bryan's Eleven against an International Eleven, lining up with many of his old team-mates including Leyland, Dobing, Vernon, Clayton and McGrath. The opposition included World Cup winners Geoff Hurst, Bobby Moore and Martin Peters as well as Francis Lee and Colin Bell which gives an indication of how highly Douglas was regarded.

There was never any likelihood of Ally not accepting his friend's invitation because, as has already been demonstrated, loyalty was something that he prized very highly.

Ayr's league form proved to be indifferent as they beat Clyde, Partick and Dunfermline but lost to St Mirren, Airdrie and in the return game at Hibs. By the end of 1969 Ayr sat in 11th place with the Old Firm having reclaimed their top-two slots.

'He had the whole town buzzing,' Dick Malone remembers today of Ally. 'He had a knack about him.' Malone's memories are of a 'very upbeat' manager who always had a positive attitude, always smiling, even first thing in the morning, but someone who could be strict when required. 'He was no mug in that department,' recalls Malone. 'Although he was easy-going, when he needed to…it was "hey you will!" and that was it. Everyone knew where they stood with him.'

Years later in 1975 Ally told the *Sunday Mail*, 'I never served under a boss who enforced the law as it should be, and when I became a manager I was determined not to make the same mistake.'

Malone insists that even at his angriest he never heard Ally swear, 'His favourite word was "Whambamaroo". Another often-used word in the MacLeod vocabulary was 'baloney' which substituted for more colourful expletives.

Ayr fans had something to cheer early in the new year when they defeated Kilmarnock on 3 January at Somerset. They came from behind to win 3-2 with a late McColl clincher in an exciting match watched by 12,722.

The Scottish Cup proved to be less eventful than the League Cup as Dundee United scored the only goal of the match to send Ayr out in the first round. Ayr lost 3-0 in the league at Rangers and were defeated twice by Celtic but overall had coped well in their first season back in the top flight. They won their last match of the season, 2-1 at home to Partick, and finished in 14th place on 30 points from 34 matches.

Ally had instilled in his players a great self-belief. In an interview with the *Evening Times*'s Peter Hendry ahead of the victory over Rangers early in the season he had explained his dilemma, 'I know we are a great team but it is difficult trying to convince the players of that undoubted fact. I am not simply trying to bolster their confidence when I tell them they are a great team.'

By the end of the season the manager's words were getting through to his players, as Dick Malone recalls, 'You actually went out on to the park feeling you couldn't get beat. He really was sharp in strategy. He worked a lot on set pieces that got us into goalscoring positions. He rarely got wound up during play.'

Elaborating on this point Malone says it would be unusual to see Ally shouting from the touchline – unless someone was not pulling their weight – as he was more likely to change things around at half-time if required.

In October of 1969 Ally had spoken to the *Daily Record*'s Alex Cameron about the difficulties of part-time football, 'As a part-time manager I have to decide how far I can push my players. I think it is more difficult than dealing with a full-time side. You have less chance to teach players and study their reaction.'

10
Full-time Boss

A LLY was not a part-time manager for much longer and was soon offered a full-time position at the club now that their First Division status had been achieved. Faye remembers as significant an occasion when Ally had called on a client for the chemical company only to find they had unexpectedly been made redundant. 'He thought, well, it could happen in any walk of life. So that's why he took the gamble to go full-time,' Faye says.

Bidding his job in Glasgow farewell, the MacLeods chose to move from Clarkston to Ayr where Ally could completely immerse himself in the new position. They bought a house on Westfield Road in the town for £9,000 and although Ally later calculated that the decision to leave Hardman and Holdman had seen him lose £1,000 a year he considered the sacrifice worthwhile.

To allow him to see more of his three children Ally would pop home for lunch during the school dinner break. They often played Ludo during lunch and Faye recalls, 'They weren't allowed to move the board. Dad would never let them win.' Her daughter Gail's memory of those lunchtimes is similar, 'He would cheat so he could win. Nobody could ever beat him.'

The real success of Ayr's return to the the First Division was a profit of £49,444 – a figure which broke all previous club records. Most of this was due to a vast increase of gate receipts from £15,251 to £66,507, an advance of over 300 per cent on the promotion season with an average attendance of 8,158 in a town whose population was just below 48,000 at the time. The entire cost of the squad the manager had assembled was £3,500 with no player exceeding £250.

That summer of 1970 Alex Ingram was sold to Nottingham Forest for £32,380 which helped to pay for floodlights that were due to be installed at Somerset Park early in the new season.

Evening Times journalist Malcolm Munro hailed the success story and drew comparisons with full-time Kilmarnock who were reported to be suffering an annual loss of £30,000–£40,000. Ally gave Munro an insight into the club's finances and his philosophy for establishing a good relationship with the supporters.

He said, 'When I took over Ayr had been in the shadow of Kilmarnock for many years. I told the directors that we wouldn't get the fans back by playing safe. We had to take chances. We had to play it flat out in attack. Well, we did that and it appealed to the fans. We've tried to encourage local youngsters. The future of Ayr United will depend on local talent. We have tried to keep a close association with the fans and we always will. When we transferred Alex Ingram to Notts Forest we went to the fans and told them that if they wanted floodlights we'd have to sell Alex. They agreed with our point of view.'

In October Ally elaborated on the policy of nurturing local talent when speaking to the *Edinburgh Evening News*. He revealed that his club had no scouts in the east of Scotland, explaining that as a part-time team Ayr had a policy of only signing players who lived locally as they had to be available to train in the evenings.

A few years later in January 1975 Ayr veteran John Murphy looked back on the changes the manager had brought to the club in an interview for the monthly magazine *Scottish Football*. Referring to Ayr's Second Division days, Murphy was blunt, 'There was absolutely no professional approach, playing and training were just a formality. The club was up for sale and we were third from bottom of the second division. Things started to improve as soon as he [Ally] took over, first as coach, then boss. He soon changed the farce that was Ayr in those days.'

Again Blackburn visited Somerset for a pre-season warm-up match which finished in a 1-1 draw. As a First Division club Ayr found themselves in a League Cup section with three other top division sides – Dundee, local rivals Kilmarnock, and St Mirren.

Ayr lost the opening match at Rugby Park and won only one of their six games, the final fixture at St Mirren. They finished third on four points with Dundee going through to the quarter-finals.

Boosted by the win over St Mirren, Ayr began their league season with a convincing 4-1 home victory against Dunfermline. The usual mix of results followed, and Ayr were third from bottom of the league in mid-November with six points.

Ally had been busy in the transfer market. After selling Dick Malone to Sunderland in October, he brought in two forwards in ex-Ranger George McLean from Dunfermline and Newcastle United's Phil McGovern. Today Malone recalls that Ally never refused another club the opportunity to speak to one of his own team and always tried to negotiate the best deal for any outgoing players.

Malone had previously taken up an invitation to visit Fulham before deciding the move was not for him after manager Vic Buckingham explained his role would be as an 'attacking sweeper'. Considering this a contradiction the youngster had returned to Ayrshire with Ally's blessing.

Malone went on to win the FA Cup with Sunderland under Bob Stokoe in the famous final of 1973 but today has no doubts as to who was the top boss in his career. 'I would like it put on record Ally was the best manager I have ever played for,' he says. 'He was brilliant at blending a team.'

McGovern did not play when his former club Newcastle came north on 18 November for a match to commemorate the switching-on of Somerset Park's promised floodlights. Ayr won 2-0 courtesy of two second-half goals, one a first for McLean, who was also known by his nickname of Dandy.

'So far as we are concerned this is just another game,' a confident Ally told Malcolm Munro of the *Evening Times* ahead of the visit of Rangers – three days after the Newcastle match. 'As you know we have beaten Rangers here and there's no reason to think we can't do it again.'

And do it again they did with a repeat of the 2-1 scoreline of the previous year. A crowd of 17,634 saw Ayr lead at half-time thanks to an Ian Whitehead header. An equaliser from Derek Johnstone seemed to give Rangers the initiative until a spectacular Quinton Young free kick 15 minutes from time won the match.

Four weeks later Celtic came to Somerset and Ayr were considered unfortunate not to gain a point in the 2-1 defeat. On Boxing Day they lost heavily at East End Park – 5-0 – as Dunfermline exacted revenge for the opening league fixture.

A boost was provided with the return of Alex Ingram to the club for £14,040 in the last week of the year, meaning Ayr had made a profit of in excess of £18,000 on the player's short break in Nottingham.

A New Year's Day victory over Morton and a draw in an exciting derby match at Kilmarnock watched by 15,240 spectators on the second day of 1971 saw Ayr climb to fourth from bottom.

Morton gained revenge by dumping Ayr out of the Scottish Cup later in the month but the Honest Men's league form improved from mid-February with four wins and two draws in their last ten matches. Two of those defeats came at Ibrox and Celtic Park, both with a 2-0 scoreline.

The team finished fifth from the bottom of the league, or 14th from the top, on 26 points from their 34 matches.

After three derby draws and one win for Kilmarnock throughout the season the two-legged Ayrshire Cup Final would decide who the real kings of the county were. The honours seemed set for Rugby Park when Ayr lost the first leg 2-1 at home on Monday 26 April. But the season ended on a high as Ally's men won 1-0 on the Saturday to tie the scores before winning the penalty shoot-out 7-6.

Ally was able to look back on another satisfactory season on the pitch for Ayr who had gone a long way to establishing themselves as a top-division club. Off the field however the board revealed a loss of £5,059 as opposed to the previous profit of over £49,000. The season's wage bill for the part-time players had been a total of £33,892.

Ayr could not have had a tougher League Cup section than the one they found themselves in for the new season. They were up against both Old Firm clubs with Morton completing the quartet. Any minimal chance of winning the group disappeared when the opening game at home to Morton finished level on 14 August 1971.

Next up was a midweek trip to Ibrox. With both Ingram and Whitehead unavailable through injury Ally had to field inexperienced forwards including 18-year-old John Doyle and his 17-year-old cousin Brian Lannon.

Despite his side's 4-0 victory Rangers manager Willie Waddell was outspoken in his criticism of the visitors' tactics. 'I seriously think it is the duty of every club to go all out in attack. Ayr passed back from the start of the game. They wouldn't come at us,' he told the *Evening Times*'s Malcolm Munro. 'We've got to give the public value for money…last night was a disgrace.'

MacLeod was quick to respond to the outburst, 'I have never at any time asked my players to go in for defensive football. Because of the absence of Ingram and Whitehead we lacked penetration. But next time these two are fit I can promise Rangers all the attacking football they want.'

To demonstrate his philosophy Ally, perhaps revealing a gift of foresight, added that he had suggested his directors ask for passing back inside the penalty area to be penalised at the next meeting of the Scottish League. 'Does that sound like someone who wants defensive football?' he asked Munro.

With Whitehead returning but not Ingram, Ayr held Celtic until half-time on the Saturday but ended up losing 3-0 with a crowd of 17,699 inside Somerset.

Rangers repeated their 4-0 Ibrox scoreline in the return match before Ayr lost at Morton (who had actually won at Celtic), guaranteeing they would finish bottom of the section. A 4-1 defeat at Celtic Park completed the schedule in a match which Alex Cameron told *Daily Record* readers, 'There was never the remotest chance of Ayr winning.'

The fresh challenge of a new league season, coupled with the signing of Ally's old Third Lanark team-mate Johnny Graham, seemed to breathe new life into the Ayr men as they took five points from their first three matches. A revenge win at home to Morton was followed by victory at Kilmarnock in the derby and a draw with Dunfermline. With these results Ayr sat joint third in the table with Aberdeen in mid-September.

Ayr then managed only one more victory before Christmas, against Airdrie, four draws and eight defeats. The manager's patience was clearly running out and he promised Jim Blair of the *Evening Times* there would be a change of personnel for the trip to Partick Thistle on Christmas Day, 'There are far too many regular first-team men who think they are automatic choices. Well there are a few who are in for a shock, for there will definitely be changes.'

True to his word six players were dropped and there were seven positional changes. The selection, which was at odds with one of Ally's golden rules, continuity of personnel, ought to have backfired on the manager. In what appears to have been something of a bizarre match Thistle could have scored three times in the opening five minutes as the Ayr players struggled to get to know each other's game. Ayr won with a late Robertson goal which struck a defender then went in via a post. David Stirling's *Evening Times* report read, 'Thistle should have thrashed Ayr United…it was one of those games when a team plays well enough to win 6-0 yet loses 1-0.'

But the two points were a welcome Christmas present regardless of the circumstances and Ayr sat in a relatively comfortable 13th position as the New Year approached.

A win at Morton, followed by two draws – with Scotland boss Tommy Docherty watching the goalless match with Kilmarnock – welcomed in 1972. A Scottish Cup victory at Clyde was offset seven days later by a league defeat to the same side.

Ayr exited the cup to Motherwell in the next round following a replay. Their joint biggest win of the season was a 4-0 triumph over East Fife in March – the club's first home win in six months – followed a few weeks later by a 7-0 hammering at Aberdeen where a single point was required to guarantee safety. The *Ayrshire Post* considered the Pittodrie defeat, 'The mother and father of a hiding.'

The players rallied to beat Dundee United before losing at Falkirk. The double was completed over Partick with Johnny Graham scoring all the goals in a 4-0 win before Ayr headed to Ibrox on the last day of the season.

Ayr took the game to Rangers and went ahead through Ingram midway through the first half only for Alfie Conn to level. Again Ingram gave Ayr the lead five minutes before the break but Rangers scored three times in the second period to win 4-2.

Ayr finished in a quite satisfactory 12th position, meaning that they had continued to improve their league standing in each of their three seasons back in the top division. Although they lost the Ayrshire Cup to Kilmarnock a couple of days later (3-1 over the two legs) the club had qualified for the following season's Texaco Cup, a trophy which Scottish and English clubs not involved in European competition competed for.

The finances of the club had seen a dramatic turnaround in 1971/72 with Ayr now back in the black with a profit of £10,807 against a deficit of over £5,000 12 months earlier. The main reason for this was an increase in attendances with gate receipts for the season now totalling £74,746, some £13,550 up although the players' wage bill had now increased by £5,000 to £38,973.

11

Mr Ayr United

ALTHOUGH Ally was employed as a full-time manager his players were still part-time. Having moved to the town Ally had begun to totally immerse himself in the club. He became involved in all aspects of Ayr United and even took on the task of temporary groundsman when the club's own man took ill following an accident when the team coach was involved in a crash.

The Somerset Park playing surface had been much maligned throughout the 1971/72 season and Andy MacLeod remembers he and his siblings helping out as their father drove a tractor reseeding the ground that summer in preparation for a new pitch.

Ally revamped the youth set-up at the club and attended many junior and reserve matches looking for players. He was determined that any promising local youngsters would not end up at a rival club. On occasion he was known to sign players and only notify the directors after the event.

He was also very keen to lift the profile of the club in the local community and attended as many school and charity events as he could to encourage the people of Ayr to come along to Somerset Park where he promised an entertaining brand of football. 'He went to any supporters' club he was invited to,' Faye remembers of her husband's commitment to the fans.

Ally had realised that he could use contacts in the press to promote his team and made himself easily accessible to journalists. Many a sports editor was able to fill an empty space on the back page after a quick telephone call to Somerset Park. Equally he could often be found holding court in the press club in Glasgow, of which he was a member, on a Thursday or Friday afternoon. He was only too aware that any stories he passed on to journalists were likely to find themselves in the sports section of the following day's editions.

Chick Young was then writing for the *Irvine Herald* and fondly remembers those days, 'It was an absolute delight to go down to Somerset Park to see and hear Ally hold court in that manager's office. He was an instantly likeable guy. He would talk and sell his teams and would back his off-field talk with results on the field.

'The entertainment was not just on the park but in that manager's office. After a match the journalists would gather there. He was a newspaper man's dream. We would all cram into the room to listen to Ally. He had us at his feet recounting story after story. He was a spin doctor for PR for his clubs before spin doctors were invented.'

The players did not always welcome this publicity as Johnny Graham recalled in a BBC Scotland documentary, *Footballers' Lives*, broadcast in 2003. Graham revealed that Ally's boasts used to annoy the players by putting added pressure on them, particularly if they were facing one of the Old Firm clubs the following day.

Faye used to scorn at some of the headlines he generated, 'I used to say to him he would get found out if he said such outlandish things all the time, but he said he didn't care as long as it got more people through the gate.'

At this point in his Somerset Park career Ally may very well have been justified should he have felt the need to change his name to Mr Ayr United.

An interesting if somewhat amusing letter had appeared within the pages of the *Scottish Sunday Express* at the end of January 1972 which demonstrated the manager's appreciation of the club's supporters. Robert MacFarlane of Glasgow was so impressed by Ally's actions that he took the trouble to pen the following to the newspaper, 'My thirteen year old son and three of his pals are very keen supporters of Queen's Park. Last Saturday the four set out by train for Forfar under the impression Queen's were playing there. They were spotted on the train in their black and white tammies by Ally MacLeod. Assuming they were Ayr fans Ally said it was encouraging to see young lads prepared to travel to support their team and gave each a complimentary stand ticket for Dundee v Ayr. At Dundee they learned Queen's Park were not playing at Forfar and enjoyed a day as VIP Ayr fans.'

In conversation with *Evening Times* journalist Malcolm Munro in July 1972, Ally said, 'So far as manager of Ayr is concerned, I've got over the first phase. We are now accepted as a First Division side. We aren't a yo-yo team. Just watch us from now on.'

Quick to point out that since the advent of relegation in 1921 it was the first occasion that Ayr had been in the First Division for four consecutive years, he also stressed the pressures on his squad of 29 part-time players, 'Obviously the full-timers have the edge. We always do well at the beginning of a season. But get into the season and have two or three injuries and you are right in trouble.'

Quinton Young had been sold to Coventry City for £40,000 during the summer break and Ayr were further handicapped by the unavailability of their ground in August while Somerset Park was being returfed. A solution was found in the town's athletics stadium at Dam Park which would host their home League Cup matches against St Mirren and Clydebank.

Before that Ally took the players south to England for two pre-season friendlies. The first match at Fourth Division side Cambridge United ended in a 1-0 loss before a 2-0 victory was recorded at non-leaguers Stevenage Athletic on 7 August.

A crowd of 5,335 watched Ayr kick off their campaign at their temporary home with a 2-1 win over the Buddies with George McLean scoring their first goal of the season from the penalty spot.

A loss at Clydebank was not the ideal preparation for the next group game at Ibrox. Although Ayr could consider themselves unfortunate to be drawn with Rangers in successive seasons, the format of the League Cup had been altered with two of the four teams now progressing to an extra round, the results of which determined the quarter-finalists.

'We'll be going all out for both points,' announced Ally, perhaps remembering Willie Waddell's criticism of the previous season's corresponding fixture.

Just two minutes of the second period had lapsed when McLean put Ayr ahead against his former club. A goal by Willie Johnston looked to have sealed a draw but the visitors were to be denied a precious point by a highly contentious refereeing decision in the dying minutes of the match.

A long kick from Ibrox goalkeeper Peter McCloy was clutched by his opposite number Dave Stewart as Derek Parlane leaped to challenge. The ball broke free and crossed the goal line after striking the Rangers forward's arm. 'At no time did Parlane touch the ball with his foot,' said Jim Blair in his *Evening Times* report. But referee Bill Anderson saw fit to award a goal, resulting in vehement protests from the Ayr players which saw two of them booked and Johnny Graham ordered from the field.

Ally too found himself reported by the referee but only after being recalled from the dressing room. He revealed to Blair that he had deliberately rushed from the dugout wary that his temperament was likely to get him into trouble should he come into contact with Anderson. One of his own players then got involved with an opponent in the tunnel and the manager was asked to intervene. It was then that he exchanged words with the referee which resulted in the manager having his name taken.

Summoned to the SFA's disciplinary panel the following month, Ally was fined £25 for his remarks to the referee while Graham had to pay £10 for his dismissal. The next time Ally saw referee Anderson he apologised for the abuse having had a couple of weeks to cool down.

Faye remembers that her husband started to smoke a pipe in the dugout in an attempt to calm him down. This succeeded to a degree but the idea was abandoned when he kept sitting down on and breaking too many pipes and on at least one occasion he had set fire to his tie!

Back in the League Cup, Ayr avenged Clydebank at Dam Park with a 5-0 scoreline but the real result of the night took place elsewhere and sent shockwaves through Scottish football – Rangers 1 St Mirren 4. Ironically, given recent events at Ibrox, all four of the Buddies' goals came from their 20-year-old striker who went by the name of Ally McLeod – and this was the correct spelling!

The implications were that both Saints and Ayr were level on four points, two adrift of Rangers, with two games to play. Ayr then won with surprising ease in Paisley, causing the *Sunday People*'s John Blair to highlight the manager's gameplan,

'St Mirren allowed themselves to be hustled off their stride and they were quickly deflated in a fashion that left no doubts about Ayr's tactical superiority.'

The win meant that a single point against Rangers would guarantee a place in the next round while victory would see them win the section on goal average.

Due to Dam Park's 10,000 capacity the match was staged at Kilmarnock where it rather ironically attracted an audience of 9,646 paying customers. With McLean injured Ayr's attacking threat was depleted and Rangers went away with a 2-1 result. But thanks to Clydebank's draw with St Mirren, Ayr went through with the Ibrox side although goal average would have been enough had the Paisley team won.

In a twist of fate the same fixture was scheduled for just three days later but this time Somerset Park was ready to host the opening First Division match. In his match programme notes the manager predicted a tough afternoon, 'Today is the third meeting with Rangers and possibly it will turn out the hardest tussle of the three as it is important for both clubs to start the league programme with a convincing win.'

Ally went on to congratulate the contractors who had returfed the pitch which he considered to be 'in top class condition'.

A crowd of 13,658 watched as all the goals went in before half-time. Willie Johnston became the first player to score on the new turf but Ayr fought back as Doyle and Ingram – with a 'bird-like header' according to the *Evening Times* – won the points for the home side. It was the third time in four seasons that Ayr had beaten Rangers 2-1 in the league.

The following Monday, Malcolm Munro paid tribute to Ally's managerial skills and shrewdness in the transfer market in his *Evening Times* column, 'Ally MacLeod "stole" this side. And it's a good one. These players from all the wee clubs and villages become ten foot tall because of Ally MacLeod. MacLeod inspires. He'd talk the birds from the trees. I'd have stripped and played for him on Saturday if it hadn't been for the traffic hold-up.'

Any inflated ideas the Ayr players may have had of their own status were soon put in perspective when they crashed out of the League Cup to Second Division Alloa Athletic. After a goalless draw at Recreation Park that Monday the teams met for the second leg just two days later, the third match both sides had played in five days. Ayr pressed for 40 minutes only to fall behind to a Willie McCulloch header. They bombarded the Alloa goal in the second half but their keeper Dave McWilliams stopped everything including an Eric Stevenson penalty.

Despite the loss of a place in the quarter-finals and the welcome revenue that would have generated, Ally was surprisingly philosophical. 'This was perhaps the most one-sided game I've ever seen,' he told Jim Blair, adding, 'I thought we played well. It was the old story of not being able to put the ball into the net… even from the penalty spot.'

Ayr delighted their supporters on the following Saturday as an Ingram goal won the derby match at Kilmarnock, leaving United with four points from their opening two matches.

Newcastle United were back at Somerset in the first round of the Texaco Cup in September. When the first leg finished goalless Newcastle's £180,000 striker Malcolm Macdonald dismissed Ayr's chances on Tyneside but the manager still felt they could progress.

Supermac's prediction proved the more accurate as the Geordies scored twice without conceding. But Ayr had far from disgraced themselves against the English First Division side.

Back in the league Ayr hit an inconsistent patch with two draws followed by a narrow defeat at Celtic. After a home win against Partick the Honest Men then took one point from three matches. After a win over Motherwell at Somerset, Ayr sat in ninth position in the table at the beginning of November.

In mid-December 1972 Ayr were in Edinburgh where Hibernian paraded the League Cup they had won against Celtic seven days earlier. It turned into a disastrous day for the visitors who conceded after just 12 seconds and eventually lost 8-1. It was their heaviest defeat since returning to the top division.

The manager's reaction was, it must be said, rather off the wall. 'The greatest team I have ever seen in all my life,' was Ally's assessment of Hibs when speaking to Malcolm Munro. 'We didn't play all that badly. But this was different class. Hibs were fantastic.'

Far from demoralising the players the Easter Road hiding actually triggered a league run of eight matches where Ayr lost only twice – 2-1 to Rangers and 3-1 to Celtic. By the second week of February 1973 they sat seventh in the league table and had disposed of Highland League side Inverness Thistle in the Scottish Cup.

Another home draw paired them with Stirling Albion in the fourth round. Winning by the odd goal in three, Ayr were now through to a quarter-final meeting with Partick at Firhill on 17 March. After falling behind Ayr roared back to win 5-1 and looked forward to their first ever Scottish Cup semi-final where they would meet Rangers at Hampden Park.

The good league form continued with four wins and only a defeat to Dundee during five league matches played in the month of March and Ayr were still seventh in the table as the Hampden date neared.

Rangers, under Jock Wallace and on the back of their European Cup Winners' Cup triumph the previous season, were playing some of their best football for years and looked capable of ending Celtic's run of seven consecutive titles that season. Interviewed by Dick Currie for the *Daily Record*, Ally sounded confident, 'We have no cause to fear Rangers. Our last four games against them have been decided by the odd goal.' He addressed Jim Blair – who noted MacLeod 'has a reputation of being a talker' – of the *Evening Times* in a similar tone, 'We are confident of beating Rangers simply because we are playing well and with the utmost belief in our own ability.'

Typically keen to gain any psychological advantage, Ally chose the morning of the semi-final to pledge his future to the Somerset Park club. This ended speculation that had linked him to the vacant Motherwell manager's position which was later filled by Ian St John.

A special train carried hundreds of supporters from Ayr to Hampden where a huge crowd of 51,625 turned up on the evening of Wednesday 4 April. There was almost a sensation as Alex Ingram headed home in the very first minute only to have the goal ruled out for offside.

Unfortunately Rangers did not ease off from their league form and Ayr were always second best for the remaining 89 minutes as they lost to two Derek Parlane goals – one on either side of the break. Hugh Taylor's *Daily Record* report summarised, 'Ayr just didn't have an answer. They stood up bravely to almost constant Rangers pressure, but they never matched their relentless opponents in ideas of individual ability.'

'I felt the first minute goal might have been allowed. But we've no complaints,' said Ally to another *Record* reporter, Bob Patience. He may have been a bad loser but Ally rarely offered excuses in defeat and generally conceded if he considered the result to have been just, although most reports were of the opinion the referee had been correct to rule out Ingram's effort.

Unbeaten in their remaining four league matches, Ayr finished the season with a win at Airdrie. Again the club had improved on their final league position to finish as high as sixth with 40 points from 34 games played.

Ayr travelled further afield than ever before for their next pre-season preparations. That July they went all the way to Newfoundland where they won each of their four matches with ease, scoring no less than 28 times. In an 8-2 victory over the Newfoundland All Stars Ingram netted four goals while McLean bagged a hat-trick.

During their stay the team were invited to banquets and receptions each day which included a civic reception with the Mayor of St John's and his council. Links between the communities of Ayr and St John's stretched back as far as the First World War when many Newfoundlanders had been billeted in Ayrshire.

Impressed by the performances and conduct of his players, the Newfoundland FA invited Ally back the following summer to set up coaching camps for local teams.

Landing back in Scotland on 5 July a jet-lagged Ally told the *Evening Times* at Prestwick Airport, 'They had four good games together and played well... Now we are all off for a good sleep.'

A few days later the *Ayrshire Post* quoted Ally's assessment of the tour, 'The main thing it gave us was the chance to live together as a team...and this is important for a part-time club. It built up team spirit and got us into the habit of scoring goals.'

A civic reception was held in the town's Marine Hotel on 12 July where Provost Campbell Howie congratulated the club on their most successful season ever. Also honoured were Ayr United Boys Club who had won two trophies in the under-16s section of a European youth tournament in Glasgow.

In a speech club chairman Tom Murray praised the manager whom he referred to as a 'a wonderful P.R.O. both for the club and the town of Ayr'.

Before long the club were off on their travels again, participating in the Lorient Celtic Festival Cup in France. The squad set off from Ayr at 6am on Monday 30 July then had to suffer a delay at Glasgow Airport.

After a sleep in the holiday camp they were staying in they faced St Lorient that same evening. The home side were tough, physical opponents and one of their players even kicked Ally on the touchline during the match. The half-time break lasted all of 45 minutes as a cycle race entertained the 6,000 crowd, probably reviving memories of Hibs' Czechoslovakian tour 11 years earlier for the manager.

Concerned at the effect of the delay on his players, Ally made them do some stiffening-up exercises. After taking a few knocks and worse Ayr left the field just before midnight having won 2-0 and headed back to the accommodation which they shared with hammer throwers, a tug of war team, tennis players and a pipe band from Kirkcaldy who were all taking part in the festival.

The party then undertook a 30-mile journey to Concarneau where they apparently made hard work of beating a poor local team 2-1. Two George McLean goals in a 3-1 win in the last game against Cork Celtic ensured Ayr were presented with the trophy by the Mayor of Lorient. All the participants in the festival then attended a banquet during which Ally is reported to have uttered a few words in French and assured the hosts that Ayr would be delighted to defend the trophy the following year.

12

A Citizen of Ayr

'**I**'M not going to say we'll win the league but as almost all our players are under 25 I believe we will go on improving. The extra year's experience behind them must show...so we have good reason to be optimistic.' Ally was speaking to Ian Fraser (who noted the manager's 'bubbling enthusiasm') of the monthly magazine *Scottish Football* about his hopes for the new season.

Ayr avoided both the Old Firm clubs in the League Cup draw which placed them in a favourable group with Hibernian, Dumbarton and Morton with again the top two qualifying.

McLean, now 30 years of age, scored both goals as the Honest Men kicked off with a 2-0 home win over Dumbarton. But they lost four of the six group matches and defeated Morton 2-1 at Somerset Park to finish bottom of Section Two. One consolation was that they had conceded just three times during the two matches with Hibs, an improvement on the eight shipped in their last meeting.

Speaking to *Scottish Football* in the March edition George McLean revealed he had played under a total of nine managers in his career, 'I say without any doubts Ally has been, overall, the best of the lot. Ally typifies everything that a manager should be. He's 100 per cent for his club, Which means he's 100 per cent behind every one of his players. He just lives for the game, he's very publicity conscious, he'll fight to the death for what he believes in...and he can be as hard as nails or a father figure, depending on the particular occasion.'

McLean also praised his manager's motivational skills, 'When we run on to the park, no matter who the opposition may be, we believe completely that we'll win.'

'You're better than him, and I know you're better,' Ally would tell a player when discussing an opponent, assuring him that if he performed to his ability he had nothing to worry about.

Supporter John Grigor has been watching the club since 1967. 'He was my childhood hero,' he says of Ally. 'He was the best manager we ever had. He gave us belief that we were going to win. It didn't matter if you lost four goals so long as you scored five. It was a strange outlook on the management side but he was able to pass it on to the supporters.'

Again Ayr found themselves up against Rangers on the opening day of the league season, 1 September, this time in Glasgow. Now gaining something of a reputation as a bogey side to the Ibrox team, Ayr ground out a goalless draw. Hunter Irvine's match summary for the *Glasgow Herald* considered that Ally's men had done rather more than contain Rangers.

'It is perhaps unfair to say "held" – they looked as capable of winning as the home side. But the reaction of the Ayr players at the final whistle suggested that they were happy enough with the scoreline.' Irvine also referred to 'an ill-tempered contest with the ball often an unwelcome intruder in a series of private feuds'.

Again accusations were labelled at Ayr's approach to the Rangers game, provoking the following response from the manager in the *Ayrshire Post*, 'I've said it countless times this week – Ayr are not a dirty side. What I do say is that we are not going to be steamrollered into the ground by Rangers or any other side. If the opposition wants to mix it then they will find that out. Ayr United have the players to take up the challenge.'

On Monday 3 September Ally secured the signature of another attacker when he signed 31-year-old Alex Ferguson who had been released on a free transfer by Falkirk. The two of them had played against each other in matches between St Johnstone and Hibs and Ferguson had watched Ally as a spectator at the Third Lanark v Rangers Scottish Cup ties almost 20 years earlier.

'I had been player-coach at Falkirk,' Sir Alex recalls today. 'The club had sacked Willie Cunningham, the manager. I phoned Cunningham to see what I was going to do and he told me to apply for the job as Willie Palmer, the chairman, liked me. But he sold the club to young guys Manson and Hardie, so I applied for the job but they gave it to John Prentice and he brought in his own assistant. When he offered me a free I took it.

'I had the pub at the time [Fergie's, on the corner of Glasgow's Paisley Road West and Govan Road] and Jim McLean phoned me and told me to come up but it was full-time at Dundee United and travel would be hard.

'I was just about to go up the road to see him when Ally phoned. Ally asked to meet up with me so I met him at Reid's tea room. This was the first time of me really meeting Ally although I was aware he had a great reputation and great enthusiasm. We discussed it and he stated "you'll really enjoy it". It was part-time which really suited me with the pub.

'I'll always remember he pulled out the fixture list. He started, "Dumbarton in the first game – we always win there. Well that's two points then it's Clyde, that's another two points." This went on match by match until we got to Hibs in November when he said, "Hibs at Easter Road, we've got a bad record there but that's due to change so two points there."

'He got to Christmas and we hadn't lost a game! "Is this guy's enthusiasm possible?" I thought. However he sold Ayr to me and I accepted a two-year contract on a good salary and signing-on fee. There was no discussion with the board, it was all done through Ally. Ally controlled the club.'

Ferguson played in a reserve match at Celtic Park against a strong home team which included Jimmy Johnstone, John Deans and Bobby Murdoch the following evening in a 1-1 draw and made his first-team debut on the Saturday when Morton visited Somerset Park.

Although they had both played for Rangers and Dunfermline Ferguson and McLean had never been team-mates until their time at Ayr. That day against Morton they struck up a formidable partnership with McLean scoring twice. One came from a Ferguson pass and the other via the penalty spot following a foul on Ferguson as the home side repeated their 2-1 League Cup scoreline.

'He teamed me up with George "Dandy" McLean,' reminisces Sir Alex. 'He said he was the only man that could control Dandy. On that note I didn't think so.'

Two Ferguson headed goals gave the Honest Men a 2-0 victory at Dumbarton (just as Ally had predicted) in their next match, followed by a 2-2 home draw with Clyde with Ferguson and McLean both scoring.

After the woes of the League Cup Ayr United were going well in the First Division and with four matches played they sat joint top of the table with Celtic.

'He had an incredible desire to win and if you didn't win...' Sir Alex says of Ally. 'All leaders have a belief, personality and desire to win and a determination to succeed. Ally had that embraced with a boyish enthusiasm. You had to admire that.'

That summer of 1973 Ally was one of the five nominees put forward for the title of Ayr's Citizen of the Year. The award had been inaugurated the previous year by the Junior Chamber of the town in association with local newspapers and the Ayr Cooperative. Ally, nominated by the *Ayrshire Post*, was up against four others including the president of the Association of Burns Clubs and a local building contractor. Ballot papers were printed in the local press and the public were invited to post them to the Junior Chamber or deposit them in one of 16 boxes located throughout the town.

With almost twice the number of votes cast as in 1972 and with ballot papers returned from as far as London and Sutton Coldfield, Ally emerged as a clear winner. 'I am not normally without something to say, but at the moment I am at a loss for words,' he said on receiving the award at a civic luncheon held in the town's Savoy Park Hotel on Thursday 13 September.

Finding his voice he expressed his belief that the honour was not just for him but for the football club, 'I have been living in the town for three years now and I find I am not a Glaswegian any more, but a citizen of Ayr.'

In years to come Ally spoke fondly of the honour as he did the people of the town. He was always keen to promote the town and its football club and during a speech to Cumnock Rotarians the following week he expressed some innovative ideas to improve football, some of which have since been implemented.

While criticising the maximum four pounds win bonus clubs were authorised to pay, he also called for changes to the offside rule, a complete ban on transfers during the season and legislation to allow home clubs to retain gate money. Ally made a point of acknowledging that the last of these would not prove popular with his directors!

Ally further boosted his profile when he was one of three managers invited to air their opinions during Scottish Television's live coverage of the Scotland v Czechoslovakia match on 26 September. The others were both former internationals, Motherwell boss Ian St John and George Farm who was in charge at Raith Rovers. A victory for Willie Ormond's team in their last match would ensure qualification for the following summer's World Cup finals in West Germany.

On a dramatic night Scotland overcame the loss of an early goal to win 2-1 and earned the right to take part in their first World Cup for 16 years. The *Evening Times* TV critic Bill Law commented, 'The panel's summing-up after the game was a deal better than their halfway summing-up. I enjoyed Ally MacLeod's view of the opposition – "a bunch of crunchers".'

Less impressed was Baillie James Cook who, giving his address as Edinburgh City Chambers, took the trouble of writing to the *Edinburgh Evening News* to express his feelings. After crediting STV for arranging the live broadcast he was damning of the panel's contribution whom he deemed 'boring and unimaginative'. Also picking up on Ally's 'bunch of crunchers' comment (but less favourably), Cook was particularly upset that the panel had on more than one occasion referred to one of the Czech players with 'the three-letter word "guy",' which he considered was, 'Not the type of language calculated to impress, unless STV were preparing an award for the most inarticulate appearance on Scottish Television.'

Back on club business Ally took his unbeaten side to the capital to face a Hibs team just two points behind them. A crowd of 8,176 ventured through the turnstiles on a cold and windy afternoon and there were shades of the previous season's 8-1 result when Eddie Turnbull's side led by four goals after 56 minutes. A late fightback made the result a more respectable 4-2 as Hibs drew level with Ayr's points total of six.

Only the brilliance of Peter Shilton and an own goal by McAnespie had prevented Ayr taking a lead into the second leg of their Texaco Cup tie with Leicester City in September, best summed up by an anonymous report in the *Glasgow Herald*, 'The English international goalkeeper undoubtedly denied United their due reward for so much skill and effort that produced so little in the end. Shilton's saves from Fleming and Graham alone were worth the admission money.'

A goal each it had finished with the crowd estimated at 12,000. Perhaps predictably the return match went the way of the home team who scored twice without reply and Ayr again went out in round one.

Early in December Ayr's home match with Falkirk was one of only three Scottish fixtures to beat the winter weather but it provided unexpected entertainment for the 3,791 fans who braved the cold. Close to half-time a five-month-old puppy named Lassie broke free from her owners and ran on to the pitch, holding up the match for five minutes as she evaded anyone who tried to catch her. Some young spectators had the audience in fits of laughter as they dived for and missed the dog.

Ally came from the dugout to help and at one point held a chequebook and pen close to the pup, intimating he wished to sign her. Eventually Rikki Fleming managed to grab Lassie and the match restarted to a cheer from the crowd.

The cheer was almost as loud when Ferguson netted the game's only goal against his most recent former club late in the game. Lassie was pictured in the newspapers reunited with her owners a few days later who advised they were still awaiting the manager's call.

Ayr then won twice more and sat in the lofty heights of fourth place in the table when Rangers came calling on 29 December. For once Ayr took nothing from the fixture but were only beaten by what was described in the *Evening Times* as a last-minute 'wonder goal' from Parlane who seemed to be developing a habit of scoring against Ayr.

'The young players used to love listening to his stories on the away game bus journeys,' Sir Alex remembers of Ally. 'He had a lot of good players coming through – Wells, Doyle, Filippi and McCulloch. A lot of managers don't give young players their time and by giving them that and their first chance there's a lot of players that will never forget Ally MacLeod.

'The loyalty they got from that would obviously stay with them especially with the like of Doyle who stayed until he went to Celtic. It was a great management art of how you develop a loyalty base by giving your time and giving yourself to them as you really surrender your own loyalty and hope you get it back. All the players had a loyalty to him as you knew what he was.'

That same December Ally's old club Blackburn Rovers found themselves managerless when Ken Furphy left to take charge at Sheffield United. Strong rumours persisted of a return to Ewood Park for Ally and when approached by the *Ayrshire Post* he did little to quash the speculation with, 'No comment!' The rumours only died when Gordon Lee took charge of Blackburn the following month.

Into 1974 and Ayr won four of their next eight league matches, drawing two and losing the same quota. Things were also going well in the Scottish Cup when following convincing away wins at Second Division Cowdenbeath (5-0) and Stranraer (7-1 – with both McCulloch and McLean scoring hat-tricks) the Honest Men found themselves in the quarter-finals again.

An away tie at Hearts on 9 March stood between Ayr and their second semi-final in successive seasons. If any added incentive were needed to win the cup then that belonged to the Edinburgh side who were celebrating 100 years since the birth of the club.

In conversation with Stewart Brown of the *Edinburgh Evening News*, Ally mulled over his side's prospects in the tournament, 'I believe we have a chance of winning it this time. Until last year Ayr had not appeared in the semi-final. But having reached that stage once, my players want to be there again.'

The journey from Ayr to Edinburgh did not quite go to plan as Sir Alex remembers, 'George McLean was late and Ally hated lateness. We had a pick-up point in Glasgow – Reids Bar in Hope Street. The bus turns up and Ally says, "Where's Dandy? Okay we'll give him ten minutes. He's fined. I'm laying down the law on this one. He's not getting away with it this time." Fifteen to twenty minutes later and Ally's going mental and Dandy's for the guillotine.

'Well eventually Dandy turned up in an open top car driven by a gorgeous blonde and pulls in front of the bus. We were all sinking in our seats awaiting the rant. Ally goes off, "Where have you been?" Well Dandy goes, "Boss, calm down."

'The directors and staff and I are now cringing, sinking more into our seats when George says in a very polite way, "Boss, I went to the Muscular Arms in Glasgow for a quiet pint when this lovely lady comes up to me and says 'Dandy I must sleep with you tonight'." The bus was in tears! This was the man Ally said he could control. It was hilarious!'

Ayr, with McLean in the starting 11, led at Tynecastle through a Graham penalty and were just ten minutes from another semi-final when an Alan Anderson equaliser forced a replay.

A bumper gate of 16,185 headed for Somerset Park on the Wednesday with the start delayed for ten minutes as police dealt with crowd trouble on the terracing.

An entertaining 90 minutes failed to produce a goal and the game entered extra time. Donald Ford's header gave the visitors the lead at the start of the second period but the part-timers fought off any feelings of fatigue and looked to have secured a third game when Fleming found the net seven minutes later. But Ford scored again with just five minutes remaining. All three of the goals had come from headers.

Publicly, manager Ally was gracious in defeat. 'I reckon we might have gone out to the cup winners again,' he told Stewart Brown of the *Edinburgh Evening News*. 'Rangers did it in their centenary, so might Hearts.'

Recalling long-gone days at training, Sir Alex Ferguson, 'He'd always come up with great ideas for free kicks. I remember one when the first player runs over the ball, then the second, then the third and the fourth player was supposed to hit it.'

When the routine was tried in a match it did not quite work. 'Right on half-time we got a free kick and all four players ran over it and no one was left to hit it! I was getting ready to run in at half-time and Big Dandy said, "Don't you effing run in. Don't hurry it will be like a war in there." So when we got in he had them all lined up against the wall and he was screaming at them and tea cups were being thrown, boots, everything! Dandy and I crept in as he was ranting and raving but he never held a grudge against anyone, that was a great quality to him.'

Back in the First Division, Ayr lost their next three matches, predictably one at Celtic Park, then finished off the season by winning three and losing only one of their final six fixtures.

They won their last game at Methil on 27 April with a Dougie Mitchell penalty the difference between them and East Fife. Those two points gained at Bayview left Ayr in seventh place and they finished on 38 points in yet another successful season for the club.

Ferguson played in the reserve fixture between Ayr and East Fife at Somerset Park on that final day and scored with a header in a 2-1 win, his last match as a player.

By the latter part of the season Ferguson had been missing matches or making the odd appearance from the substitutes' bench, the result of recurring groin injuries. Possessing the same work ethic as his manager the player was uncomfortable with this and went to Ally's office.

'Boss,' he said, 'I'm toiling with groin injuries and letting you down.' Ally assured Ferguson that he was far from letting him down as he had scored goals for the club. The player then insisted that he really felt as though he was toiling. Ally then told Ferguson that there had been enquiries from Queen's Park and East Stirling with the view to him taking up management positions. Asked for his opinion, Ally advised to at least attend the interviews particularly as Ferguson had played for Queen's Park.

'I went along and every person in the boardroom I had played with,' Sir Alex recalls. 'I interviewed badly as I was nervous and in the end they gave the job to Davie MacParland.'

'That happens,' Ally consoled him but added that East Stirling were still interested. Again the player asked for his manager's thoughts and he still remembers the advice given to this day. 'The only thing I can say to you is that if you are out of the game for two minutes you can be forgotten about. Take the job if it's offered to you, you will do well in management,' Ally said, adding that had he been in Ferguson's position he would take it. Ferguson then met with the club chairman Willie Muirhead and was offered the manager's position but decided he needed a couple of weeks to think about it.

This time Ally advised Ferguson to take his time and not to take it for the sake of being in a job but added that if he felt it was right he should say yes to the offer. Again Ferguson listened to his manager and mulled over the opportunity.

That summer Ally was one of a number of managers and club officials who travelled to the World Cup in West Germany on a Scottish League sponsored flight. He considered his role more as an observer and 'a bit of a fan' according to the *Ayrshire Post* and was keen to learn from the experience.

Also in the party was the East Stirling chairman Willie Muirhead and Sir Alex recalls him flying back early to persuade him to accept the post that would start his career in management. Whether or not Ally had spoken to Muirhead recommending Ferguson is unknown but far from unlikely given his nature and the fact he was aware of the situation.

13

Top Ten Target

DURING the second week of August 1974 and just days ahead of the new season Alex Ferguson was getting ready to open his pub when there was a knock at the door. He takes up the story today, 'Ally bounced in and said, "Put the kettle on." I said, "Okay boss." So we sat chatting in the alcove of the pub having tea and he was asking how it was at East Stirling. I said "we've no players" and he asked if I had money for players. I said they were trying to arrange a board meeting to see if they could raise some money.

'He said, "I'll see if we have any players you could use." And then he stuck his hand in his inside pocket and said, "Here's your salaries that you're owed." He gave me ten weeks' wages! I said, "What are you doing? I left in April, I'm not due that. What will the directors say?"

'Ally said, "Never mind the directors. Don't worry about them, you've earned it. You're my player – I pay you not the directors and you deserve it." Honestly, brilliant. I talk about earning loyalty – in that moment he earned my loyalty. From that moment on I will never ever forget Ally MacLeod.'

In the 1974/75 season Ayr were drawn in Section Four of the League Cup which provided tough opposition in the form of Celtic, Dundee United and Motherwell with only the group winners advancing. They lost the first match on 10 August in Dundee when two Andy Gray goals helped his side to a 3-1 victory during which the *Evening Times*'s scribe noted, 'The game was held up for a few minutes as the referee dashed to the Ayr dugout to lecture manager Ally McLeod for shouting.' Although most journals had by now grasped the correct spelling of Ally's surname there was still the occasional slip.

Despite his impressive home record against Rangers Ally had still failed to gain the upper hand over Jock Stein when Celtic came to Ayr on 14 August. 'Victory here tonight could give us a great chance of qualifying for the later stages of the competition,' the manager wrote in the match programme. The opposite proved to be the case.

The crowd of 7,766 certainly got value for their money. New signing Doug Somner struck first blood for Ayr after 14 minutes but a Steve Murray goal brought Celtic level. A Mitchell penalty restored Ayr's lead at the interval but back came Celtic again with George Connelly equalising in spectacular fashion from 25 yards.

But the home side were not finished and Ingram headed in a free kick on 65 minutes to claim the League Cup points. The result was achieved against the odds with Graham, McAnespie and McLean all unavailable through injury.

It was in fact Ayr's first win over Celtic in 14 years. Having achieved that long-awaited victory they then failed to win another match in the section but did finish their last game on a high by fighting back from two down to draw 2-2 with Dundee United at Somerset, although Ayr finished bottom of the section with just the three points. Celtic incidentally gained revenge for their defeat with a 5-2 win in the return match.

Change was in the air that season and Ally's priority was the same as every other manager in the First Division, other than the Old Firm bosses who had title ambitions. It was essential that Ayr finished in one of the top ten places as only those sides would take part in the following season's inaugural Scottish Premier League where they would compete with each other four times during the course of a campaign.

This of course promised the golden honeypot of twice as many fixtures against the Glasgow giants, guaranteeing extra income through the turnstiles and more television exposure and revenue. On past form of course a top-ten finish was quite achievable but with every other club eager to finish as high as possible every precious point would have to be fought for. To finish 11th or lower would be nothing short of disastrous for part-time Ayr.

Again Rangers were due at Somerset early in the season, in the opening league game. And again Ayr took something from the match with a McCulloch goal cancelling out Sandy Jardine's opener for a point each. Bobby Tait saw ten minutes of action when he was sent on during the second half only for the manager to substitute the substitute following the equaliser.

The post-match press conference found the Ayr manager in entertaining mood. 'We should have had the game won,' Ally enthused. 'Did you see the chances we missed in the last 20 minutes?'

Someone pointed out that Rangers too had missed chances and should in fact have had the points in the bag shortly after half-time. Ally thought this over then responded, 'Well, of course I'm a bit biased when it comes to Ayr United… but I still think we should have won.'

Defeat in the derby at Rugby Park in their next match was the first of four consecutive losses. By the end of September, after conceding five times at Celtic Park again, Ayr were marooned at the very foot of the table with one solitary point and their dreams of a Premier League place receding on a weekly basis. They had also crashed out of the Texaco Cup in the first round again, losing 3-0 at Birmingham City and managing only a scoreless draw in the return.

The league revival started on 5 October as Ayr scored five goals against Partick Thistle. Although they went down at Aberdeen the following Saturday, Ally's men lost only twice more that year, at Easter Road and Ibrox.

Wins were recorded against Airdrie, St Johnstone, Dumbarton, Arbroath and Dundee.

As 1975 dawned the remarkable turnaround in Ayr's fortunes had seen them climb to the aspired position of ninth place with 16 points on the board.

January saw an inconsistent spell. The period began well with a 3-2 derby win against Kilmarnock at Somerset on the first day of the year. As he always did if they had a match on the first, Ally made sure the club arranged for the players to stay overnight in a hotel in Girvan on Hogmanay. This was a lesson he had learned from the party he had held for his Blackburn team-mates at Livesey Branch Road all those years earlier.

A heavy defeat at Motherwell (5-1) was followed up by a home victory over Clyde. Ayr then lost five goals to Celtic for the third time in the season – they had also scored nine times against the Glasgow side during the four matches – and suffered the humiliation of a Scottish Cup exit at home to Scotland's only league side who were still amateurs, Queen's Park.

After Graham had missed the chance to force a replay when his penalty kick stuck a post, the Somerset faithful sensed it was not to be their day and burst into a chorus of 'What a load of rubbish'. 'I don't want to take anything away from Queen's,' Ally told Jim Blair after the match. 'But if we'd taken all our chances it could have been a cricket score.'

A February home win over Aberdeen lifted spirits and at the end of March, following victory at Arbroath, Ally's men were clinging on to ninth spot. But it was tight with St Johnstone level on 28 points and Kilmarnock just one behind.

Ayr again made the sports headlines early in March following the ordering-off of Johnny Doyle in the home game against Airdrie for a retaliatory foul on Paul Jonquin. The manager was of the opinion that the red card could have cost the club their top ten place. 'When Doyle went off it meant we had to play for 32 minutes with ten men,' he was quoted in the *Evening Times* where he credited the rest of his team for holding on for a 1-0 victory.

Ally's strict disciplinary code came into effect when he fined Doyle the not insignificant amount of £100, stressing that the punishment was not specifically for being sent off, but for throwing his chewing gum at a linesman as he left the pitch.

Ally set his players a challenge of winning their last three matches which would make sure of finishing at least tenth in the table.

The first of these games was an exciting affair at Dens Park on 12 April where Ayr came away with a 3-2 win. Next was a home fixture against Dunfermline where, after losing an early goal, Ayr fought back to again win 3-2 despite a rather nervy finish. The results of other matches played that afternoon benefitted Ally's team and their top-ten status was confirmed with one match still to play.

Ally was perhaps more laid back than might have been expected when he spoke to the *Evening Times* on the Monday, 'Three games ago we set ourselves a target of winning all three games…I knew four points would be enough but I wanted to be sure.'

Only a late equaliser deprived Ayr of victory in the 1-1 draw at Morton while three other clubs walked a tightrope for the last two Premier League places on the season's final day. Ayr finished the season in a very respectable seventh place having collected 36 points.

During the summer the manager added midfielder Jim McSherry to his squad. McSherry was one of the players who had just been freed by Kilmarnock following their failure to finish in the top ten. Like many of Ally's dealings the signing was not quite routine. The player had to get on a train to Glasgow and meet Ally at Central Station. McSherry remembers the events of that Friday well and expected to be taken to the press club where Ally was meeting his friend Davie MacParland, then the Queen's Park manager.

'He asked me "how are you" as we walked across the road to the Bank of Scotland. He told me the terms of the contract and a few things, then asked, "Oh…do you have a passport as you're going to Canada in the next fortnight as John Murphy has pulled out of the trip and you're now going."

'He handed me some papers and told me to sign them which I did. The documents were signed on a shelf at the bank which people used to write cheques. "Congratulations, you are now an Ayr United player," he said.'

And with that McSherry's new manager left him standing outside the bank and walked off to meet MacParland at the press club.

Ayr had been invited back to Newfoundland that close-season and, with the problems associated with the release of part-time players for two weeks overcome, had arranged to take part in some matches in Canada on the way. Ayr won all their matches save for a 2-2 draw with a Canadian All Stars who were really the Olympic team preparing for the Montreal Games the following year.

Following a two-hour boat trip to Saint Pierre, a French-speaking island, the manager promised his players they could have a night out if they managed to score 13 times against local side Miquelon. Helped by four from Doyle and a Graham hat-trick the players racked up a score of 14-0 to qualify for the promised reward. But not all of Ally's instructions had been carried out.

At 14-0 Ally had passed word to his players to let Miquelon score or to at leas concede a penalty kick. Sure enough the home side had the chance to score from the spot with keeper Ally McLean under instructions not to save it but to look as though he was trying. The manager was reported to be furious when the ball struck McLean on the head and bounced over the crossbar. He then ordered his men not to score any further goals before they headed for their night out.

During the tour they also renewed their friendship with St John's, beating them 8-1, and hit eight goals without reply against a St Lawrence select side.

The more competitive Premier League presented a new challenge for Ally as he entered his tenth year of management. Did he harbour ambitions of managing a bigger club? He certainly never sought out such positions and in his autobiography claims to have turned down a number of offers to stay at Somerset Park as he 'felt that I could satisfy all my football ambitions right there'. Were those ambitions limited to a place in the top division or did he believe that cup success with Ayr was a possibility?

Faye does remember a US coach visiting the house in Westfield Road to offer Ally a position in Denver, Colorado which he rejected, concerned at the disruption such a move would cause his children's education.

Like her brothers, Gail insists she never felt neglected by her father although she was aware that Ally was no ordinary dad, 'It was a kind of strange childhood because everybody wanted a piece of him. You couldn't go anywhere but people wanted autographs and pictures taken. Deep down he was quite a shy man but he did enjoy the attention. We called him Ally a lot of the time as everybody else called him Ally.'

Before the first ball was kicked in the new set-up the players had to face the challenge of the League Cup. Ayr had a decent section containing Hibs, Dunfermline and Dundee. Although they only lost once, at Hibs, three draws proved costly and Ayr finished second to the Edinburgh side which ended the club's involvement in the tournament.

The match at Easter Road had been a midweek affair and local newspaper reporter and Ayr fan Bob Shields had intimated to Ally that he would struggle to get home by train. The manager told him not to worry as there would be room on the team coach if he was stuck. During the match Shields bumped into a local hotelier and accepted his offer of a ride back to Ayr.

Shields answered the telephone in his office the next day. 'You held everybody up!' Ally ranted, before advising that the club had decided to withdraw any future travel facilities from the press.

A few weeks later Ally asked Shields if he was travelling to Tannadice for a league match. The journalist was unsure and said he had to check the timetables at which Ally said, 'Oh, just come back with us then,' and with that the Easter Road incident was forgotten.

Ayr kicked off their Premier League season with a 1-1 draw at Motherwell which prompted the manager to point out in the following week's match programme that Ayr had been the only away side to earn a Premier League point in that first week.

St Johnstone then lost to a second-half Doyle goal at Somerset and with three points in the bag Ayr were off to a good start. They then lost narrowly at Hibs, saw off Dundee by the odd goal in three at home then lost away matches at Aberdeen and Dundee United. In between they had exited the Texaco Cup – by now the Anglo-Scottish Cup after the end of Texaco's sponsorship – to Mansfield Town of the English Third Division by an aggregate score of 3-0.

Ingram was sent off before the end of the second leg at Field Mill with three other Ayr players booked, including skipper Johnny Graham. As well as the defeat the manager was disappointed with the lack of discipline and made a point of telling his team just that during the after-match meal in their hotel.

Skipper Graham asked the manager if the players could have a beer but was told soft drinks were the order of the day after which Graham apparently bought himself a pint. According to Jim McSherry, 'Ally then took the captaincy off him in no uncertain terms and made Rikki Fleming skipper.'

As they approached their home game with champions Rangers on 11 October Ayr were in a credible sixth place in the new league with five points on the board. Rangers were top and unbeaten with twice United's tally.

What happened that afternoon at Somerset Park is still remembered by older fans of the club as one of the greatest days in Ayr's history. A crowd of 18,638 witnessed the club's most comprehensive result yet over the Ibrox men who had broken the Celtic monopoly of nine successive league titles at the end of the previous season.

Two goals scored within a minute by McCulloch and Ingram around the half-hour saw Ally's men in control and a second-half Graham volley from a Doyle cross was the icing on the cake for a 3-0 victory. BBC Scotland had selected the match for televising and those watching *Sportscene* that Saturday evening saw a thoroughly deserved home win followed by an interview with a jubilant and excited manager. That match and the resulting media coverage propelled Ally firmly into the public eye and anyone who hadn't known who he was certainly did now.

Bob Shields composed the following for the *Ayrshire Post*, 'A MacLeod ear to ear grin which flashed across the nation's television sets on Saturday night summed it all up for United fans who could only have dreamed about a match like this…Rangers were not only beaten but severely thrashed in every department of the game.'

After seven matches part-time Ayr United sat proudly in fourth position of the new Premier League table behind only Celtic, Rangers and Hibernian.

At the time no one could have foreseen the consequences that the Rangers result and subsequent publicity would have for Ayr and ultimately Scottish football.

On that same day, as Ayr were running riot against Rangers, Celtic chalked up a 2-1 victory at Pittodrie. The defeat left Aberdeen joint bottom of the table in a league that would see two clubs relegated at the end of the season. The Dons had won just one of their seven matches – against Ayr – and gained four points. Three days later manager Jimmy Bonthrone resigned, a decision which the Aberdeen board attempted to talk him out of. Almost immediately, with Ayr's weekend win still being talked about, Ally was one of the names rumoured as a possible replacement for Bonthrone.

The Ayr players were brought back down to earth seven days after the Rangers game when losing their next match in Edinburgh to Hearts but then overcame Motherwell 2-0 at Somerset on Saturday 1 November.

On the Monday Aberdeen made their move and Ally, refusing the offer of a contract, agreed to take over the Aberdeen job but not for another seven days and not until he had taken charge of Ayr for one last time. Aberdeen chairman Dick Donald later told the *Aberdeen Evening Express*'s James Forbes, 'It was such an amicable meeting that it took only half an hour for us to agree on terms.'

'We always felt there was a possibility he would move on at some stage,' recalls defender Davie Wells. 'Because he had been so successful I felt he would progress and move on to better himself.'

The approach almost came too late as Ally had recently attended an interview in London for a £15,000 job away from the game and was giving it consideration. The post was as territorial manager looking after the Scottish interests of Alpine Glazing and Ally was tempted, but the chance of working with a bigger club and full-time players was too great to reject.

The following evening Kilmarnock hosted the first leg of the Ayrshire Cup Final in front of a crowd estimated at 7,000. Ally's farewell present to the Ayr supporters was a 3-0 win, rendering the Somerset leg a formality. One of Ally's last acts as Ayr manager was to reinstate the captaincy to Johnny Graham whom he had replaced after the Mansfield defeat. Jim McSherry remembers that although Rikki Fleming was a great player he did not command the same respect as a captain from his team-mates.

Is it conceivable that Ally might have seen out the rest of his management days at Somerset Park had his head not been turned by Aberdeen? Faye believes he did have ambitions beyond Ayr at that point, 'I think at the time he thought if he wanted to win anything he really had to leave Ayr. He had gone as far as he could by taking them into the Premier League.'

During Ally's tenure at Somerset Park his home record against Rangers, bearing in mind Ayr's part-time status, was an impressive four wins, two draws and five defeats in 11 league and cup matches. The statistics of Celtic's Somerset Park appearances during the same period tell a different story. Ayr lost nine of the ten league and cup matches with just the one League Cup victory between August 1966 and the end of October 1975.

Significantly this period coincided with the rise of Jock Stein's all-conquering Celtic side which won 19 out of 27 domestic trophies available including nine league titles.

Celtic's Davie Hay recalls that his club had to fight for those victories against Ayr, 'You always got a game at Somerset Park against Ayr. They were always hard games and Ally had a good team there.'

Two days after the Ayrshire Cup match Ally was revealed to the press as the new manager of Aberdeen Football Club.

Aberdeen were something of a sleeping giant in Scottish football and having won the Scottish Cup in 1970, and very nearly the championship 12 months later under Eddie Turnbull, were now a club deep in relegation trouble who saw Ally as the man to get them out of it.

14

A New Don

'I FIRMLY believe Aberdeen can win something and I see the job as a big challenge. It is my opinion that keeping Ayr United in the Premier League is a more difficult thing to do than help the Dons win a trophy.' Ally MacLeod was speaking to Frank Gilfeather of the *Aberdeen Evening Express* just after his appointment. Again he promised entertaining football, 'I think the fans want excitement and goalmouth incidents. The Dons' style of play must be based on this.'

Two days before officially taking up office Ally was in the directors' box at Fir Park to watch his new side take on Motherwell, who they had defeated at Ayr seven days earlier. A 2-0 deficit for the Dons saw the manager head for the dressing room at half-time to air his observations. He was then seen to take his place in the dugout for the remainder of the game. A penalty kick sealed a 3-0 win for the Steelmen leaving Ally somewhat bemused.

'This must have been Aberdeen's worst performance of the season,' he told Joe Hamilton of the *Glasgow Herald*. 'A lot of hard work is in front of me. The situation is serious and we do not have a lot of time…But give me three weeks and I'll have sorted out a lot of the problems.'

Ally's optimism was already starting to shine through despite his concerns over the performance. Much was made of his dressing room intervention and subsequent appearance in the dugout but it had actually been pre-planned as he had hinted to Gilfeather on the eve of the game, 'As far as I'm concerned I become Aberdeen boss at midnight tonight. Let's just say I don't think I'll be in the stand after the first 45 minutes. If I see one or two little things that can help the side I'll let them know.'

His first official match in charge, on 15 November, already had a 'must-win' look about it. Dundee United were two points clear of the Dons and defeat would increase the gap. Previewing the match for the *Evening Express* he told James Forbes that he had been happy with the way things had gone during his first week with the players but that there was still a lot of work to be done, and he added, 'This team is capable of great things.'

United had home advantage but it took only four minutes for Billy Williamson to put Aberdeen ahead from a penalty. The manager later revealed that his gameplan had been for a frenzied attack on the opposition goal and the tactic had clearly been successful.

United levelled after the break only for Jocky Scott to quickly restore the lead with what proved to be the winner though the Dons had the disadvantage of finishing a man short following the dismissal of Drew Jarvie.

'His enthusiasm has already begun to rub off on the players,' Gilfeather noted in his *Evening Express* column on the Monday.

The reserve players certainly became aware of the manager's enthusiasm that week then they were ordered to do an extra afternoon's training after letting a 1-0 lead end in defeat with the loss of two late goals – in a practice match.

There was a buzz about the city in the build-up to Ally's first home game the following Saturday against Hearts. As well as looking for a house in the area Ally spent much of that week enthusiastically promoting the match, appearing on Grampian TV and in the newspapers to urge the public to turn up to support their team with the promise of attacking football.

Just as in his Somerset Park days he knew the importance of breaking down any barriers which isolated the boardroom from the supporters. 'My first concern is to get the team winning regularly in the next few weeks,' he told Bill McAllister of the *Aberdeen Press and Journal*, 'so that we can get into contention for the Premier League title.'

On the Friday, James Forbes penned the following in the *Evening Express*, 'It looks as though they will have the support of a much higher crowd than usual. People are again "talking football" in the city.' Dons supporter Tommy Petrie remembers Ally attending a meeting of the Northern Lights Supporters Club within days of his appointment and was immediately stuck by his enthusiasm. 'His exuberance for the club was something else and he was a real character. A great appointment and a really nice man,' Tommy recalls.

In his match programme notes the new manager told supporters, 'I see myself as a motivator getting the best out of the players. They [Hearts] have been playing well and justify their position in the league table but as I have said, if we believe in ourselves and the players selected "die" for me I am convinced that not only will we win today, we can win this first Premier League.'

Although the Hearts match ended without a goal Aberdeen climbed to third-bottom after Dundee United lost to Motherwell. The attendance of 12,378 was over 5,000 in excess of the last home match with Dundee. The revival, it seemed, had begun.

An excellent piece by 'a special correspondent' in the following Monday's *Scotsman* captured the moment the supporters first caught sight of the new manager, 'He is moving up the table and fast. For Ally MacLeod read Aberdeen – they are already interchangeable. In a mere fortnight MacLeod has achieved total identification with the club. When the Aberdeen players took to the field on Saturday they were hailed with a respectable roar.

Ally, extreme left, back row, in the school team at Queen's Park secondary 1947/48. (MacLeod family archive)

A keen all-round sportsman, Ally, third from right bottom row, also turned out for the school cricket team. (MacLeod family archive)

Living the dream, Ally signed
as a professional for his
beloved Third Lanark aged
18 in 1949. (MacLeod family
archive)

Ally scores for Third
Lanark at Pittodrie in 1952,
a ground where he would
later spend his happiest days
in management. (Evening
Citizen)

Ally's best match. He marries Faye in Glagow in October 1956. Best man John Anderson later became a TV personality as the Judge in *Gladiators*. (MacLeod family archive)

Bedecked in balloons and his football strip Ally is carried from the wedding reception bound for the overnight train and a short honeymoon in London. (MacLeod family archive)

His happiest playing days were at Blackburn and here Ally scores the winning goal against Liverpool in the FA Cup quarter-final March 1958. (Mirrorpix)

The MacLeods at home in Livesey Branch Road, Blackburn. Faye, Ally and Simon. (Soccer Star magazine)

The Blackburn Rovers team for the 1960 FA Cup Final (Back row) John Bray, Matt Woods, Harry Leyland, Louis Simpson, Derek Dougan, Dave Whelan, Mick McGrath. (Front) Eddie Thomas (reserve), Peter Dobing, Ronnie Clayton, Bryan Douglas and Ally MacLeod. (Getty Images)

Ally, closest to the camera, waits to be introduced to the Duke of Gloucester ahead of the Wembley final. The thick tracksuits unsettled the Blackburn players. (Getty Images)

Ally and Simon. He named the poodle after the lead character in *The Saint* novels before the books were adapted into a television series. (Getty Images)

Ally was made captain of Hibs and his two seasons there allowed him to sample European competition in the Inter Cities Fairs Cup. (Herald and Times)

Ally and his first son Andrew outside their home in Clarkston, Glasgow in 1967. (MacLeod family archive)

A rare photograph of all the MacLeod family together. Faye, Ally, Andrew, Gail and David on holiday in 1969. (MacLeod family archive)

Only his suit and tie distinguish the manager from the jubilant Ayr United supporters. Here Ally celebrates as his part-timers score in the defeat of Rangers in September 1969 shortly after their return to the First Division. The 2-1 victory was witnessed by Somerset Park's record home attendance of over 25,000. (Mirrorpix)

Ally with his Ayr United squad and the Ayrshire Cup, 1971/72 season. (Eric McCowatt)

Drew Jarvie heads Aberdeen level in the 1976 League Cup Final... (SNS)

... and Davie Robb nets the winner in extra time. (SNS)

Full time at Hampden and after an enthralling 120 minutes Aberdeen have won the League Cup. Ally and his backroom team rush from the dugout whilst Jock Stein gets ready to console his players. (Eric McCowatt)

The proud manager watches from the pitchside as his team are presented with the cup. (Eric McCowatt)

Ally with the League Cup. He turned Aberdeen into trophy winners less than a year after taking charge of a relegation-threatened club.
(Eric McCowatt)

"*That's three games without defeat and the championship. Probably the wise thing would be to go back to Aberdeen and ask for my old job at Pittodrie.*" Just as at Aberdeen Ally delivered immediate success with Scotland. Here with the British Championship trophy June 1977. (Herald and Times)

Don Masson is the coolest man in the cauldron of Anfield as his penalty kick sends Scotland on their way to the World Cup finals on a dramatic night against Wales. (Getty Images)

Argentina here we come! Full time at Anfield and Scotland have qualified for the 1978 World Cup. (Herald and Times)

His darkest hour. Ally has just witnessed the anger of the Scotland fans after the draw with Iran in Cordoba. Worse was to follow when the team bus was held up outside the stadium. (Herald and Times)

No sign of a lynch mob as Ally signs autographs on arrival at Glasgow Airport from Argentina. One bystander points the finger of blame in his direction. (Herald and Times)

Blackburn Rovers
Football & Athletic Co. Limited

REGISTERED OFFICE:
EWOOD PARK . BLACKBURN BB2 4JF
TELEPHONES: 55432 & 55433   REGISTERED No. 53492 ENGLAND

Mr. A. McCleod,   Our Ref:- WHB/EA.
1, Corfe Hill Place,
AYR,
Scotland.   31st October, 1978.

Dear Alistair,

I make no excuse whatsoever for writing to you to reiterate my plea
to you to come down and manage Blackburn Rovers. Because I have
blue and white eyeballs I have a duty to perform, and I am
authorised to make the following offer to you regarding a
proposed contract :-

1) A fixed salary of £17,500 per annum paid in fortnightly
   instalments on the second Tuesday of every fortnight.

2) £1,000 if the first team shall remain in the Second Division
   of the Football League.

3) £1,500 if the first team finishes the season in the first
   eleven of the Second Division.

4) A whole series of bonuses ranging from £250 to £5,000 with
   regard to the Club's involvement in the Anglo-Scottish Cup,
   the F.A. Cup and the Football League Cup.

5) All travelling and out-of-pocket expenses etc. incurred by you,
   including a period of three months whereby the Club would pay
   all expenses incurred by you at a Hotel of your choice in the
   district, whilst settling in and negotiating the purchase of
   a house.

6) A new blue 'T' registration Ford Granada for your exclusive use.

I deeply respect your point of view with regard to your present position
with Ayr United Football Club, and I trust you will think none the worse
of me for making you this offer in writing. Speaking personally I would
dearly love to welcome you back to Ewood Park after all these years,
because I feel certain you will not only lift the team, you will lift the
town and I think you will even lift the board, which by the way at the
moment of writing have an average age of 48 years (so you can see some
changes have taken place here).

Should there be any merit in my suggestion of a meeting I
would appreciate a call from you on 0254/665243(which is
my private ex-directory number at home) or on 0254/57706
which is my business number.   Incidentally we are playing
Fulham in London on Friday evening, and consequently I will
be away from Blackburn from Thursday lunchtime to Saturday
lunchtime, but I trust I am not being too optimistic in hoping
to hear from you one way or another at some time in the
future.

Yours sincerely,

WILLIAM H. BANCROFT, CHAIRMAN.

Even in the immediate aftermath of Argentina there was no shortage of job offers. (MacLeod family archive)

Leaving the SFA at Park Gardens for the last time to return to Ayr United less than a week after taking charge of Scotland in Austria, 26/09/78. (Herald and Times)

Ally is named Scottish Brewers Personality of the Month for August 1984 after his Airdrie side defeated Scottish champions Aberdeen in the League Cup.

'Da Ya Think I'm Sexy?' Ally meets up with his old friend Rod Stewart in Paisley prior to the Scotland v Australia match in 1985. Then in his third spell at Ayr United discussions took place that evening with a view to the singer investing in the club. (Mirrorpix)

Champagne celebration. April 1988 and Ally toasts his Ayr United players who have just secured the Second Division championship as well as promotion.

Ally with some of his former Ayr players at his testimonial dinner in February 1992. Left to right - Davie Wells, Jim Cowell, Dougie McCracken, John Sludden, Ian McAllister and Ally. (MacLeod family archive)

Smiling until the end. One of the last pictures of Ally taken in 2002. Still with that optimism shining through despite suffering from Alzheimer's. (MacLeod family archive)

'But there was a veritable explosion of noise three minutes later when MacLeod appeared and made his way to the dugout. He was acclaimed not only by the young…also dour old season ticket holders in the stand stood and cheered. Here was the man they had all been waiting for.'

The piece sums up both the renewed expectations of the Pittodrie crowd as well as the charisma of the man entrusted with those hopes.

Bill McAllister penned a similar tribute in his *Press and Journal* column, 'Ally MacLeod is the only man who can get a standing ovation from over 11,000 people for simply putting one foot in front of the other. He proved that on Saturday by strolling to the dugout minutes before the kick-off…and the whole stand rose as one and the crowd seemed to go berserk.'

The local Saturday night results paper the *Green Final* launched a 'Meet Macleod' competition for 60 winners to attend a function in the city and in keeping with the manager's ambitions the club began to think bigger. Acting on a suggestion of Ally's, Aberdeen chartered a 50-seater aircraft to fly to Prestwick for the game at Ayr United, a venture partly funded by supporters in the Pittodrie 50 Club.

Dons secretary Jim Rust hinted this was something which may be repeated for other games in the west of the country and all being well the party hoped to be back in Aberdeen around 6.30pm, hours earlier than a coach trip would allow.

Ally is reported to have been given a good reception by the Ayr fans in the crowd of 5,187 where Alex Stuart was taking charge for the first time. Embarrassingly for Ally the Dons lost the game to a freak goal on the 50-minute mark. Murphy hit a speculative 40-yard lob high into the penalty area which goalkeeper Andy Geoghan caught, then let slip, and the ball bounced over the line. Geoghan had only taken over in goal from injured club captain Bobby Clark the previous week.

In Willie Miller's autobiography, *The Don*, he recalls the manager was 'furious' in the dressing room after the match, tearing into each and every one of the players whom he felt had humiliated him. Publicly he was more diplomatic. 'We made mistakes but I thought we were worth a draw,' was Ally's post-match assessment in the press room.

In Clark's absence Miller had been made skipper and the manager decided to let the central defender retain the captaincy once the goalkeeper returned.

'It was pretty simple as I had injured my knee just before Ally arrived,' Clark recalls. 'I was on the sideline in his first game because of this and had to go in for surgery [cartilage removed]. Since I had been the captain he had to find a new one and picked Willie Miller. There was no big deal about it as I could not play at the time and, as history has shown, it was an excellent choice.'

The following week's match on 6 December proved to be one of the most significant of Ally's reign at Aberdeen. The Dons had not beaten Rangers in any competition at Pittodrie since a League Cup match in August 1965. The last home league victory had been a few months before that in March, a period of ten long years. Although factually accurate this statistic does not tell the full story of the fixture. In the ten First Division meetings at Pittodrie since 1965 half of them had ended in draws and in the same period Aberdeen had beaten Rangers four times at Ibrox in the league, drawn twice, and also won a Scottish Cup replay there just nine months earlier.

Yet the Pittodrie fans had been deprived of that elusive home win and one man planned to change that and lay the bogey to rest at the earliest opportunity.

'I am looking forward to Saturday's game because I know my players are going to fight until they drop,' Ally told Andy Melvin of the *Aberdeen Evening Express*, adding, 'If they don't I'm going to be on top of them like a ton of bricks.'

His match programme notes echoed those sentiments, 'I can assure you that every game played at Pittodrie will be worth the admission fee – failing this I will make sure the players realise the fans' feelings.'

Goalless with six minutes remaining, the game appeared to be heading for another draw when the Rangers defence failed to deal with a long lob into their penalty area. As they hesitated the ball broke kindly for Drew Jarvie who stabbed it beyond Stewart Kennedy from six yards, sending the home fans delirious.

Ally leapt from the dugout and ran to celebrate with his players at the end as the home fans in the 20,557 crowd rejoiced in the 1-0 victory. 'I can't underestimate the value of that win, both from the players' and the fans' angle,' a still-bubbling Ally told the *Evening Times*'s Alan Davidson. 'Did you see the way the players rushed towards each other at the end? We've got a great rapport going now.'

Looking ahead he boasted, 'We're going to need Concorde to take all the fans who want to travel to Glasgow for the game with Celtic next week.'

That was the way the fixtures worked out for the Dons, who were meeting both the Old Firm sides on successive Saturdays.

Aberdeen supporter Scott Bremner remembers the significance of the Rangers result, 'The win over Rangers at Pittodrie acted as a catalyst for the club to prove they were heading in the right direction. He was never scared to show his emotions with a win and at that point in my opinion the seed was sown for the Aberdeen of the 1980s as the fans had renewed belief in someone.'

'We haven't even talked about Celtic and we hardly talked about Rangers last week either,' Ally disclosed to Andy Melvin, before expanding on his psychology with, 'I'm trying to make my players believe in themselves. I'm not going to bog them down with worrying about the opposition. We may have a ten-minute chat about Celtic tomorrow and that will be it.'

It took Jarvie just six minutes to open the Dons' account with Arthur Graham doubling the tally before half-time. Celtic failed in their efforts to find a way past Geoghan and 2-0 it finished.

In his first attempt with Aberdeen, Ally had beaten Celtic in the league – a feat beyond him in 14 First Division matches when in charge of Ayr.

'Ally's Army marches on!' read Allan Heron's *Sunday Mail* report, which continued, 'Not only did the MacLeod men outmanoeuvre and outmaster the pride of Parkhead, but they also had Celtic fans queuing to leave fifteen minutes from the end.'

The Dons had now stepped up to fourth from bottom in the league, seventh from the top and just six points behind leaders Celtic. In a few short weeks the manager had turned a gloomy season around with a new optimism sweeping through the city. When Ally had taken over the main priority was to establish a place in the new league for the following season, but to beat Rangers AND Celtic was beyond even the most optimistic of supporter's dreams.

This charismatic new manager seemed to have the Midas touch and was already adored by the Aberdeen public. The question on every Dons fan's lips was – just how far could Ally MacLeod take Aberdeen?

Bobby Clark looks back fondly on Ally's early days at Pittodrie, 'Ally loved having a headline for the newspapers and got the entire town very excited. He was not a tactical coach like Eddie Turnbull had been but was much more of a motivator. He was an entertainer and brought great spirit and belief.'

In the programme for the next home match, against Hibernian, the manager wrote, 'What a double – Rangers and Celtic in two successive weeks. A real team effort with everyone playing their part.'

The Hibs match ended in a draw as did meetings with Motherwell and Hearts, but wins against both the Dundee teams and a revenge victory against Ayr kept the momentum going into 1976.

'I honestly believe that I can make Aberdeen the best-supported team in Scotland,' Ally had told Dixon Blackstock of the *Sunday Mail* in December 1975. Such a target would now be viewed as quite ludicrous but the quote is a good example of how one of Ally's statements can be misrepresented today.

Before it was made an all-seated stadium in 1978 Pittodrie could accommodate up to 35,000 fans and the Dons had been the fifth-best supported club in Scotland the previous term behind the Glasgow and Edinburgh teams. The average gate at Ibrox in 1975/76 was 31,319 and on one occasion Rangers played to a mere 11,000 spectators while Celtic averaged 26,227.

At the time Aberdeen not only had an entire city to themselves, but as far as league football was concerned they had the whole of the north of Scotland as a potential fan base. Taking all these factors into account Ally was not aiming for the unachievable.

Having brushed aside Alloa Athletic in the Scottish Cup the Dons faced a trip to Ibrox in round four, but not before the two sides met in the league on 7 February, seven days ahead of the cup tie.

In the league game Rangers held a two-goal lead at half-time and looked comfortable with the Dons offering little threat. It was not until a 78th-minute goal from substitute Billy Pirie that the visitors started to come to life. By the end Rangers had gone from looking convincing winners to praying for the final whistle but time ran out on Aberdeen and the home team left the field to muted cheers.

Despite the result Aberdeen had finished the stronger side and felt they could improve for the cup game.

'For once a big cup tie at Ibrox won't be dominated by the Rangers fans,' Ally told the *Daily Record*'s Hugh Taylor on the eve of the game. 'There's so much enthusiasm in the north that I estimate at least 8,000 of our own supporters going south. The players are full of confidence because they reckon they should have won the Premier League game last week. And with the armada of supporters behind them, the boys feel they just can't lose.'

The newspaper picked up on the manager's words and christened the travelling fans 'Ally's Armada'.

The Glasgow newspapers made more of Ally's match predictions than those in the north which gave greater coverage to the travelling supporters. The *Evening Express* informed that 15 coaches carrying 600 fans had set off before 8.30am with another 400 or so following by train in a football special while a group of fish merchants chartered a plane at a cost of £22.80 each. The team themselves flew out of Aberdeen airport at 10.45am.

Having stressed to his players the need to compete from the start, Ally's gameplan seemed to be working in front of the 53,000 crowd as the match approached half-time without a goal. Then it all fell apart as first Derek Johnstone put the Glasgow side ahead, and just 30 seconds after the restart Alex MacDonald doubled the advantage.

As they had done in the league the Dons hit back to reduce the leeway through Joe Smith but Rangers too had learnt from the previous match and scored twice more to seal a 4-1 win. The scoreline was a fair reflection of the play and long before the end a chant of 'Ally, Ally shut your mouth!' was sung repeatedly on the Copland Road terracing.

In Monday's *Daily Record* Ally offered no excuse, 'Rangers were the better team and we never played as we can play.' Hugh Taylor was unable to resist turning the armada quote around, 'The Dons were sunk and Ally's Armada never stormed in with all guns firing.'

Pessimism poured from the pen of James Forbes in his column for the *Aberdeen Evening Express* on the same day, 'So the honeymoon is over for the Dons! Full marks to them for the revival they staged after the arrival of Ally MacLeod as manager, but successive matches against Rangers have shown there is still a long way to go. Aberdeen's tactics have had me puzzled.'

The cup exit became more than a temporary setback and confidence dropped when Celtic won at Pittodrie the following weekend. In their next match the Dons won comfortably against bottom club St Johnstone but then hit an alarming sequence of five successive defeats. After a good run prior to the Scottish Cup defeat Aberdeen suddenly found themselves slipping back into relegation danger.

They almost came unstuck for a second time at Somerset Park in April where, having been reduced to ten men, Jarvie scrambled an equaliser for a point with three minutes left. Aberdeen now had four games left to save their season with the first two of those against the Old Firm.

League leaders Rangers headed north on a Wednesday night and with both sides desperate for points and fearful of losing, the goalless draw was perhaps no surprise. Again the Dons finished a man short following Davie Robb's dismissal on 51 minutes.

A trip to Celtic Park three days later saw yet another sending-off with Miller dismissed at a similar time to Robb for bringing down Roy Aitken. But again the Dons clung on for a vital point in a 1-1 draw.

Three draws and three red cards had at least stopped the run of defeats and a quick look at the league table saw the Dons looking safe in fifth place. Closer inspection revealed they were four points clear of second-bottom Dundee with two games to play. But Dundee, along with Hearts, Ayr and Dundee United, who separated the two, had two matches in hand over Aberdeen. This meant that even if the Dons won both of their matches each of the other four were capable of at least equalling their points total.

'That first season of the Premier League was a dog eat dog affair,' remembers Bobby Clark. 'With only ten teams in the league and with two being relegated you could be halfway up the league and still be in relegation trouble. I think, going into the final game, there were five or six teams who could be relegated. That is a big percentage in a ten-team league!

'It was a very nerve-wracking time. Ally had promised me that on my recovery from my knee surgery I could go out to America to play the summer in the NASL with San Antonio. This was when we looked safe from relegation but when the team slipped into a precarious position he put me back in the starting line-up and told me I had to wait until we were safe. This, of course, never happened until the final day so my US sojourn was delayed.'

Addressing the three red cards with James Forbes, there was a hint that the manager was feeling the pressure as for once he conceded that he may have made errors, 'In normal circumstances I would have dealt with these players but they have been under a lot of strain recently. Some of that could have been my fault.'

Disaster struck when after taking points from both Old Firm clubs Aberdeen went down at relegated St Johnstone who had only previously won twice all season.

Approaching their final match, a home game against Hibs on 24 April, other results had aided Aberdeen to the degree that if they won they would escape relegation. Equally it brought home the fact that a win at Perth would have meant avoiding the last-day scenario and the pressure it brought with it. The task seemed straightforward enough but this was a team who had not tasted victory since the last day of February and the situation was completely at odds with the optimism of December and January.

A very nervous match was played out in front of 11,961 spectators and the tension increased when an early Robb penalty kick was saved. Clark recalls the pressure on the day, 'The game itself was the most nerve-wracking of my career. Cup finals, league deciders, etc., had nothing on this. The thought of being part of the first Aberdeen team to be relegated was a huge weight to carry around during those final weeks.' A Jarvie goal after half an hour helped calm things and the Dons went on to record a comfortable 3-0 result. They finished fourth-bottom, matching both the Dundee clubs on 32 points. Only superior goal difference ensured another season in the Premier League for Aberdeen and United with Dundee joining St Johnstone in the First Division.

15

The King of Aberdeen

D URING the summer Aberdeen fans wondered which of Ally's teams they would be watching in the new term, the one he kick-started in November or that which capitulated after the cup defeat at Ibrox. In the meantime the manager was busy releasing some players and adding others like Falkirk full-back Stuart Kennedy and a young central defender called Alex McLeish to the squad. He also brought in midfielder Dom Sullivan from Clyde and secured the return of fans' favourite Joe Harper following an unsettled time for the striker at Hibernian.

Harper had no hesitation in signing for two reasons. Firstly he had fond memories of his previous days at Aberdeen and he also rated the manager highly. Harper remembers driving to meet Ally in an Arbroath hotel where he was waiting with a pot of tea and some biscuits.

'I want you to sign for Aberdeen, son,' was enough for Harper to hear. 'I put my hand out and shook hands with him. I never asked about wages or anything like that because I knew he was an honest man and he would look after me,' he recalls. The striker soon began to benefit from Ally's psychology. 'He was a great motivator,' Harper reminisces. 'There was nothing that he could see that you couldn't do if you put your mind to it.'

The early signs were promising. Aberdeen topped their League Cup section above Kilmarnock, St Mirren and Ayr, losing only once at Rugby Park. In the match programme for the opener at home to Killie the manager was in optimistic mood ahead of the new season, 'My aim as Aberdeen manager is to produce a team capable of bringing honours to the club. Everyone on the playing staff has been warned that I will not tolerate laziness on the field and I expect our "wonderful" support to be well rewarded this season with some entertaining and thrilling soccer.'

Typically of Ally there was no mention of the troubles of last season and two of his most consistent traits, entertaining the fans and the need for strict discipline, were evident.

The eccentric training methods which used to frustrate many of the part-time players at Ayr continued to wind up the full-timers of the Premier League.

Harper remembers five- and seven-a-side matches in the Pittodrie car park, 'You could be 6-1 down and Ally would say "next goal's worth seven"!' The manager would then call time once his own side gained the advantage.

Bobby Clark used to mark the correct score on the gravel behind his goal and got frustrated when new rules were suddenly implemented, 'His team would be losing by four goals so he would shout out that the next goal was worth five. He also could deduct goals, usually from the opposing team, for a bad miss. By the end of the game nobody really knew the correct score but somehow Ally had manipulated the score so his team won.

'I always used to keep the correct score regardless of Ally. His practices were all about small-sided games which had conditions – two-touch; one-touch; can only pass forward; pass and follow your pass, etc. He would always play in these games and would manipulate the score and rules so that his team always won. He certainly kept us competitive and gave everyone belief.'

Harper also remembers the manager having them play head tennis in the car park with a foot of snow on the ground and games of football on the beach, kicking the ball around in water because Ally never bothered to check if the tide would be in or out.

'He wanted to win all the time, whatever the game,' Harper says. If one of the players was getting the better of Ally at table tennis or snooker there would invariably be a message delivered by a youngster on the staff that there was a "phone call for Mr MacLeod"! He always had an excuse if he was getting beat to walk away.'

Harper's most abiding memory is of 'a very humble man, the most loyal man under the sun'.

Fan Scott Bremner has good reason to remember one of his hero's training sessions. He says, 'Back then the Dons trained in Seaton Park and me and a couple of wee pals were hanging about watching. MacLeod came over and asked us to be ball boys as he joked Bobby Clark couldn't save a thing and the balls were whizzing past him! As a six- to seven-year-old I was in total awe that the AFC manager came and asked us personally to help with training. At the end he let us take a few shots at Clark and, I think, John Gardiner.'

Aberdeen got off to a good start in the league and were unbeaten after five matches, albeit with three of them ending in draws.

The League Cup quarter-final draw was kind with two games against Second Division (or Third Division proper) side Stirling Albion all that stood in the way of the semi-final. Aberdeen made hard work of the home leg and, having only a Harper goal to show for their efforts, were barracked by their own fans before the end. The goal meant that Harper had scored in every one of the League Cup matches to date but it was a slender lead to take to Annfield.

Stirling embarrassed Aberdeen, winning by the same margin, and were considered unfortunate not to have won the tie which required a third game. The semi-final draw paired the winners against Rangers or Clydebank, with the Ibrox men also unable to dispose of a lower division side over two matches.

The Stirling replay was staged at the home of Dundee where the Dons finally disposed of the underdogs 2-0. Rangers required a fourth match to separate them from the Bankies but the expected Aberdeen v Rangers showdown was confirmed for 27 October at Hampden Park.

On the preceding Saturday the Dons were at home to Celtic in the league. A Kenny Dalglish penalty put the visitors ahead before a Harper double gave Aberdeen the points and the perfect boost before the Rangers game.

Ally, as noted by *Evening Times* journalist Jim Blair, had been more subdued this season, a conscious decision on the part of the manager. 'I've purposefully kept quiet this season,' he told Blair, elaborating that the Dons fans had been built up and then let down.

'At first when I came to Aberdeen I did a bit of shouting, but this season I decided to let the results speak for me, and we've done all right.'

When asked to predict the result of the semi-final his response was an uncharacteristic, 'That's not my style. Well not this season anyway...' Perhaps remembering the 'Ally's Armada' episode which had sparked the demise of his team's form, Ally appeared to have taken the advice of the Rangers fans on board and literally 'shut his mouth'.

The manager's pre-match team talk at Hampden is remembered to this day by Joe Harper who recalls it was purely motivational with no discussion over tactics, 'I know you're a better team than them. They know you're a better team than them. It's up to you to go out and prove to yourselves you're a better team.'

What happened that night in Glasgow will never be forgotten by the hundreds of Aberdeen fans in the 20,993 crowd. Only three minutes had lapsed when the Dons took the lead through Jocky Scott. Scott scored again although it was back to 2-1 by half-time. Harper restored the two-goal advantage just after the hour before a Jarvie effort made the score an incredible 4-1. There was still time for a fifth following a free kick move which allowed Scott to complete his hat-trick. The free kick itself, Harper remembers, had only been tried the week before in training and had been practised maybe four times but it worked to perfection on the night.

Bobby Clark recalls another of the manager's training routines which produced dividends that evening, 'Ally used to play a small-sided game where every time you played a pass to someone you had to overlap him. It was a game that produced overlaps and brought a lot of movement and third man runs. That night the team had great mobility and really played with a relaxed confidence.'

Aberdeen 5 Rangers 1. Just in case anyone harboured any doubts that result and performance proved that Aberdeen and Ally had well and truly arrived. The score also went one better than the Scottish Cup defeat when Rangers had scored four (the following season Rangers went one better with a 6-1 home win over the Dons in a League Cup tie).

The Aberdeen coach stopped off at the BBC studios in Glasgow's Queen Margaret Drive where the triumphant players watched the match highlights on *Sportscene* before heading north.

The evening's events were best summed up by Alex Cameron's *Daily Record* headline in the morning, 'Clobbered'. 'They walloped the holders in the semifinal last night – destroying them in ninety minutes of humiliating anguish,' Cameron summarised.

Although Rangers were going through a bad spell at the time it is worth remembering that just a few months earlier Jock Wallace's side had completed the clean sweep of honours by winning not only the first Premier League title but also both cups.

It was another Old Firm double and, as with the season before, it instilled in the players the belief that they were capable of beating any side in the country.

On the following Saturday a huge crowd of 19,557 turned up at Pittodrie where the Dons continued their good run by beating Dundee United by the odd goal in five. The manager's programme notes that day consisted of just one word in large print to sum up the semi-final – 'MAGIC!'

On the Monday, 1 November, Ally was named as Football Personality of the Month in recognition of the wins over Celtic, Rangers and Dundee United in the space of eight days. He was presented with a £100 cheque and a gallon of whisky from the sponsors MacKinlay and McPherson. The runner-up was St Mirren manager and one of his former players, Alex Ferguson. Ally was only the second recipient of the award with Jim McLean, the Dundee United boss, the inaugural winner.

Another home win over Motherwell on the Tuesday, where Ally played, and risked, ten of the 11 of his cup final team for the Saturday, lifted Aberdeen to the top of the table having lost just once in the opening nine matches. The attendance of 16,086 for the Motherwell match was almost three times the crowd of 5,500 that had watched the same fixture little over a year before under Jimmy Bonthrone – and this for a midweek game! Looking down on the rest of Scottish football, the Dons players could now turn their attention to the League Cup Final on the Saturday.

'I'm amazed at my side's confidence,' the manager told the *Evening Times*'s Alan Davidson on the eve of the match. 'In all my time in the game I've never handled a side who play with so much belief in themselves.' It was as though Ally had surprised himself at how successfully his motivational skills had been applied to the players.

Ally chose the MacDonald Hotel in Newton Mearns as the club's base for the Hampden occasion, the same venue where a few years earlier he had left the American client who had such a passion for the banks of 'Loch Lomond'.

Heading from the MacDonald towards Hampden, the party were approaching the roundabout at Eastwood Toll when they caught sight of the Celtic coach en route from their base in Troon. At this Ally sprang into action and ordered the driver to hit the roundabout first to give them a head start on their rivals. The driver was then instructed to motor at a speed of 25mph all the way to Hampden with Ally keen to exploit the psychological advantage of arriving at the ground first.

The Aberdeen players recall Ally's behaviour for the last leg of the journey as running up and down the bus drumming it into them that they had one over on Celtic already.

Celtic were taking part in their 13th consecutive League Cup Final. What was at odds with this consistency was the fact that since Ally's Ayr United had taken them to a replay in the semi-final seven years earlier Celtic had developed an odd habit of losing in this particular fixture. They had actually been runners-up in five of the last six League Cup finals yet strangely had not once fallen at the semi-final stage.

The bookmakers had Celtic as slight favourites and seemed to have got it right when they took an early lead through a Dalglish penalty just as they had done a few weeks earlier in the league match. The Dons fought back and a Drew Jarvie header sent the teams in level at the interval. Celtic dominated and really ought to have scored in the second half with the Aberdeen goal at times under siege but the whistle came at the right time for the Dons and a bad time for the Celtic players.

Before the start of extra time Ally could be seen out on the pitch with his tired players, motivating them for that final push. 'I just couldn't wait to get out there at the end of 90 minutes. I thought we were panicking a bit at that point and I told them to calm down,' he later told the *Sunday Mail*, adding, 'They followed my advice and it worked.'

And work it certainly did. Just two minutes into the extension and Aberdeen led for the first time when a cross was diverted to Davie Robb who netted from close range right in front of the majority of the 17,000 Dons supporters. Aberdeen held on to win the cup in what had been an exciting match and although the corner count had been 16 to one in Celtic's favour this had no bearing on the destination of the trophy.

Just as in the recent Premier League meeting the Dons had recovered from a Dalglish penalty to win 2-1. The margin of victory might have been even greater when Harper found himself clear on goal only to see his shot rebound from a post as Celtic pressed in the closing minutes.

When the referee ended the match Ally was pictured on television running on to the park in his blue suit leaping about like a madman, hugging his players but still finding time to shake Jock Stein's hand. Even some of the Aberdeen contingent will admit that they rode their luck in the final. Willie Miller says as much in his autobiography and, while adamant that the award of Celtic's penalty was unjust, Joe Harper today concedes, 'They played us off the park that day. I have to say we got the breaks.'

Speaking to the press the manager was in buoyant mood and pointed out that his side were now the only team capable of winning the treble that season.

The team coach, no longer motoring at 25mph, took the victorious squad to Perth where a victory banquet was held at the Station Hotel. The Lord Provost Robert Lennox (father of Annie Lennox, later to find fame as a singer with Eurythmics before enjoying a successful solo career) and Lady Provost were present with the celebrations only interrupted by the match highlights on BBC1.

On the Sunday the players returned to Aberdeen where they were again greeted by the Provost at the Town House before travelling to Pittodrie on an open-top bus as thousands lined Union Street and the route to the stadium. There was some controversy as the team were apparently ahead of schedule and many locals were disappointed after finding they had left when they arrived in Union Street. The explanation given was that the team's arrival at Pittodrie had to coincide with a live television broadcast from the ground on STV and Grampian.

Some 25,000 fans inside the ground cheered as the players held the League Cup aloft on their home pitch. For once Ally was keeping in the background, preferring to let his players enjoy the limelight until Bobby Clark and match-winner Robb chaired him across the pitch, raising the loudest cheer of the afternoon.

Ally, his voice hoarse from the excitement of the last 24 hours, could manage only two words for the *Press and Journal*, 'Just magic!'

In the space of 12 months Ally had transformed Aberdeen from a relegation-threatened side to trophy winners, a team capable of beating both Rangers and Celtic in their own backyard. The Aberdeen public loved him and he loved them. He was a hero like no previous manager to the supporters now known as 'Ally's Red Army'. Indeed he was like no other football manager and had a star charisma about him as far as his followers were concerned.

The distance from the players' tunnel at the end of the main stand to the dugout at Pittodrie is considerable and before each home game Ally's walk along the track was accompanied by a novelty record called 'Muhammad Ali' from the stadium's PA system. At that particular time Ally was the undisputed King of Aberdeen.

Just as in his Ayr days Ally always made time to stop and talk to supporters when he bumped into them. He was conscious of how important the bond between a team and its fans was and wanted them to feel part of the club. He attended as many supporters' club functions as was possible and it was not unusual to see him in the local press photographed visiting sick fans in hospital.

But there was more to his actions than mere publicity. Ally genuinely liked the fans, he liked people and of course he enjoyed the adulation being manager of a successful local football team brought.

'Ally had that west coast bravado not associated with Aberdonians,' Dons fan Scott Bremner remembers. 'But he got away with it as he gave instant belief plus he had no Old Firm connections. Folk who knew the club, like my grandfather who had been a season ticket holder for the previous 20 years, really took to him (or maybe because he was a MacLeod too!).'

Ally also possessed a rather unique gift of making boastful statements in such a way that he was not perceived as arrogant or big-headed when others might have been...he was just being Ally. With his optimistic, smiling, positive nature Ally was a very difficult man to dislike.

One of the often-repeated myths about Ally is that his side won the League Cup one year to the day after he took office at Pittodrie. This is a great story but is not quite accurate given that he started two days after the Fir Park defeat which was on 10 November when the League Cup Final was on 6 November the following year. Even if we take his first day in charge as the Motherwell match he still secured the trophy less than a year after the appointment.

He is often said to have promised a trophy to the Dons fans on his appointment but the closest I can find to such a claim is the interview with Frank Gilfeather where he considered such an achievement ought to be simpler than avoiding relegation from the Premier League with Ayr.

Ally took his side to play his old club Blackburn at the beginning of December, a match arranged to inaugurate Rovers' modernised floodlights. Home manager Jim Smith and Ally received a warm welcome from the supporters as they walked on to the pitch ahead of the kick-off. The journey proved worthwhile as the Dons won 2-1.

The MacLeods were now living in Milltimber, six miles to the west of the city, where they had bought a house at number 73 Colthill Circle, just a few doors along from where Drew Jarvie lived.

In December the manager decided to hold a Christmas party to celebrate the previous month's League Cup win. It turned into quite an event which included Ally and the players staging races in the street between the MacLeod and Jarvie households. Andy MacLeod recalls waking the next morning to find the League Cup lying on its side underneath the Christmas tree. Still half full of flat alcohol, one of Scottish football's most prized trophies lay there like a discarded toy!

As a result of bad weather the friendly at Ewood Park proved to be one of only two matches Aberdeen played in the month of December the other saw Celtic share four goals at Pittodrie on Boxing Day.

But the training continued and during a five-a-side match 20-year-old Willie Garner found himself in the same team as Ally. When a penalty kick was awarded – by Ally – there was a debate as to which of them should take it. Young Garner was eager to impress and assured his boss that he had never missed from the spot. Ally's logic was that if he missed himself he would just order a retake but if Willie did not score he would be required back at the ground at 8pm for a 20-minute run around the pitch.

The youngster persisted and Ally relented but Garner then missed the kick so they both returned to Pittodrie in the dark that evening. Neither of them knew how to switch on the power so Garner changed by torchlight and started his punishment run as the manager watched from the entrance to the tunnel.

In the dark he eventually decided to walk for a bit. With no sound, other than his own breathing and footsteps in the darkness, Garner got the fright of his life when Ally jumped up from behind a wall on the opposite side of the ground and tore into him. Joe Harper remembers that on the following morning Ally's footprints could be seen in the snow leading across the pitch to the wall.

After the first round of fixtures of 1977 Aberdeen were still top of the Premier League, two points clear of Celtic, and had lost only two league matches all season.

Following successive draws with Ayr United and Partick Thistle the manager was perhaps experiencing feelings of déjà vu for the second half of the season and questioned the players' commitment when speaking to the *Sunday Mail*, 'There is not enough fight, not enough work…they want to win, but is that desire burning?'

A third drawn match saw Aberdeen let a 3-1 home lead over Rangers end 3-3 in mid-January but this time the manager's response was surprisingly upbeat, almost dismissing the late cave-in. 'You have just watched the team who should represent Scotland in the European Cup,' he told Jim Blair of the *Evening Times*. 'We don't fear Celtic or Rangers. We may not win the Premier League but we should because we are everything that is good in Scottish football.'

In another interview that month of January he predicted an end to the dominance of the Old Firm. 'Celtic or Rangers might win the title again this season,' he conceded to Jason Thomas in an unknown publication. 'But I'll tell you this – their monopoly will be broken within the next two years.'

Newspaper speculation linking Ally with the manager's post vacated by Gordon Lee at Newcastle United drew a cryptic response when the *Evening Express*'s John Gibson raised the subject at the end of January, 'If I received a phone call from Newcastle I would listen. I would be very interested indeed but I won't be applying for the job.' He added that he was flattered to be linked with the position.

That telephone call never came and a couple of days later Richard Dinnis was named as Lee's successor. Ally had previously been linked to the Newcastle job when at Ayr prior to Lee's appointment.

In the Scottish Cup a hard-earned win at Dunfermline was followed by a shock defeat at home to First Division side Dundee in a replay with a young player by the name of Gordon Strachan inflicting most of the damage. That ended any more talk of a possible treble for that season at least.

The cup exit generated even more headlines a couple of weeks later when the *Sunday Mail* learned that Grampian Police had launched an investigation following allegations that three Dons players had placed large bets at odds of 8-1 on Dundee winning the replay. It was publicity the club and the manager could clearly do without and the newspaper highlighted the scandal on Saturday night television advertisements and used the story on its front page.

Following their enquiries the police concluded that there was no evidence whatsoever to support the claims but the episode had been an unpleasant experience.

Aberdeen held a press conference after being cleared. 'There were 14 players in my pool that night and all of them have been smeared by this dreadful article,' the manager told the assembled journalists. 'It's the worst thing I have had happen in 28 years of professional football.'

It transpired that the story had been initiated by a member of the public who was not from Aberdeen but had apparently overheard one end of a telephone conversation while queuing to use a public kiosk.

Ally agreed to a televised face-to-face meeting with the journalist who broke the story, Nick Hunter, on Grampian's *Sportscall* but the club directors asked him not to take part.

After losing to a last-minute penalty at Ibrox on 19 February the Dons had slipped to fourth in the table. They won their next league match 2-1 – at home to Celtic. 'We keep beating Celtic…but who else is doing it?' the manager posed at the post-match press conference. The Dons then dropped four points to Dundee United with one of those fixtures a rescheduled match.

Any lingering hopes of the championship had already gone by the time an in-form Celtic achieved their first win over Aberdeen of the season on 20 April, a convincing 4-1 result.

While it would not immediately appear relevant the resignation of Hearts manager John Hagart on the same day as the Celtic defeat would prove to be the next significant step in the rollercoaster career of Ally. Hearts had been relegated the previous Saturday and along with Kilmarnock would be consigned to at least one season of First Division football.

Aberdeen won their last two matches, firstly defeating Motherwell at Fir Park, then rounding off a memorable season with a 2-1 Pittodrie victory over Rangers on the last day of April. The Dons finished in third place on 43 points, 12 adrift of champions Celtic but only three behind runners-up Rangers.

Although there had been defeats in matches with the Old Firm, Ally's overall record with Aberdeen against both Celtic and Rangers in all competitions makes impressive reading. In 17 matches the Dons won seven (including one in extra time), lost six, drew four, scored 25 goals and conceded 23.

Headed 'Ally MacLeod Looks Back – and Forward' in what proved to be his last contribution to the Aberdeen match programme, for the Rangers game, Ally had taken stock of the fact the club had risen from third from bottom of the league to third from top but was still not satisfied, 'But we have still to become, in my eyes, true champions.' He concluded that the supporters 'should have a tremendous amount to look forward to in the next few years'. Even he could not have imagined just how true that last statement would prove to be but he would not be around to witness Aberdeen's golden era.

Just as during his last days at Ayr, a series of events would conspire to alter both Ally's life and Scottish football.

16

A Wembley Winner

THE period from 1973 until the end of 1977 is now regarded as something of a golden age by fans of the Scottish national team. This covers all of Willie Ormond's time in charge of the side plus the first half of Ally's tenure.

There were however times when Ormond was given little credit and his position was often the subject of speculation. Due to Leeds United's involvement in the European Cup Final of 1975 Ormond had lost four leading players for the Home International series. After losing five goals to England it was widely believed that defeat to Romania in a European Championships qualifier eight days later would lead to the manager's dismissal. A last-minute goal salvaged a point in Bucharest but the speculation over Ormond's future refused to go away.

What now seems a bizarre editorial in the 27 February 1975 edition of *Scottish Football Weekly* contained the following, 'Argue that Willie Ormond is the wrong man for the job, protest that he has really done nothing for the Scottish team bar beat England since he took over. Who for example can deny that it was the crowd who took Scotland through against Czechoslovakia in the World Cup?' In that piece he was being denied any credit for qualifying for and returning unbeaten from West Germany.

The uncertainty over his future must have had some bearing on Ormond's decision to step down and take up the position vacated by John Hagart at Hearts.

In what seems a contradiction Ormond performed two functions in his capacity as Scotland manager on Thursday 5 May 1977. One was to name a squad of 22 players for the imminent Home International Championship plus a three-game South American tour in June. His second act was to offer the SFA his resignation and request to be released from his contract with immediate effect to allow him to fill the post at Hearts.

Permitted to relinquish his duties, Ormond did agree to take charge of a Glasgow Select side against the English League at Hampden Park on 17 May as part of the Silver Jubilee celebrations.

Stating that he missed the every-day involvement of club management, it was not for another six years that Ormond, in a *Sunday Mail* interview, broke his silence on the issue, 'Basically it was about money and subsequent events have proved me right.' He revealed that Hearts had made an approach with an offer which was considerably more than the SFA were paying, a sum he admitted to being astonished by.

Although Ormond's resignation was a surprise to some, it was not completely unexpected as it had been reported that he had spoken to the Hearts chairman Bobby Parker the previous week. The timing of the announcement did however seem odd.

With little over three weeks until Scotland took on Wales, finding a replacement for Ormond was a priority and two names were the first to be linked with the position. Not surprisingly Jock Stein was the front-runner with the little-known Andy Roxburgh, who had been gaining results with the under-21 squad, another contender. Ally's name was not in the mix at this point.

The approach from the SFA came on Friday 6 May when the Aberdeen chairman Dick Donald was asked for permission to speak to their manager. Ally had not been their first choice. Stein had been sounded out but he had recommended Ally for the job. It is believed Stein had concerns that the forthcoming World Cup was being held in Argentina, a country where he had experienced troubled times during the World Club Championship in 1967.

Ally claims that the request came completely out of the blue and that he had never considered himself a candidate for the national job. He saw his future at Aberdeen where he felt his task of making them the top team in Scotland was progressing well but far from finished.

The Dons' season was not quite over. An end-of-season friendly in Yugoslavia against OFK Kikinda was scheduled for Sunday 15 May, with plans for a second match abandoned.

Ally agreed to attend an interview in Glasgow on his return from Yugoslavia although he could not immediately decide if he wanted the Scotland job at this point in his career. He was enjoying his time at Aberdeen and his family had settled happily there. The city was a good place to be at that time with not only a successful football team but the boom of the North Sea oil industry.

Evening Express journalist Ron Robertson caught up with the Aberdeen party as they prepared to fly out of Aberdeen Airport on 11 May. With rumours starting to leak out regarding Ally's future Robertson was given the following response when he raised the matter, 'As far as I am concerned my name being linked with the Scotland job is pure speculation. I have no comment to make on the matter… in fact there is nothing to say.'

For once Ally was grateful there were no journalists travelling with the party, the only newspaper reports being supplied by two of his players, Miller and Jarvie.

Delays with a connecting flight from Dubrovnik to Belgrade resulted in the Aberdeen squad being transferred from the airport to a nearby hotel in the early hours of the morning. They were assured they would be able to board the flight at 6am, 11 hours later than scheduled. The match was due to start at 4.30pm and the party faced a two-hour coach journey from Belgrade to Kikinda.

Choosing to stay on his feet, it was while pacing up and down in that hotel foyer that Ally made the decision which would ultimately change his life. 'I argued with myself for hours,' he later revealed in his autobiography. He was torn between the challenge of finishing a job in an environment he enjoyed and the possibility of leading his country to the following year's World Cup finals.

Also playing on his mind was the memory of how that Scottish Cup replay with Third Lanark all those years before had forced his withdrawal from the Scotland B team and the one chance he had had of international honours. He was aware that should he turn down the SFA's offer the opportunity may never come his way again.

But there was a niggling doubt that maybe it was just too soon for him. Barely 18 months earlier he had been in charge of part-time players and he felt that his work at Aberdeen had just begun.

Eldest son Andy says, 'It was one of the hardest decisions he ever made. He didn't want to leave Aberdeen. He had built a team that he thought would go on and compete with the Old Firm.'

'He did a lot of soul searching,' wife Faye recalls, and she remembers he had doubts about the timing with Scotland halfway through their qualifying campaign. Eventually Ally decided that if the SFA agreed to his terms at the interview he would accept the offer. Now he had to tell his Aberdeen players.

The match with Kikinda was a farce due to torrential rain, thunder and lightning. The pitch resembled a swamp and the overall feeling was that had the Scottish side not travelled so far the referee would not have allowed the game to start. Kikinda won 2-1 with the most notable aspect of the game being the debut of 18-year-old Jim Leighton as Aberdeen's goalkeeper. Continuing the farce the winner was deflected in by Willie Miller with Leighton going in the opposite direction.

Joe Harper recalls that Ally picked the moment for his farewell team meeting with the players. The squad were told to meet in the hotel restaurant at a specified time.

'What do you want to drink?' the manager asked each of them which drew the usual milk, coffee or orange juice response. 'No, no. Do you want a beer, a vodka or a whisky?' Harper remembers being surprised at this. It turned into quite a long drink with the players not spending a penny and Harper knew then, 'It was the end as far as Aberdeen was concerned.' Although the manager did not apparently say so in as many words they all knew he would be moving on.

Bobby Clark recalls he had mixed emotions at the news, 'I suppose there was excitement for me as Willie Ormond had picked me in the squad to play in the home internationals and to tour South America. I wondered where Ally would see me and if I would make the World Cup squad. The team itself was surprised and, as whenever a team changes leader, there is an air of uncertainty. Those that are established wonder if they will still retain their positions and others, the ones on the outside, perhaps see an opportunity.'

Back in Scotland the press now had confirmation of the SFA's approach and were desperate to learn if Ally had come to a decision. When changing planes in Heathrow on the way home Ally found reporters waiting to ask if he was the new Scotland manager. For one of the few times in his life Ally had nothing to say to the media. The players too were approached but knew not to give anything away.

Ally drove from the family home in Milltimber to Glasgow on the morning of Tuesday 17 May and entered the offices of the SFA at 6 Park Gardens after knocking on a side window. Once the association's secretary Ernie Walker and three members of the executive committee had agreed to his conditions he was offered a contract for the £14,000-a-year job as manager of the Scottish international team. Just as he had done at Aberdeen he turned down the contract offer.

Later that day Walker was at Hampden to watch the Glasgow Select defeat the English League side 2-1 in Willie Ormond's last duty. There he informed the journalists present that he had arranged a press conference for 11am the following day.

In Park Gardens the secretary announced to the assembled journalists what they already knew, 'The SFA have invited Mr MacLeod to become Scotland's manager and he has accepted.'

The man at the centre was in top form and did not disappoint when giving his reasons for accepting the post, 'I have always relished a challenge. I'm a bit of a nationalist...and I want to prove that I am the best manager in the world. People might laugh at that, but I firmly believe I was born to be a success.'

When quizzed over his refusal of a contract he explained his way of thinking, 'Personally I always prefer the right to leave a job without hitches if I am not happy in it.'

He paid tribute to Willie Ormond, acknowledging that the squad his predecessor had selected was much the same as he would have picked. 'But this will be Ally MacLeod's team,' he insisted. 'I have always been my own man – and I will do this job my way.'

That same day Aberdeen vice-chairman Chris Anderson told the *Evening Times*'s Alan Davidson how disappointed his club were to lose their manager. Anderson revealed there was nothing his board could have done to retain Ally's services once he had reached a decision, 'It was not a question of money, as far as Ally was concerned fame was the spur for him.'

Anderson stressed the club's intentions to continue in the direction Ally had pointed them. Ally's successor at Somerset Park, Alex Stuart, was hotly tipped to once again follow in his footsteps.

Dons fan Tommy Petrie took the news badly, 'I was gutted when he left for the Scotland job. Winning the League Cup against Celtic was the pinnacle but he kicked off the start of many great years for the support.'

'It was a shame he left,' says fellow Aberdeen supporter Scott Bremner. 'I am sure he would have built a team to challenge the Old Firm, nobody will ever know if that would have been akin to Alex Ferguson but by hell it would have been fun I am sure, as the club were in good hands and would have backed him.

'We were obviously disappointed to lose him but who better to lead our country at the time? It was a proud moment really when the new Scotland manager had come from Aberdeen FC. Regardless of what happened in 1978 he is fondly remembered in Aberdeen for sure and time and time again folks still say that he built the foundations for Sir Alex.'

Ally had found it hard to leave Aberdeen. He would later say that his happiest playing days had been at Blackburn and his favourite period in management had been the time spent at Pittodrie.

He personally wrote to each branch of the Aberdeen Supporters' Club, thanking them for their 'wonderful support' and apologising that, due to his swift appointment to the Scotland job, he had been unable to visit them in person.

He threw a party in Colthill Circle for the staff of the club and friends he had made since moving to the area. No expense had been spared and there was even bunting in the street with loud music blaring from number 73. Arriving guests were issued with straw hats and there seemed to be no limit to the supply of alcohol and food.

During a speech Ally announced he had a gift for the players before presenting each of them with a bottle of slivovitz. He had brought back a supply of the spirit from the recent trip to Yugoslavia and insisted that each player had to drink a glass there and then to celebrate his appointment as Scotland manager. Speeches, memories and much drinking went on until the small hours as the manager enjoyed the evening. Soon it would be time for him to get back to work again.

Seven days after the press conference Ally was back in Glasgow to meet up with the home-based Scotland players before travelling to their base near Chester to prepare for the match with Wales in Wrexham on 28 May.

Chester was the first time he had met many of the 'Anglos' and they were left in no doubt as to the new manager's ambitions when he spoke to them. 'My name is Ally MacLeod and I'm a winner,' was how he introduced himself. Ally later explained those carefully-chosen words were designed for maximum impact in case any of the southern-based players did not take him seriously with the first game just 48 hours away.

Conscious that he was now dealing with a higher calibre of player than at any time in the past, Ally had superstars from many of the top English clubs of the day in his charge. Leeds, Manchester United, Derby County, Aston Villa and Everton were all represented in the squad Ormond had selected. When two of the players arrived a few minutes late this gave the manager the perfect opportunity to emphasise the standards he expected them to meet. 'That is the last time anyone will be late for me and get off without a fine,' he imparted.

Another chance to show he would be doing things his way was, just as he had done with Willie Miller at Aberdeen, to announce a new captain.

Archie Gemmill had been Ormond's skipper but Ally was of the opinion Gemmill was in the 'Billy Bremner mould'. Bremner, later voted into the Scottish

Football Hall of Fame, will always be a legend to Scotland supporters who saw him play. But he had not been a popular figure within the SFA hierarchy following more than one episode of indiscipline and there were those in the press too who felt that the Leeds captain had become too big for his boots. It was said he had enjoyed too much influence over Ormond, a situation Ally would never have tolerated.

Ultimately misbehaviour had cost Bremner his international place following an incident in a Copenhagen nightclub two years earlier which resulted in him and four others being banned from representing their country. Ally would later apologise to Gemmill, saying he had been wrongly informed as to the type of captain he was.

He chose Bruce Rioch of Everton as skipper for the Home Internationals with the intention of replacing him with the injured Martin Buchan should he be fit for the South American tour.

Ally opted for an attacking 4-4-2 formation for the game in Wrexham with at least as many Scottish fans in the crowd of 14,469 as there were Welsh supporters.

One banner prominently displayed behind a goal contained the message 'GOOD LUCK ALLY, ABERDEEN STILL LOVES YOU'.

Wales dominated the match and Danny McGrain kicked a Deacy header off the line in the first half while a late Joey Jones effort smacked the crossbar. In between Alan Rough had performed well in goal and it actually looked as though the Scots were playing for a draw which would have been completely against Ally's attacking ethos.

Yet for all that Scotland almost committed an act of daylight robbery when, in the final minute, Kenny Burns put through Asa Hartford who looked sure to score, but he sent the ball wide of the post. It had been the clearest opportunity for either side but the game finished without a goal.

Ally's own notes on the match are interesting and reveal he had indeed set out to avoid defeat, 'As this was my first international I played very safe and the side selected achieved the aim required. A good start to the defence of the home championships. Could have won before the end. Nevertheless a 0-0 result was most satisfactory.'

The squad headed north for the Northern Ireland game the following Tuesday at Hampden Park, an area the manager knew so well from his childhood. Already there was renewed optimism among the Scottish supporters. This was largely due to the exuberant nature of the new manager whose personality could not have been more contrasting to Ormond's, but also the forthcoming fixture with England on the Saturday at Wembley.

There was something about the Scottish psyche which seemed to take on new confidence every year when the England match came around regardless of form, and past disappointments were brushed aside.

'Ally, Ally, Ally MacLeod,' sang the crowd as the game kicked off. This time the manager delivered as Scotland won by a 3-0 scoreline for the third successive year in the fixture. Two Dalglish goals and one from Gordon McQueen sent the fans into a chorus of 'Why are we so good?' before the end with the rest of the singing concentrating on the forthcoming trip to 'Wem-bi-lee'.

This was actually the first year Scotland fans had picked up on the old Doris Day 'Que Sera Sera' standard which had been heard down south at that year's FA Cup Final.

The England match at Wembley was set for Saturday 4 June, the weekend of the Queen's Silver Jubilee celebrations. Street parties and events were planned for towns and villages throughout Britain, but nowhere would the event be more celebrated than in London. Union flags and red, white and blue bunting decorated streets with pictures of the monarch displayed in many windows.

As was traditional tens of thousands of Scottish fans descended on the capital in the days leading up to the match. The SFA's allocation of 30,000 of the 100,000 tickets printed was a fraction of the supporters who travelled. Many Scots acquired tickets from friends living in England and of course many exiles living over the border were able to exploit this loophole.

There seemed to be just as many Scots seeking tickets as those who had them and it would not be an exaggeration to state there were at least 90,000 Scottish supporters in London that weekend and quite likely in excess of 100,000, some of whom would not gain entry to the stadium.

One supporter from Edinburgh died on the Friday evening after diving from the upper plinth of one of the fountains in Trafalgar Square, unaware the depth of the water was a mere 18 inches. Witnesses at the scene reported there were just as many people enquiring if he had a match ticket as there were those concerned for his welfare.

The Saturday saw London bathed in beautiful sunshine as the last of the supporters already dubbed 'Ally's Army' on the back page of the *Scottish Daily Express* poured off overnight trains and coaches. Scotland had not won in London for ten years and in that period had suffered a number of heavy losses including the 5-1 reverse under Ormond two years earlier.

England were going through a bad spell and had lost their last two home matches, to Holland and to the Welsh the day after Scotland defeated Northern Ireland. Manager Don Revie was a man under pressure to get a result although Ladbrokes had England as slight favourites.

But there was something different about the optimism of the tartan hordes in London this time. There was a real sense of belief that Scotland had a side capable of ending the Wembley hoodoo rather than the misplaced nationalism of before rooted in an arrogant 'Wha's like us?' mentality.

The manager was confident too. Ally told the *Express*'s John MacKenzie, 'I think we have better players and a more settled formation than Don Revie can offer, but it is important my players don't get carried away with themselves.' MacKenzie too predicted a tartan triumph.

Consistent with his club days, Ally named the same 11 who had beaten the Irish before seeing Revie's line-up. 'Nothing Don Revie did was going to change my mind,' he insisted.

The teams walked out to a stadium overpacked with Scottish supporters. Some of the gates had been stormed and there were still thousands outside seeking tickets or less legitimate means of entry. It may as well have been a home match for Ally's team as they looked around at the cluster of the red and yellow and blue and white flags on all sides of the stadium. The crescendo of noise was ear-splitting as Ally took his seat in the dugout in the old stadium which had given him his biggest disappointment as a player in the FA Cup Final 17 years earlier.

Alex Cameron of the *Daily Record* had arranged for the manager's family to be flown down from Aberdeen and Andy MacLeod recalls he was sitting directly in front of Rangers manager Jock Wallace. 'He kept asking me if I wanted a drink from his hip flask,' Andy remembers. Wallace certainly had faith in Andy's father, 'Dinnae worry Andy there's no way that Scotland are gonae lose today. Ally will make sure o' that!'

Andy's mother Faye was surprised to find herself sitting along from a former Third Lanark season ticket holder she had not seen since her husband's playing days.

The match went well. Without completely dominating Scotland were the better side in the first half and took the lead just ahead of the interval. Hartford sent over a free kick from the right which McQueen rose for. The big centre-half reached an incredible height to head the ball which was soon bouncing around inside the net.

The expected England fightback never materialised with Rough having little to do. Scotland looked home and dry when Dalglish forced the ball over in the 61st minute after which a track-side BBC cameraman captured Ally leaping from the dugout throwing both arms in the air to celebrate. But there was to be a dramatic end.

The Hungarian referee awarded England a contentious penalty with just three minutes left which Mick Channon scored with ease. Rough was then required to make his first real save of the afternoon when he fumbled a Channon header over and he confidently clutched the resultant corner as it swung into the box. The referee added no time and Scotland had won 2-1 but in the end Channon's header had almost forced a draw – it had been that close.

Hundreds of Scottish supporters spilled on to the field to celebrate and skipper Rioch was carried on the shoulders of some of those fans. Other players quickly made for the tunnel where the manager stood digesting the results of his afternoon's work. The hundreds turned into thousands of invaders and at one point it actually looked as though there were more people on the pitch than the terracing singing their new 'Que Sera' song.

The temporary three-foot barriers proved no deterrent to the jubilant fans as they carved up pieces of turf to take home for souvenirs while others scaled both goals, causing the crossbars to break under the weight of bodies. The cost of the damage was later estimated at £15,000.

Fifer Jock Vila was among the pitch invaders that day. Approaching 22 he had never attended an international match before despite football occupying a large part of his life having followed Dunfermline Athletic home and away for a number of years. Encouraged by the new manager's optimism Vila booked on a Wembley trip which he recalls was around £40 for the coach and two nights in a London hotel. He worked alongside 19-year-old Stuart Adamson at the Elliotts electronics factory in Cowdenbeath and had a notion he wanted to learn to play the guitar. His work-mate gave him his old acoustic model in return for Jock paying for his trip to Wembley.

That very summer Adamson would form punk band Skids and would later enjoy global success with Big Country, ensuring that Vila's £40 investment paid dividends. As the fans celebrated on the pitch Vila and Adamson briefly debated whether to join them before making their way down to the field where Vila wandered around with a bare-chested Adamson on his shoulders savouring the occasion.

As they were heading away from the ground singer Rod Stewart's coach was making its way through the crowds, 'His bus was crawling down the road as we were going down and I just remember jumping on the back of it as they had the emergency door open and I said hello to him. He gave us a 24-pack of Tennent's lager, maybe just to get rid of me. It was quite a good day all in all for my first Scotland game,' Vila recalls.

That evening in the team's base, the St Ermin's Hotel near St James Park, Ally spoke with Jim Reynolds of the *Glasgow Herald*. 'Maybe I should quit now,' he joked. 'That's three games without defeat and the championship. Probably the wise thing would be to go back to Aberdeen and ask for my old job at Pittodrie.'

With the benefit of hindsight his next statement proved to be chillingly prophetic. 'I have had only good times in my short spell as Scotland manager… but, as in everything else, the bad times have still to come.'

After just three matches in charge Ally had produced what thousands of Scots had waited years for, victory at Wembley. History was repeating itself. Just as at Aberdeen the new manager had delivered immediate success. In a whirlwind period of 20 months he had gone from working with part-time players at a provincial club to winning an international championship, stopping off on the way to reignite a dying team and delivering a trophy. Now he had the drive and ambition to become, in his own words, 'the best manager in the world'.

Ally at that time must have felt blessed. And who in all honesty could possibly blame the man?

If anyone had any doubts regarding his appointment to the Scotland job they were surely now convinced that Ally was the right man to take the national team forward. He now had a whole nation behind him as the wider Scottish public came to the same conclusion that Aberdonians already had.

Ally MacLeod could walk on water.

17

On the March

THE Scotland party set off from Glasgow Airport the following Thursday on a 23-hour journey to South America. The first stop was Gatwick where the 'Anglos' joined the party. A delay added another three hours to the journey before they boarded for the flight to Santiago. Some journalists complained that the conditions on the British Caledonian 707 aircraft were too cramped while a handful of supporters even followed the team on the tour.

On the same day the squad had set off Aberdeen announced Clyde's Billy McNeill as Ally's replacement. An approach to lure Alex Stuart from Ayr had been unsuccessful and even Denis Law's name had been linked to the post. McNeill told Andy Melvin of the *Aberdeen Evening Express* he wanted the Dons to take over from his old club Celtic at the top of Scottish football but was quick to point out, 'I'm no Ally MacLeod.'

The new Scotland manager had put paid to any thoughts of withdrawals, insisting that anyone who did not want to take part in the tour would not be considered for the forthcoming World Cup qualifiers. There were some grumblings about money with each squad member given an allowance of £5 per day plus £100 for each match they took part in. The non-participants would receive £50 for each game with no bonus payments to be made which was strict SFA policy for friendly matches.

In Santiago some of the players held a meeting with the manager regarding bonuses for the upcoming qualifiers and suggested the incentives may be increased to £300 per point. The payments for the Home Internationals had been £100 a point, a maximum earning of £500 for playing in all three games. The meeting was an amicable one and the manager agreed to speak to the secretary supporting the players' suggestions. It would not be the last time the players went to the manager with a grievance over bonus payments and they now felt they had a sympathetic ear.

The game in Chile was not until the following Wednesday but had attracted some controversy due to the choice of venue. In 1973 a military coup had removed the country's left-wing government and the Santiago Stadium had housed a prison for political prisoners where many had been tortured and a number executed. There were calls from trade unionists and political activists in Britain for the SFA to refuse to play there and supporters at the Wales match in Wrexham had been handed leaflets expressing those concerns.

But the match went ahead and Scotland's good form continued, scoring three times in the first 37 minutes through Kenny Dalglish, Lou Macari and Asa Hartford, eventually winning 4-2. If anything the margin of victory ought to have been greater as a number of chances were squandered. Martin Buchan had started but Rioch had remained captain.

'We were brilliant for 55 minutes,' MacLeod told Ewart Butler, reporting for the *Aberdeen Evening Express*. 'We played some real dream stuff.' He added that he felt Scotland had their best side in 30 years but that they may struggle to overcome their next opponents and the following year's World Cup hosts – Argentina.

Scotland's performance had impressed other South American nations and while in Buenos Aires the SFA delegation were approached to extend their tour with offers of matches against Bolivia and Peru. Both were declined although subsequent events were to prove a game against the Peruvians might have proved beneficial.

The match in La Bombonera, the home of Boca Juniors, proved to be far more than a friendly in front of a hostile crowd of 57,000. With Rioch out through injury this time Buchan was given the captaincy. Argentinian right-back Pernia was booked after just six minutes for his second foul on Willie Johnston. Two further assaults on the winger merited nothing more than a telling-off by the Brazilian referee Filho and 11 minutes into the second period Pernia punched his opponent to the ground. The referee was away from the incident but decided to send both players off. This mirrored events in the same stadium just six days earlier when a Uruguayan official had ordered off England's Trevor Cherry along with the home side's Bertoni in a similar incident.

Don Revie had considered Cherry to be 'the unluckiest player in the world' and had apparently warned Ally of what to expect.

Scotland were awarded a penalty kick on 77 minutes which Don Masson coolly converted. A mere three minutes later, and in what looked like an attempt to even things up, Argentina were given a penalty when substitute Trossero was adjudged to have been fouled by Tom Forsyth but television replays showed the decision to be a farce. Passarella equalised and Scotland were denied a famous victory. Skipper Buchan later revealed that the Scots players had at one point felt like walking off over the way the match had been officiated.

The Scottish reporters were less tolerant than the players during the after-match press conference. After being refused any straight answers from Argentinian manager Cesar Menotti about his team's antics, the journalists walked out.

Ally absolved Johnston of any blame, adding that had he been guilty his international career would have been on the line. Argentina had not been a pleasant experience although there were worse events to follow for both Ally and Johnston in the same country 12 months later.

In Rio de Janeiro the Scots boss watched on television as the final tour opponents defeated Poland 3-1 in Sao Paulo the following day. On the Tuesday Ally was interviewed on Brazilian television and wooed the natives when he considered their side were favourites to win the following year's World Cup, adding, 'In fact Thursday night's match could be a dress rehearsal for the final.'

The *Glasgow Herald* journalist Jim Reynolds reported a conversation he had with the manager which hinted Ally may not have been completely joking during his television appearance. 'Winning the British Championship gave me a thrill, but really the World Cup is what it's all about,' Ally told the reporter. 'People may laugh when I say that is our aim, but I am deadly serious.' He added that the Brazilian press had advised him they considered Scotland among the top three sides in Europe. 'I think we are even better than that,' he told Reynolds.

Is it possible Ally was now starting to believe in his own publicity with inflated ideas about his and the squad's capabilities? Yet there is no denying he had a number of quality players at his disposal who in just a matter of months would destroy the European champions.

Rioch returned to captain the side although Buchan retained his place as did Johnston. Ally surprised everyone when he chose Gemmill as his lone striker when substitute Derek Parlane would have been more suited to the role.

Scotland failed to win a corner and posed little attacking threat but held out until the 71st minute before conceding twice in quick succession. Zico's free kick beat Rough and five minutes later the game was over when Cerezo completed the scoring. After what had gone before, the defeat and lacklustre attack did end the tour on a bit of an anti-climax but there was no disgrace in losing to Brazil. The manager's notes offered little excuse, 'Well beaten by a better team. Humidity seemed to drain our midfield. Never in the game in the second half.'

Despite the events of Buenos Aires the tour had been considered a success. 'A tremendous experience both for players and staff,' Ally typed in his report where he also praised Rioch as captain, 'His example on and off the field was first-class.'

Perhaps tired of aeroplanes, Ally planned a family holiday in Nairn on his return, but only after speaking to Billy McNeill regarding some inside information he may find useful at Pittodrie.

With the dawn of a new season there was optimism among supporters of the Scottish national team with two vital World Cup qualifiers looming. Before then there was time for another challenge match with East Germany in Berlin on Wednesday 7 September, just two weeks ahead of the first qualifier.

The team flew out by chartered jet on the Monday night with only 17 players following a number of call-offs, including skipper Rioch. 'I don't believe in friendlies,' Ally told Jim Blair. 'The object of this exercise is to build towards the next two games – not to impress the East Germans. If we can beat them in the process so much the better.'

Although Rough was available Ally played Leeds and former Ayr goalkeeper Dave Stewart and sprang a surprise by making Masson captain ahead of Buchan. Scotland lost the match 1-0 to a Schade goal but it took a number of saves from Stewart, including one from a penalty kick, to limit the damage.

The Scots too had missed chances, particularly in the early part of the game, but the main talking point once again was the rough play of their opponents.

Jim Reynolds's *Herald* report singled out Konrad Weisse as the main culprit who was apparently guilty of 'chopping down Joe Jordan with sickening regularity'. For once the manager did not mince his words after the match, telling the journalists at the press conference, 'They are the dirtiest international side I have ever seen – even worse than the Argentinians. They committed an amazing number of off the ball fouls that went unpunished.'

Back in Glasgow the reason for Masson's choice as captain was revealed in the *Evening Times*. Buchan had told Ally he did not want the responsibility and repeated his concerns to Blair, 'In Argentina the captain will be under tremendous pressure. A lot of publicity will surround him.' When confronted by Blair the manager said little more than that the player had explained his position and that he accepted the situation.

Under Willie Ormond two points had been collected from two World Cup qualifying matches. This left the same number of fixtures to fulfil in the three-team group with two wins guaranteeing Scotland a place in Argentina.

Czechoslovakia were due at Hampden for the first of the vital games, an encounter which evoked memories of the night when Ormond's team had qualified for West Germany and Ally had been on the STV studio panel.

The Czechs had improved in the intervening four years to the extent they had won the European Championship in 1976, albeit in a penalty shoot-out against West Germany, and had beaten Ormond's team in the group's opener.

The visitors' travel plans were disrupted due to an air traffic controller dispute which meant their aircraft was three hours late leaving Prague. When they arrived in Heathrow they had missed their connection to Glasgow and had to travel into central London for the overnight train. With no sleepers available they sat with the other passengers and arrived in Glasgow, somewhat weary, early on the Tuesday morning before heading to their accommodation in Erskine. A request for the match to be postponed for 24 hours was rejected by FIFA on the grounds they were in the country more than one day ahead of the kick-off.

Ally had no sympathy. 'I'm more concerned with what Scotland do than to worry about the Czechs' excuse,' he told Blair.

The manager had called for patience from the capacity 85,000 crowd but just as he had done four years earlier Jordan headed into the net with 18 minutes on the clock. On 35 minutes Hartford scored a second and it looked all over. A second-half Dalglish header capped a glorious night countered only by a late Czech goal which completed the scoring at 3-1.

It was almost the perfect Scotland performance and eliminated the Czechs, leaving a straight fight between the Scots and the Welsh for that one qualification slot.

Around 60,000 of the crowd stayed behind anticipating a lap of honour but they didn't shout for Scotland. Instead the chant was 'We want Ally!' The manager had already succeeded in establishing a rapport with the supporters that no other Scotland manager before or since has come remotely close to. The crowd saw him as one of their own, another fan. In less than six months Ally had risen from his throne as the King of Aberdeen to be crowned King of all Scotland.

But there was no lap of honour, a decision taken by the manager as he explained to the *Daily Record*'s Ken Gallagher, 'We would have looked stupid if we had gone back out, taken the applause, and then failed against the Welsh. No, our lap of honour will come at Anfield when we win.'

Ally could not stop raving about Masson's performance when interviewed by Alex Cameron for STV. 'What about Masson?' was his reply to an unrelated question.

The manager's post-match celebrations were typical of Ally in that they were just a little bit different. He met his family at Hampden before heading for Faye's mother's in the nearby Croftfoot district. There they queued up in the Linn fish and chip shop with other fans who had been at the game (some apparently did not recognise the manager) before heading to Mrs Dunwoodie's. Ally was certainly brought back down to earth when his mother-in-law asked if it had been a good result! It was around 5am before the MacLeods arrived back in Milltimber, tired but happy.

Between the two matches full-back Danny McGrain suffered an ankle injury which would keep him out of not just the Scotland team but also the Celtic side for 16 months.

Anfield, the home of Liverpool Football Club, was the venue chosen by the Welsh FA to host the crucial match, a decision which was to backfire on them. Their 'lucky' ground at Wrexham was unavailable due to sanctions imposed by the football authorities following crowd trouble in a match against Yugoslavia the previous year. It was also where Scotland had struggled just a few months earlier.

Cardiff and Swansea were overlooked in favour of maximising revenue at the 51,000-capacity Anfield stadium which suggests Wrexham may have been ruled out on the same grounds anyway. Villa Park and even Wembley Stadium had been considered but Liverpool was chosen due to its closer proximity to the Welsh border.

The SFA had received an allocation of just 12,000 tickets which had all sold out within 30 minutes at various outlets throughout the country on the Monday ahead of the Czech game.

The Scottish allocation was for some seats and the Anfield Road end of the ground with the larger Kop terrace deemed the 'home' or Welsh end. 'The Kop will be full of Scots,' Ally predicted in the run-up to the game.

A draw may have been enough for Scotland but Wales had the advantage of a game with the Czechs still to play. If the match ended level a Welsh victory in Prague would see them top the group on goal difference.

There were tens of thousands of Scots in Liverpool, some with and many seeking tickets. Gates were stormed, walls scaled, gate men bribed, police lines repeatedly broken and even tickets stolen with an estimated 10,000 locked outside as the match kicked off. Some ticket holders arriving at the ground close to the start failed to gain entry as there were so many people already inside. This was the game that just about everyone in Scotland wanted to see.

Just as they did every other year at Wembley, and as Ally had predicted, the vast majority of the crowd were made up of what was now referred to as Ally's Army. Anfield was a cauldron of noise, a home match for Scotland.

Jock Vila had a ticket for the Anfield Road end and witnessed one group of enterprising fans who had a plan to scale the stadium walls, 'There was about eight or nine guys going along the street with a big ladder with scarves and flags over it as disguise. I never found out if they were successful, but they were going to have an attempt.'

The level of chaos Vila encountered at the ground around 15 minutes ahead of the start was unprecedented, 'I remember going up towards the turnstiles. It was jam packed and nothing seemed to be moving and we thought "we're never going to get into this game".

'The police came along on horses and a lot of folk got shunted to the right then they came back and a lot of folk went away to the left and I just missed getting pushed in with the others. We just went forward and I was suddenly at the turnstile from being about 20 yards away and seconds later got in. The police were going mental, pushing folk about.

'Every second turnstile was shut, filled up with confiscated drink. I've never seen so much drink lying in a heap at a football ground in my life. All piled three or four feet high with crates of lager, bottles of beer…you got searched as soon as you got through the turnstile and if they found anything they were just piling it up in the turnstile that was closed next to it.'

At the other end the few thousand Welsh fans in the Kop had been forced into a corner. Tommy Collin was one of a dozen supporters who travelled by minibus from Eyemouth to the game. A friend of Collin's had an uncle who was on the Welsh FA so 12 Kop tickets were gratefully acquired.

'The only time you saw a Welshman was inside the ground and they were getting hemmed into a corner,' he remembers. 'They were chucking bottles and there was a little bit of bother but it soon died down when they realised they were well outnumbered. There were Scots all around…it was amazing we got so many tickets for that end.'

An exciting but nervous match reached the interval without a goal. Two incidents in the second period determined the result. A John Toshack lob on 58 minutes looked net-bound before Rough leapt and got just enough on it to touch the ball on to the crossbar and behind. Then with 12 minutes remaining Willie Johnston sent a throw-in into the box where it clearly struck an arm. The French referee Robert Wurtz immediately signalled for a penalty kick and Masson prepared to take it.

'A penalty kick to Scotland and I can hardly look!' was how STV commentator Arthur Montford described the moment. Seconds later Anfield erupted into bedlam.

Montford's opposite number for BBC Scotland, Archie MacPherson, described the moment with the immortal words, 'He has done it and the Scottish supporters are going mad. You have never heard noise like this in all your life!'

There was further drama when Dalglish, now a Liverpool player, headed home a Buchan cross almost at the end to seal a 2-0 victory and World Cup qualification.

Again the crowd stayed with the continued chant of 'We want Ally!' But the fans were denied the lap of honour the manager had promised on the orders of the local police. It is likely the pitch invasion earlier that year at Wembley had a bearing on the decision.

Although there had been some rumblings from the Welsh camp, it was not until days after the game that a press photograph in the *Sunday Mail* suggested the offending arm in the penalty incident may well have belonged to Joe Jordan. Further examination of television footage seemed to back up the claims although to this day Jordan has refused to confess.

In truth the Welsh had every right to feel aggrieved at how the game was decided but over the 90 minutes, and unlike the Home International in Wrexham, Scotland had been the better side and had at times in the second half laid siege to the Welsh goal. That is not to say that the Welsh played badly, merely that spurred on by the crowd, Scotland performed the better of the two.

Ally was quoted in *The Scotsman*, 'It was a real battle…the only real disappointment was that we were not allowed to do a lap of honour. We'll just have to save that for when we bring the cup home next year.'

The *Liverpool Daily Post* headlined the day's events as 'The Night The City Will Never Forget' and reported 300 injuries, 107 arrests and one fatality due to a heart attack inside the ground. The response of the locals to the visiting hordes was mixed with some criticising the chaos and disorder while others praised good-natured fans.

After the Wembley pitch invasion there had been an element of scaremongering on Merseyside about what to expect from the Scots. Schools were closed early and people living around Anfield warned to stay indoors while pubs in the area remained closed. Tommy Collin remembers his party walking back to their minibus after the game and a woman in her 60s or 70s standing on her doorstep offering one of them a cup of water. 'Our throats were absolutely killing us,' he recalls.

Before long thirsty fans were queuing up as she kept going back and forwards to the kitchen for more water. Running out of cups, a milk bottle was welcomed and Collin remembers at one point 'a pan of water getting passed round. She was laughing and fair enjoying herself and there were other doors open as well. They were all at their doors, it was magic. Just all out to see the fans going past.'

At the end of November in that eventful year of 1977 Ally and SFA secretary Ernie Walker travelled to Argentina to look at facilities and accommodation. They visited all five of the venues and made provisional bookings in the best hotels they could find, ready to confirm the reservation at the relevant location once their schedule became known. This appeared to be a case of good forward planning on the part of the association.

Expanding on the purpose of the excursion the secretary explained to the *Evening Times*, 'The trip was invaluable and we both feel that the finals will be a great occasion. We were both struck by the enthusiasm and efficiency of the Argentinians.'

Over the following six months the World Cup coverage on television, radio, newspapers and all manner of media increased as the tournament drew closer. Centre stage in many, but not all, of these events was the manager, now a folk hero in his own land.

Ally appeared on television four times in as many days over the New Year period. He guested on *Hogmanay Sportscene* on BBC1 followed by a spot on Grampian's *Welcome to the Ceilidh*, heralding the start of 1978. Ally was then in the *Scotsport* studio the following afternoon and on the Tuesday he discussed his musical tastes with Kenneth McKellar on STVs *Sounds and Sweet Airs* with both sporting tartan bonnets.

'His emergence as a showbiz personality does not seem to have harmed the Scottish team's progress,' pondered TV critic Tom Shields in the *Glasgow Herald*, continuing, 'Just think, when we win the World Cup we'll be seeing even more of him.'

Ally also appeared in a couple of adverts (most famously one for Scotland Argentina rugs made by J. Ross and Co.) and even had a stint as a disc jockey on Radio Clyde. That training as a sales representative all those years earlier had after all been worthwhile.

He was a guest on the BBC programme *Blue Peter* and had a regular slot alongside Ian Archer each Sunday afternoon on *Scotsport* titled *The Ally MacLeod File*. Most of this promotional work had been arranged by an agent recommended to Ally by Jock Stein who had, of course, suggested Ally for the Scotland job.

By now the MacLeods had moved from Aberdeen back to the west of Scotland but not to Glasgow, instead to Corsehill Place in Ayr where the family felt very much at home. 'The automatic thing would be to live in Glasgow but he just wanted to come back to Ayr,' daughter Gail remembers.

The eagerly awaited draw for the tournament was screened live from Buenos Aires on both STV and Grampian on the evening of Saturday 14 January. From the 16 finalists four groups of four were drawn with the top two from each progressing to the last eight.

To quote Ian Archer's commentary on the night, 'Holland, Iran, Peru, and Scotland. The best draw in the world for Scotland. Surely a passport into the last eight. Iran and Peru the two minnows, it could be that when we get to Holland we've both qualified already.'

Speaking to the *Sunday Post* by telephone from the Argentinian capital, Ally was pleased, 'It couldn't have worked out any better if I'd planned it myself. We must have a fair chance of moving into the later stages. And just to add the icing on the cake we'll be able to live in the hotel we really wanted. It has tennis courts, a golf course, a swimming pool and it is easily the best one we looked at when Ernie Walker and I were over there just before Christmas. That should suit the players right down to the ground, it dispels any fears of them suffering from boredom between games.'

Skipper Rioch was also quoted in the *Post*, 'Marvellous. We couldn't have asked for any better. I reckon we can win the first two games then we're through.' Don Masson was even more confident, 'We are certs to go through to the last eight.' It is interesting to note that at this point the manager was the more cautious of the four quoted although his enthusiasm regarding the accommodation would later seem misplaced.

Walker and Ally headed to Cordoba the following day to confirm the reservation they had made in November. When they arrived at the Sierras they found that the Iranian squad had been there ahead of them and tried to bribe the hotel manager to cancel the SFA booking and let them stay there.

Seven days later when the pair changed flights in London on the way home the manager gave an interview which would later come back to haunt him. In a VIP lounge at Gatwick he spoke to a number of Scottish journalists including Alan Herron of the *Sunday Mail* which published the following, 'I'm now feeling really optimistic about achieving some success in June. I'm certain that we'll be among the medals and if we get the right break of the ball who knows? All we need are two 1-0 wins out of our three group games and we are into the last eight.'

The quote was part of a larger article focusing on the return from Argentina in which Ally also mentioned that he planned to watch Iran's match with France in May.

All Premier League matches were postponed due to bad weather that Saturday with only two First Division games going ahead so the opportunity was there for a sports headline regarding Ally's mention of medals. But although reported, little was made of the claim at the time with the *Mail*'s article typical of how the Sunday papers featured Ally's return home.

In another interview Ally had been asked what he would do should Scotland win the World Cup, to which he replied in his flippant manner, 'Retain it!' This was typical of Ally's quick wit and at the time was viewed in the same way as when he had said that Aberdeen were the only side who could win the treble following their League Cup triumph. That and the medals comment are two isolated quotes from countless interviews given by the manager over the next few months but they proved to be among the most damning.

18

The Summer of '78

ALLY had been seeking to enter the licensed trade in his home town for some time but when a deal for a pub in the centre of Ayr fell through he looked further afield and purchased the Old Tudor Inn in what would not so very long before have been the enemy territory of Kilmarnock early in 1978. The MacLeods paid £28,000 for the premises in the town's Titchfield Street, not the reported figure of £50,000, and Ally's brother-in-law initially ran the bar.

Scotland were unable to play again until 22 February and even then the match was almost called off. On the preceding Saturday only three Scottish Cup ties had beaten the weather due to a series of frozen pitches and the SFA had to make a decision that day as to whether Bulgaria should travel to Glasgow on the Monday or whether to call the game off. They chose to go ahead in what was a £25,000–£30,000 gamble as that was the estimated compensation the SFA would have to pay their opponents should Hampden Park be unplayable.

A thaw followed by heavy rain on the day of the match forced English referee Pat Partridge to delay a pitch inspection until 5pm, just three hours before the game was due to start. This created a real dilemma for fans travelling from outside of Glasgow but the match was given the thumbs-up and in spite of the circumstances a huge crowd of 59,524 made it to the game.

The figure would have been even greater had it not been for poor organisation on the night. With many turnstiles closed there was little in the way of ordered queuing, and mass congestion would probably be a more appropriate description of the scenes outside the ground. It took some fans 30 minutes to pay their way in long after others had given up and gone home.

SFA secretary Ernie Walker later admitted to being 'astonished' at the size of the crowd. 'I think that it's a reflection of the huge interest there is in the international side in the World Cup finals this year,' he told Alan Davidson of the *Evening Times*. The gamble had definitely paid off.

The match was just as dramatic as the events surrounding it with the vociferous crowd refusing to be silenced when the Bulgarians took an early lead. The Scots – fielding only six of the Anfield 11 due to call-offs – levelled through a Gemmill penalty kick just ahead of the break.

The winner came in the very last minute of the match through substitute Ian Wallace, sending the fans home happy but wet.

One song sang repeatedly from the terraces that evening was 'Ally's Tartan Army', often referred to by its opening lyric of 'We're on the march wi' Ally's Army.' The disc had been recorded by Glasgow comedian Andy Cameron and it is testament to the amount of interest brewing at that time that it had already been released and was in the music charts. When asked for Ally's opinion of the record Faye's recollection is, 'He found it humorous,' and she remembers their grandchildren singing it in later years.

Dozens more of these novelty discs were issued in the coming weeks as budding Sydney Devines grasped the opportunity to make a fast buck. Some of these were quite decent while others contained, frankly, dreadful lyrics but it was all part of the fun of the World Cup experience.

Both Cameron's and the official squad's records ('Ole Ola' with Rod Stewart) actually entered the top ten of the UK chart.

ITV's popular *This is Your Life* planned a show featuring Ally in the run-up to the World Cup but had to abandon the idea when news was leaked to the 'surprise' guest.

There was no shortage of gifts for the national manager that year with one of the most unusual being 100 trees from the Jewish National Fund commission in February. The trees had been planted in a Jerusalem forest although he never did get to see them. Ally was also made an honorary member of Turnberry Golf Club.

The players too were able to exploit the marketing opportunities which increased as the weeks passed. Some of the squad took part in a television advert for Chrysler Avenger cars which was said to be worth £20,000 and there was no shortage of offers to make public appearances. It was quite common to see pictures of the manager or one of his players holding a replica of the World Cup trophy just as Willie Ormond had been photographed doing four years earlier.

Andy MacLeod is adamant that despite accusations that his father had not bothered to watch Scotland's World Cup opponents this was down to the SFA refusing to fund trips rather than Ally's indifference. 'On many occasion he said to the SFA he wanted to go and watch opposition but they wouldn't fund trips so he had to rely on video,' says Andy.

Ally did have an ally when seeking information on the group rivals in ITV Sport presenter Brian Moore. Andy recalls Moore 'bent over backwards to help', regularly sending up video recordings of matches that he felt may be of use whether it be of World Cup opponents or club matches involving Scottish players.

Another, perhaps unlikely, ally was Nottingham Forest manager Brian Clough. Clough's assistance even extended to asking if Ally wanted him to play Kenny Burns and John Robertson in any particular way and Andy recalls him regularly calling the family home in Ayr with updates on the players.

Less helpful to Ally's cause proved to be Tommy Docherty who rarely played Don Masson and Bruce Rioch in the Derby County team during the run-up to Argentina, as of course it was his prerogative as a manager to do. In March that year the Doc placed Rioch on a two-week suspension as well as the transfer list following a row between them although the ban was subsequently halved and the player then reinstated.

Andy remembers long car journeys travelling hundreds of miles with his father to watch matches checking on who to include in the World Cup squad. 'It was father and son bonding time as he was away a lot,' Andy reminisces, thinking back to trips to Villa Park, Goodison and the like where he remembers 'the clubs' hospitality towards Ally was fantastic'.

Andy recalls one journey to watch Everton play Newcastle towards the end of 1977, 'We were sitting outside Goodison before the game in the officials' car park listening to the radio and Everton goalkeeper George Wood's recorded interview was on about his possible Scottish call-up. He said that it was an honour that he was in consideration and that if Ally was down to watch him he hoped he didn't know he was there to watch. After the interview was over Ally and I got out to go in and promptly bumped into George Wood in the car park!'

Ally's match notes reflected the player's concerns, 'Everton 4 Newcastle 4. Woods: A shaky game. Possibly reacting to knowing I was at the game. Need to see him several more times.' The visitors' Tommy Craig caught his eye and was noted as 'a possible deputy for Masson'.

Others who impressed the manager on these spying missions but never made it to the initial squad of 40 were youngsters Graeme Payne of Dundee United and Bobby Russell of Rangers, who were both marked down as future internationals.

Another manager who was keen to help was Welsh boss Mike Smith who supplied a dossier on Iran who Wales had beaten in a friendly prior to the World Cup. The report highlighted the fact Iran had been unbeaten in their last 13 matches of 1977 and played to a 4-3-3 formation.

From his original 40 named in March, Ally announced his chosen World Cup squad of 22 on 3 May with six players listed as reserves. Addressing the press at Park Gardens he sympathised with those left out, explaining, 'I have built a unit and I could not let loyalty rule my head.'

The listing of Andy Gray as a reserve surprised many. Ally offered the following explanation, 'Jordan and Derek Johnstone are both left-sided players and that is the reason I have left out Andy Gray, another left-sided man.'

With Joe Harper also in the squad there was no shortage of strikers and other forwards such as Kenny Dalglish were capable of scoring but the omission of Gray still puzzles some and the truth regarding his exclusion can now be revealed.

Ally rated the striker highly and had gone to watch the player on a number of occasions. He was later to claim that Gray had twice called off from matches he was planning to attend and more than once had been unable to complete the 90 minutes when he had been present, as reported in the *Evening Times* on 2 September 1978.

The deciding factor was a telephone call to Corsehill Place shortly before the squad announcement from Gray's manager at Aston Villa, Ron Saunders. Saunders intimated that his player was not fit enough to compete in the World

Cup and expressed concerns over the striker travelling all the way to South America. This reinforced Ally's doubts and he left Gray out but never told the player about his manager's intervention.

This is consistent with Gray's autobiography, *Gray Matters*, in which he relates that one of the reasons he was given for non-selection was that Ally had not been convinced of his fitness which backs up the telephone story. The closest Gray would get to Argentina would be the ITV studios in London where he formed part of their World Cup panel.

Ally chose John Hagart, who now had a coaching role at Fir Park, as his assistant manager for the World Cup, which was ironic considering it was he who had sparked the chain of events which led to Ally becoming Scotland manager. Hagart's departure from Tynecastle had of course led to Willie Ormond leaving the Scotland job. Explaining the choice of Hagart, the manager told John Mann of the *Scottish Daily Express* that there would likely be conflict had he taken another manager such as Jock Stein or Jim McLean who were used to being in charge. Hagart, Ally explained, was ideal for him as he was used to working under Roger Hynd at Motherwell. His duties were to include taking charge when the manager was dealing with the media and when, as Ally put it, 'I disappear as I certainly intend to do now and again.'

As the domestic season concluded the focus intensified on the national side to an unprecedented level. Billy McNeill had carried on Ally's work in his own way with Aberdeen who had been runners-up in both the Premier League and Scottish Cup to Rangers, but had finished a massive 17 points above Celtic in the table. But McNeill would be gone by the end of May with Alex Ferguson appointed his replacement on the first day of June. Within two years the Dons would be crowned Premier League champions and go on to win a European trophy, but for now it was all about Scotland.

To bridge the week-long gap between the Scottish Cup Final and the start of the Home Internationals the *Scottish Daily Express* carried a five-part in-depth feature supposedly from the manager, but ghost-written by John Mann who would later do the same with Ally's autobiography.

One of the articles was accompanied by a photograph of Ally at home in Ayr with a Philips video player and a pile of cassettes presumably supplied by Brian Moore. He explained how he often stayed up until the small hours viewing the tapes, looking for weaknesses in the opposition. Another instalment gave his assessment of each of the squad players but the most damning piece of that or any other article was printed on the first day of the series, Monday 8 May.

'You can mark down 25 June 1978 as the day Scottish football conquered the world. For on that Sunday I'm convinced the finest team this country has ever produced can play in the final of the World Cup in Buenos Aires…AND WIN. We have the talent. We have the temperament. And the ambition. And the courage. All that stands between us and the crown is the right kind of luck.

'I'm so sure we can do it I give my permission here and now for the big celebration on 25 June to be made an annual festival…a national Ally-day!'

Even by his own standards this was breaking new ground. A 'national Ally-day'? Had he really become that egotistical or had the article been written for him? At the very least Mann would have embellished the piece as the series was not presented in the form of interviews but as articles from Ally himself. It is certainly a quantum leap from any other predictions he made including the comment regarding medals back in January but is the closest Ally ever came to saying, 'Scotland will win the World Cup.'

All three of Scotland's Home Internationals were scheduled for Glasgow that year and were made all-ticket affairs, probably as a result of the chaos at the Bulgaria friendly. Minus Dalglish and Graeme Souness, who were playing in the European Cup Final for Liverpool at Wembley that evening, the Scotland squad met up at Dunblane on Wednesday 10 May. This put paid to the manager's previous plans to watch Iran play in France the following night.

The first game against Northern Ireland on 13 May was officially an away fixture but the two had met at Hampden Park every year since 1971 due to the reluctance of the SFA to travel to the province during the sectarian troubles. A crowd of 64,433 attended the Saturday game which ended in a lacklustre 1-1 draw with goals from Martin O'Neill for the Ulstermen and a headed equaliser courtesy of Derek Johnstone.

As a spectacle it had been rather ordinary but no worse than the tournament's opener in Wrexham the year before. Interviewing the manager for *Sportscene* after the final whistle, Archie MacPherson suggested that he may have perhaps underestimated the opposition. This prompted the response of, 'I never underestimate anyone!' from Ally.

The Wales game on the Wednesday night attracted an even greater audience of 70,241. Again it was Johnstone who scored, this time with a spectacular diving header, connecting with a cross from Gemmill inside 12 minutes. The visitors came close to equalising when McQueen stopped a Phil Dwyer shot on the line but in doing so fell awkwardly and collided with a post, damaging his knee. After a delay he was forced to leave the field and replaced by Tom Forsyth.

It was still 1-0 when in the 86th minute Forsyth handled in the area and this time the Welsh were the beneficiaries of a penalty award. Scotland had played well, much better than on the Saturday, but looked to have blown it until Brian Flynn's effort struck a goalpost to the relief of the crowd.

The Scots then committed soccer suicide with just seconds of the game remaining. Goalkeeper Jim Blyth rolled the ball out to full-back Willie Donachie, expecting him to pass to a team-mate. But Donachie sent it back to the unsuspecting Blyth and it ended up in their own net.

So it was another 1-1 draw, but a win on the Saturday against England would provide the perfect send-off before the squad headed for South America.

While acknowledging the improved performance, the manager did express some concerns when speaking at the post-match press conference, 'It was a big improvement on Saturday…but I consider we missed too many chances and that is something we must work on.'

Johnstone's goal had been his 40th of the season with 38 league and cup goals for Rangers and the two in internationals – and that from a player who did not take penalty kicks.

The squad stayed at the Dunblane Hydro during the Home Internationals and the subject of bonus payments and whether the players would be paying UK tax on rewards earned overseas reared its head at a team meeting with the manager.

Joe Harper recalls, 'We had a meeting about money. When we were told what we were getting and what the bonuses were, depending on how far we went, Lou Macari stood up and said, "That's ridiculous! I can make more money out of my fish and chip shop in one weekend in Manchester." That's when Bobby Clark, myself and Stuart Kennedy got up and walked out of the room because we weren't going to listen to anybody.

'We weren't there for the money. It was the Anglos were the ones that caused the money problems…the boys that were on better money, maybe three or four times more money than we were getting as players in Scotland.'

Ally then had to go to the SFA hierarchy and act as a middle man. 'The manager's job is to look after players and get the players to do their best on the park. It's not to talk about money. He should never have been put in a position where he had to talk about money to any player,' Harper insists today.

Andy MacLeod recalls that even on the eve of the World Cup his father was so incensed at being left to deal with such non-football matters that he seriously considered resigning that week. He was the team manager after all, not a financial adviser.

'He was left to carry the can between the players and the SFA because there was a question over tax,' Andy says. Ally telephoned the family home in Ayr and after a chat with Faye decided against quitting. 'He had to be talked out of resigning. That's the only time we've been able to change his mind about anything,' Andy reflects.

Naming his team on the eve of the England game, Ally surprised everyone by bringing in Jordan with Johnstone, who Arsenal were sending a representative to watch, relegated to the bench. He explained his decision to the *Herald*'s Jim Reynolds. 'Derek Johnstone played very well in his two games. But Joe Jordan has had only half a match so it is important that the gets a run against England. If Jordan had been fit in midweek I would have played him against Wales and Johnstone would have been in tomorrow.'

Jordan had indeed limped off at half-time against Northern Ireland and put in those terms the decision was not inconsistent with giving Blyth a game against the Welsh in place of Rough with World Cup preparation given priority.

As Scotland aimed to complete a hat-trick of wins over England and with the World Cup just two weeks away excitement was at fever pitch. Following a police raid on a printing shop in Glasgow's Buchanan Street thousands of forged tickets had been seized earlier in the week and several thousand more were believed to be in circulation. The forgeries – all for the same stadium section, 'O' – had been offered in bars and workplaces throughout the west of Scotland for up to £5 each, more than three times the face value of the genuine briefs which was £1.50.

On a beautiful summer's day the teams walked on to the Hampden pitch with the loudest cheer reserved for own-goal sinner Donachie. Scotland dominated possession but in truth rarely looked like finding a breakthrough. The crowd grew restless in the second half and called for Johnstone to come off the bench but the manager would not be swayed. There was almost a sense of inevitability when Peter Barnes crossed, Rough – who had been little more than a spectator – fumbled and Steve Coppell netted the game's only goal with seven minutes left.

What followed was quite remarkable. Rather than slump into silence the crowd sang louder and continued singing a good 20 minutes after the final whistle with few heading for the exits.

'To stand there and cheer when you've seen your team beaten takes a special kind of supporter,' the manager later told Bobby Maitland of the *Scottish Daily Express*, before adding, 'The team and the fans have got something going together.'

Skipper Rioch was stunned, 'I thought I had seen and heard it all…that's the Scottish support for you. They're the best in the world.'

Commenting on the game at the press conference Ally was, well, just Ally. 'I thought England were outclassed,' was his assessment, adding that he felt his team had played better on the day than at Wembley the year before. Looking ahead to the World Cup he had this to say, 'Everything that has happened has convinced me of what I must do in Cordoba. On the whole I am satisfied with the gradual improvement in our play. The pattern was there to see against England again, and the hope is that we will reach our peak at the right time.'

The squad were due to fly out from Prestwick Airport the following Thursday evening but there were some interesting distractions in the intervening days. On the Tuesday evening Jock Wallace resigned as manager of Rangers, just a couple of weeks after securing a domestic treble. Within days Wallace was appointed manager of Leicester City, who had just been relegated from the First Division in England.

Ally then received a telephone call from Rangers' general manager Willie Waddell offering him the Ibrox manager's job. Although interested, Ally explained that he had promised to take Scotland through the World Cup campaign so declined. Had the offer come during the bonuses row a week or so earlier the response may possibly have been different.

Ally had earlier been tipped for the Leicester post with a *Sunday Express* reporter, Norman Wynne, claiming that the Filbert Street board were awaiting his return from the World Cup before making their move.

On the Wednesday, the day before the Scottish party were due to fly to South America, Rangers' Derek Johnstone handed in a written transfer request to Waddell.

A few days earlier at Dunblane, Johnstone had approached Ally. Although he had scored 40 goals that season his preferred position was at centre-half and, perhaps trying to capitalise on Gordon McQueen's injury, he told the manager he was available to play either up front or in defence.

Ally said something to the effect he would decide what his best position was and no more was said on the matter. This conversation was relevant enough for the player to mention it in his autobiography *DJ* in which he recalls, 'As I walked away I could sense his rage. I think he felt I was too big for my boots.'

When Andy MacLeod asked his father about the Johnstone situation some years later Ally explained that he felt the player only wanted to play at centre-half and not in attack. Andy recalls that Ally genuinely rated Johnstone highly and, on the basis he had brought him into the squad as a striker, had no intention of playing him at centre-half. He is also sure there was no argument as such between the player and manager at any time despite rumours to the contrary.

The seeds of the manager's assessment of Johnstone's ability had been sown even before the team had qualified for Argentina. Ally's own notes for an Old Firm match on 10 September 1977 contain the following, 'Rangers 3 Celtic 2. Tremendous game, good advert for Scottish football.

'Several players have enhanced their reputation. Derek Johnstone – started at centre half, did not play well. Moved to centre forward at start of second half, had outstanding game and was instrumental in Rangers winning.'

Celtic had incidentally led by two goals at half-time, a scoreline which required a change of tactics. This from Ally's notes dated 5 October 1977, 'Rangers 6 Aberdeen 1. Derek Johnstone – Leads the attack well. Makes space for other forwards to run into. Gradually reaching international form.'

Ally also tells in his autobiography how Johnstone sought him out for a private chat before the Bulgaria friendly in February, confiding that he saw his future in the game as a centre-half and believing he had limitations in a striking role. 'I have told Rangers, as I am telling you now, that I'd prefer to compete for a place in the defence,' is how Ally recalled that particular conversation.

Ally had sent Johnstone on for the last 25 minutes of the Bulgaria game as a replacement striker for Jordan and had clearly been impressed as his own match notes document, 'Caused quite a stir up in the Bulgarian ranks – a satisfying performance.'

In the five-part *Scottish Daily Express* series the manager's assessment of the player reads, 'He's player of the year. You can't have a better credential than that. He might be even better if he really believed that centre forward was his best position.' This suggests Ally's view was that the player lacked confidence in the striking role just as Johnstone had apparently hinted in their conversation prior to the Bulgaria game.

On the day the squad were due to fly to the World Cup – one day after John Greig had been announced as Rangers' new manager – a full-page story appeared in the *Evening Times* where Johnstone told Crawford Brankin of his reasons and the timing of his transfer request.

He explained he had wanted the transfer in place before he came back from the World Cup to dispel any rumours that his head had been turned by the money the Anglos claimed to be earning when in Argentina. At least he didn't do a Derek Dougan and make the request on cup final day! A paragraph highlighted in large bold type in the article read, 'I see myself as a centre-half and I hope any teams which bid for my signature regard me the same way.'

Whether or not Ally saw the *Times* article is impossible to say. Certainly the newspaper was on sale that afternoon before the team flew off and it is not inconceivable that there were copies among the squad or available on the flight. Equally Ally would have been rather busy that day but there is no question that Johnstone's desire to play at centre-half greatly reduced his chances of playing in Argentina. To be fair to the player he acknowledged that Jordan was rightly the first-choice striker but as they set off there were still doubts over Jordan's fitness.

'I'll either come back a hero or a villain,' were Ally's last words to Faye as he set off to the World Cup. Was the team's indifferent form in the Home Internationals causing him concern at this late stage?

The SFA arranged a World Cup Gala Night at Hampden Park to allow the fans to cheer the players off as they headed to Prestwick Airport for the journey to Argentina. This turned out to be one of the most controversial events associated with the Argentina fiasco and was later interpreted as a victory parade.

A crowd of 22,732 paid 30 pence each to wish the players good luck with many more watching the event live on STV. Andy Cameron introduced each player as one by one they appeared from the tunnel and made their way through a guard of honour of bagpipers and drummers to the centre circle. The squad then boarded an open-top bus of the type normally reserved for cup-winning teams and drove around the pitch before heading for the road to Ayrshire.

Another Ally myth is that he filled Hampden for the occasion when, as the above figure shows, the stadium was far from full. Many of the attendees that evening were women and young children who would not normally be found on the football terraces of the day.

The MacLeod family have always insisted the event was not Ally's idea and certainly looking at his body language he does look rather embarrassed. Unprompted, Joe Harper offered the following, 'He hated it. He was the most embarrassed person under the sun…That had nothing to do with him. That was the SFA.'

The event had indeed been arranged by the SFA following concerns raised by Strathclyde Police regarding possible overcrowding at the airport when the team arrived.

Well-wishers lined the route to Prestwick with families bedecked in tartan waving from gardens and Scottish flags draped from bridges along the 27-mile journey. Another 4,000 supporters were waiting at the airport where the squad were piped on board the British Caledonian aircraft which 20 hours later landed in Buenos Aires. Once there an Argentinian Air Force plane carried the party to Cordoba where they were transferred by coaches to their hotel 40 minutes away in Alta Gracia.

19

Argentina

THE locals of Alta Gracia lined the streets to welcome 'Escocia' and some of the players had to walk through those crowds to the Sierras Hotel after their coach broke down in the town. It was not the perfect end to the marathon journey, but perhaps the writing was already on the wall.

This was the fourth time in a year that Ally and Walker had been in the country counting the match in Buenos Aires, the trip to evaluate accommodation and the World Cup draw.

With eight days to fill before Scotland's opener against Peru the squad soon found themselves bored after returning from their daily training sessions. Sure the hotel had a swimming pool – with a large crack across it – and a tennis court but unfortunately there was no tennis equipment or water in the pool.

Armed guards surrounded the hotel complex which did little to contribute to a relaxed environment. Presumably referring to the security rather than the accommodation Ally at one point described the players' base as 'like Colditz'.

Joe Harper's memories of the hotel are straight to the point, 'Where we stayed in was a disaster, an absolute disaster.'

But Bobby Clark offers a surprisingly different perspective on the Sierras where he made sure he was always occupied, 'I did not mind it. I was somehow busy. There was a golf course, tennis courts, and I had to churn out 600 words a day for the *Aberdeen Evening Express* and I needed to write these myself. I also like reading so I don't recall it being too bad. Possibly the most inconvenient part was that we had a long bus ride (approximately 60 minutes) to go to practise in Cordoba. This was two hours sitting on a bus every day and I felt that was a little boring.'

The players were given permission to leave the hotel for a couple of hours on the Saturday evening so Sandy Jardine, Alan Rough and Derek Johnstone paid a visit to a nearby casino. With the curfew approaching the trio were unable to find the entrance to the Sierras and chose to scale a fence where they walked straight into armed security men.

As the players' official accreditation had not yet been issued their identity was only confirmed when SFA officials were summoned but the matter was blown out of proportion in the local press which suggested the players had returned home drunk.

A few days later the squad surprised Stuart Kennedy with a birthday party in the players' lounge. Photographs taken that evening show the attendees drinking from Coca-Cola bottles but the event was still reported as another booze-up for the squad.

Interestingly the manager did not use the same controversial training routines with the national squad that he had at club level. Clark says, 'With the Scotland team he was very different. I wish he had been the same Ally MacLeod that he had been at Pittodrie. He perhaps tried to be different and I felt that it was his extraverted personality with Aberdeen that made him successful. I am not sure if he felt the big names in the Scotland squad might have rebelled.

'At Aberdeen Ally would join in the games at training. There was always a fun feeling around the games and I think he became much more serious. The practices were fine but Ally seemed more subdued than he had been at Pittodrie.'

On the eve of the opening match the manager confessed he was feeling the pressure to the *Express*'s Ian Archer, 'Yes the tension really is beginning to get to me. I feel it right in the pit of my stomach.'

Speaking to the *Herald*'s Jim Reynolds, Ally's comments make interesting reading today, 'I am not the least bit worried by Peru. I am only concerned with ourselves…my job is to have my players mentally and physically attuned. We will let Peru do the worrying. But it will not be easy…I have never thought that way. They are a very good side going forward. If I had to pick out one danger man from their side it would have to be Munante. He is very fast on the break. It will be a close match, but I'm confident we will get the right result.'

Though at times dismissive the interview does suggest some homework had been done on the opposition although a pre-match ITV interview with the players is telling. The interview was between STVs Arthur Montford and three non-playing squad members, Harper, Robertson and the suspended Donachie.

Donachie expressed his disappointment at not taking part while Harper described the dressing room atmosphere as pressured but having 'an electrifying atmosphere'. Montford then turned to Robertson and asked, 'What do the players know of Peru as a team?' This drew the response, 'Very little actually. We've only seen one videotape recording of them against Argentina. That's all we've seen.' He then repeated his manager's observation, 'They look very good going forward actually.'

As well as Donachie, Ally was without another two first-choice defenders in McGrain and McQueen, whose injury had worsened during the flight. The manager had been advised McQueen was likely to regain full fitness during the tournament and Ally had decided against replacing him in a display of loyalty to the player who had served him well. Back home, Andy Gray could have been forgiven for being less then sympathetic at the inclusion of an injured player in the travelling party.

Although the match was to be played on a Saturday there was still a long wait for those watching in the UK with the game not starting until 8.45pm. Off licences and sports shops selling tartan tammies and scarves as well as television rental shops enjoyed sales booms. A spokesman for Agnew's, the chain of liquor stores, told the *Daily Record* that takings had been similar to at New Year.

Some 7,000 miles away in Cordoba the manager's thoughts drifted back to Scotland and the expectations of him and his players as he told Jim Reynolds, 'You know the thing I'll miss most is not being with all the fans back home. I've been wondering what it will be like for them. The streets of Scotland will be empty, the beer will be brought out and every eye will be glued to the television. I certainly hope we don't let them down…we are all very conscious of the fact that we have a nation willing us to do well.'

The locals had been impressed by the few hundred Scottish fans (the official figure for Scottish supporters travelling on package deals was 540) in Cordoba; nobody really went there and their presence had increased interest to the extent a crowd of 47,000 were in the Chateau Carreras Stadium. And it started so well as Jordan fired Scotland ahead after just 14 minutes. Playing in an all-blue strip the Scots looked comfortable as the interval approached before the defence was caught out, allowing Cesar Cueto to beat Rough and change the mood of the match.

Peru then took control of the second half and were on top when the Swedish referee gave the Scots a lifeline in the 63rd minute. Diaz fouled Rioch in the area – not the most obvious of penalties – but a penalty it was. Just as in Buenos Aires and Liverpool it would be Don Masson's responsibility. But this time Quiroga turned the ball round the post and the Peruvians regained the initiative.

Cubillas scored twice in the space of three minutes and it was all over – Peru 3 Scotland 1. The players in blue looked shattered as they walked from the pitch but just when it seemed things could not get any worse, they did.

In a televised interview with Arthur Montford broadcast live on ITV less than half an hour after the game, Ally blasted the suggestion he had underestimated the opposition, 'I never underrated them. We did our homework on them. I've said all along that Peru were no easy meat.'

Conceding it was not a normal Scottish performance he now cut an edgy, nervous, defensive figure with no sign of the bubbling enthusiasm of before. There was not even a hint of optimism when answering what Montford introduced as 'the crunch question…Can Scotland still do it?' 'That remains to be seen. It would be stupid to say we could do it after losing to Peru but funny things happen in football, and we'll just have to soldier on.'

Around the time of the interview two players from each side were selected for a urine sample with Kenny Dalglish and Willie Johnston chosen. Archie Gemmill had actually gone ahead of Johnston in error but had been unable to provide the sample. The results would not be known until the following day.

Having attended the game at Wembley the previous June, Jock Vila was now a fully paid-up member of Ally's Army. Thanks to a combination of both saving and borrowing he amassed the £1,395 – a small fortune in 1978 – required to book on the Thomas Cook World Cup charter which included 24 nights' accommodation and tickets for ten matches including the final itself.

The initial quote he recalls had been closer to £900. 'I was quite confident that we had one of the best sides in the tournament,' Jock says and even though there was defeat in that first match he recalls not being too despondent. 'Obviously we were all pretty peed off with the result but I remember we were marching around the square when we got back to the city centre. They were still pretty upbeat, most of the guys, and because we had got such a good reception from the locals we were determined not to go back and be miserable because we'd got beat.

'It was one of those squares with, if you can imagine, a St Andrews Cross pathway through it so we were marching through the square, marching round diagonally, going round in a square and all that, hundreds of Scots fans all going about chanting just trying to put on a show for the locals. Just to show that we were pretty keen that we were still going to do something. We weren't at that time thinking "that's it, we're out the World Cup".'

There was an uneasy atmosphere as the reporters assembled for the manager's press conference in Alta Gracia on the Sunday morning. Journalists that Ally had always made himself available to, even at club level, fired questions about his resignation and his approach to the Peru game. 'I cannot understand it,' he shrugged. 'In the opening 15 minutes I was sure we were on the way to World Cup glory.'

In Monday's *Daily Record* the manager was accused of passing the blame on to the players. Ian Archer, who had been so optimistic when commentating on the World Cup draw, composed a list of six questions in the *Scottish Daily Express*. 1. Why were Rioch and Masson in the side when Souness and Gemmill had a better season? 2. Why did the manager wait until 73 minutes before making any substitutions? 3. Why were Peru's wingers marked by a 'novice and an absolute beginner' (Buchan and Kennedy)? 4. Why 'for heaven's sake' did no one mark Cubillas? 5. How much homework was done on the opposition? 6. Why did Scotland slow down after taking the lead?

Although he would not see the *Express* article at the time it was the personal nature of Archer's piece which Ally's family remember hurt him more than any other criticism. Ian Archer had every right to condemn the team and the manager over the Peru game but if Ally was being accused by some of blaming the players then Archer was doing the opposite, almost absolving them of responsibility.

The two of them had sat side by side presenting the *The Ally MacLeod File* each Sunday afternoon on *Scotsport* and eldest son Andy remembers of the journalist, 'He was always phoning the house looking for stories.' Equally Archer had been responsible for penning a number of articles feeding the wave of World Cup euphoria that was building in the lead-up to Argentina.

Andy says of his father, 'He felt the *Express* article was a turning point in his relationship with the press. He felt betrayed by Archer. He was intensely disliked by our family during and after Argentina.'

Andy's sister Gail is equally unforgiving, 'He crawled to my dad constantly and then just turned on him. To this day that hurt has never left me.' Ian Archer never did telephone the MacLeod household again.

The squad were attending a reception with the Sports Minister Dennis Howell in Alta Gracia that Sunday evening when the news broke that Johnston's urine sample had proved positive.

The next day the player was driven to Buenos Aires to catch the next available flight home after being told he would never play for Scotland again. This was not quite what Ally had had in mind when he had predicted 'Willie Johnston will be the revelation of the World Cup' some weeks earlier.

It transpired that Johnston had taken two Reactivan tablets which were widely used by players in the Football League at the time. It has been described as a mild stimulant and it is believed at least five other Scottish players may have taken the same drug on the day of the Peru game. There was, and still is, some sympathy for Johnston from many of his team-mates just as there had been under different circumstances in Buenos Aires 12 months earlier.

Johnston's room-mate Masson then told the manager that he too had taken the pills. Appearing before an SFA committee in the hotel the player later retracted the 'confession'. Masson was told that his international career too was at an end but he was not sent home to avoid the SFA further embarrassment. The player then sold his inside story of the events of Alta Gracia to the *News of the World*.

To a degree the Reactivan episode had rendered the Peru result irrelevant due to a FIFA ruling which stipulated that any side found guilty of a doping offence would forfeit the relevant match which would show as a two-goal deficit, and that was exactly how the game turned out. Had Scotland performed to win the match Johnston may well have been viewed less sympathetically and probably as the man who had cost the country vital World Cup points.

Stories then began to appear in Argentinian newspapers about Scottish players drinking heavily and womanising between matches. This can largely be explained by supporters who were regularly asked to sign autographs for the locals in Cordoba and often quite innocently adopted the name of a favourite player. But these reports got back to the SFA and had to be denied. Bobby Clark says, 'It was the time when replica shirts were, for the first time, coming into vogue. The rumour was that fans were posing as members of the squad.'

Concerned at morale within the squad, SFA president Willie Harkness took the unusual step of breaking with protocol and spoke directly with the players. Harkness appealed for them to raise their spirits and approach the remaining two matches with the spirit expected of Scottish players.

A previous request for such a meeting in Alta Gracia to discuss the issue of bonuses had been refused and no sooner had the president finished than he was hit with questions over the incentives by some members of the squad.

On the subject of team spirit during the tournament Clark reflects on the task the manager would have been faced with compared to dealing with a club side, 'Possibly the biggest difference at international level is that players do not know one another as well and with Scotland there was always the Old Firm group, the Anglos, and the others. Having said that, I felt that our team got pretty close as we had the home series in 1977 followed by the South American tour.

'With many of the same players involved we again had the Home Internationals prior to the World Cup. It was a pretty close group and I never felt any problems among the players. The press tried to say discipline was poor but I thought the squad was very well behaved. There was very little trouble that players could get into in Alta Gracia. From my viewpoint the discipline was very good.'

One day ahead of the Iran game a press conference was held after a training session at the Cordoba Stadium. The manager tried to sound upbeat but there was none of the old Ally on display, 'We seem to be the target for abuse from the foreign press, but to hell with them all. Every one of us knows that to play in the World Cup finals is the chance of a lifetime. Because of this the boys are more determined than ever to do well in our remaining two matches. We aim to show everyone that we're no mugs.'

Ally would not have been fully aware of exactly how the Scottish press were reporting events back home although his strained relationship with reporters would have given him an indication.

The manager made five changes for the Iran match, two of them enforced due to the bans imposed on Johnston and Masson. Harper and Derek Johnstone were substitutes with only the Aberdeen player called into action, coming on for Dalglish in the second half. What followed is still considered to be the worst ever performance by a Scottish international side, taking the standard of opposition and importance of the game into account.

The players looked as though they would rather be anywhere than on the pitch but were given a break when they went ahead through an own goal on the stroke of half-time. Even the locals had lost faith and only around 8,000 were in attendance, around a sixth of the crowd against Peru.

The goal did nothing for team morale as the lacklustre second half continued the same pattern until the hour-mark when Danaie Fard equalised after sloppy defending. The body language of the Scottish players speaks volumes as Kenny Burns stands with hands on his hips, and a look of horror on his face while shaking his head.

Yet for all the poor play Scotland still did enough to win the match particularly when a Jordan effort from a Hartford free kick forced a diving save.

When there was a break in the play, the Argentinian television director would cut to a close-up of the Scottish manager. With each visit the actions of the once optimistic extrovert became more painful to watch. First he can be seen shouting encouragement and clenching his fist. Then he is shaking his head as the minutes tick away, becoming increasingly agitated.

Finally in the last minute Ally was seen with his head in his hands, an increasingly isolated figure. He looked ill and it was as if the life had been sucked out of the man. Peru had been bad, but this was ten times worse. As the players made their way to the tunnel a group of the 600 or so Scotland fans jeered them from above with some making the ultimate sacrifice of throwing scarves and replica tops down on them.

Again Arthur Montford had been granted an interview with the manager inside the stadium and to Ally's credit he faced the cameras. He looked a broken man and as Brian Moore observed, close to tears. Struggling to justify the display he uttered, 'I was so sure in the dressing room they would play well. Everyone looked as though they were dying to get out…but we never really played as well as Scotland can.'

Assessing the team's chances of progressing in the tournament which required a three-goal victory over Holland in the final match, he conceded, 'It looks an impossible task.' Worse was to follow as the team coach got held up outside the ground and a group of 30 to 40 angry Scotland fans subjected the squad to a torrent of insults with some spitting at the bus windows.

'No Mendoza!' (the venue for the Holland match), 'We want our money back' and 'What a load of rubbish!' were some of the more printable chants aimed at the team with much of it personal towards whoever happened to be sitting by the nearest window regardless of whether or not they had played that night. There was even an aborted attempt to overturn the coach at one point.

I know that many of those involved in the incident had travelled overland 'the hard way', leaving home in February or March and spending weeks hitchhiking through the Americas and travelling on buses to get there. Apart from the results, what annoyed those fans most was that they had to do it all again to get back. They knew that the players sitting in the comfort of the coach would fly home in a matter of hours whereas they had no idea of how, when or even if they would reach Scotland.

Other fans got heavily into debt to finance the trip and their anger was fuelled by rumours of players demanding higher bonuses.

'I never saw much of that,' says Jock Vila. 'The Iran match was just such a deflating game that everybody left the ground pretty quiet. We were all on organised transport so we just left the stadium and got on a bus back to the centre so we didn't see much of the protest going on at the stadium.

'It was a pretty quiet night that night, just one of these low-key sort of things, well it was pretty dull. Everybody just sort of realised we'd have to go and beat Holland by so many goals, we didn't know how much at the time and that was gonae be pretty much mission impossible.'

If any questions still lurked within Ally over the Scottish public's reaction to the team's performances he would have been left in no doubt after the squad's ordeal outside the stadium. It would have really hurt to see the supporters now turn on him and his players with such venom.

The collective lack of conviction among the players against Iran is something that can never be fully explained. Obviously the low morale caused by previous events had taken its toll but the team had a chance to make amends for the Peru result and were apparently confident of doing so.

On this occasion the manager had undoubtedly been unable to inspire his players, and to say otherwise would be denying the obvious. Motivation was, after all, one of Ally's greatest assets as a manager.

Meanwhile, back in Glasgow someone put a brick through one of the windows of 6 Park Gardens. The following day the owner of I and N Records in Dundee offered copies of the Andy Cameron disc for sale at one pence and reported some customers had smashed their purchase on the shop's counter. Chrysler then pulled their television advert, which claimed that the Scotland players and their Avengers 'both run rings round the competition', from the schedules.

In his final press conference in Alta Gracia the manager again rejected questions over his position with a defiant, 'I won't quit here. You have to wait until we get home.'

There was a small protest by some supporters who took the trouble to travel the 24 miles to Alta Gracia the next day although they never got beyond the gates of the Sierras.

Some of the fans who had hitchhiked to Argentina stuck to their 'No Mendoza' pledge – Mendoza is approximately 400 miles from Cordoba – and either remained in Cordoba or started the long trek home. A handful did not reach Scotland until the autumn while a couple never came home at all, at least not for some years.

One supporter, Billy Belcher, was quoted in the *Evening Times* as packing his bags and spending £1,200 on a flight home rather than wait until the end of his package. 'I'm not staying here like a dummy to represent that shower,' he said.

The players were not sorry to leave the Sierras – which still had no water in the swimming pool – as they flew to Mendoza and the San Francisco Hotel. They saw less of the manager as Hagart took training and Ally withdrew to his room when they needed him most. This was perhaps not the circumstances Ally had meant when he had said he would leave his assistant in charge when he 'disappeared now and again'.

Bobby Clark recalls, 'It was a tough time for Ally. I certainly felt very sorry for him. I cannot really remember if he went AWOL. I just remember walking past his room and seeing a very sad Ally. The door was open and he looked very dejected so I went back and had a conversation as I felt he needed some company for a few moments. I can't remember what I said outside of trying to cheer him up.'

Ally was so far from the one person he could confide in, Faye. Telecommunications were not nearly as advanced then from Britain to the rest of Europe let alone South America and Faye's recollections are that he only telephoned home from Argentina on a couple of occasions, 'I remember asking him if he had anyone he could talk to out there as he just looked absolutely miserable.' She remembers him saying, 'I know who my friends are now,' and that he was going to be more careful who he spoke to in future. Of Ally's mood during those conversations Faye says, 'He tried to be cheery…but he wasn't.'

It was not the images of her husband on the bench during the Iran game that caused Faye the most distress but the sight of Ally sitting stone-faced, looking from the coach as it pulled away from the stadium having experienced the wrath of the fans. 'He just looks so gaunt and miserable…that's the one that haunts me,' she says of the picture.

'I have had only good times in my short spell as Scotland manager…but, as in everything else, the bad times have still to come.' Did those words, uttered as Ally basked in the glory of Wembley only 12 months earlier, come back to haunt him as he sat alone in self pity in his room?

Just a couple of weeks since leaving home he had clearly put on weight and looked stressed with his face visibly tightened.

There were further calls for Ally to be sacked – it was pointed out that this would be a straightforward process as it was known he had not signed a contract. But his job was safe for another few days at least.

Lou Macari gave an exclusive interview to one of the ITV companies in which he was highly critical of the SFA's organisation of the trip. He also condemned the fans who had abused the team bus and who had accused the players of only turning up for the money. The broadcast was considered to have overstepped the mark and Macari too found himself banned from international football indefinitely. First Johnston, then Masson, now Macari.

In Mendoza, skipper Bruce Rioch spoke to the manager alone and they discussed the approach to the Holland game. For once Ally listened and agreed to a 4-4-2 formation to try and beat the Dutch and maybe, just maybe, stay in the competition – Scotland were now 500/1 to win the World Cup.

Bobby Clark recalls there was a confidence among the players ahead of the match, 'I think the squad felt they could play with anyone and although the results against Peru and Iran were not what we wanted I think we were ready for Holland.'

With a midfield of Rioch, Souness, Gemmill and Hartford, Scotland took to the field – and played.

From a Souness cross a Rioch header thumped against the crossbar, then Dalglish scored only to have it ruled out for offside. But the Dutch were awarded a penalty from which Rensenbrink scored.

Were the Gods against Scotland too? Even when playing well they now had a four-goal mountain to climb.

It got better. Dalglish netted right on half-time and it was game on. Seconds after the restart Souness went down in the area and the Austrian referee awarded what could be described as a debatable penalty. Gemmill scored. On 68 minutes the same player beat three men, drew the goalkeeper and scored a famous goal – but no one stopped to admire the beauty of it at the time.

'Scotland are in dreamland,' exuded David Coleman, commentating for the BBC. All they needed now was just one more goal and there was ample time to get it. But it didn't last as Johnny Rep beat Rough from 25 yards for the game's final score.

'I remember when Gemmill scored that goal,' says Jock Vila. 'It felt like we were chanting and singing for five or ten minutes but when the Dutch scored that goal it was only three or four minutes later but we were still singing away.'

There was just time for Forsyth to head over an open goal before full-time but Scotland had at least won 3-2 and restored some pride and ultimately only failed to progress on goal difference.

Vila was unimpressed with the opposing supporters who numbered well below 100, 'I do remember at the game thinking these Dutch guys who were there were pretty low key compared to Dutch fans I have seen since. They were well-off Dutch that went to the World Cup, not like these days. They weren't making much of a noise even though they had qualified.'

After one of their worst performances Scotland had followed up with one of their best, albeit too much too late. The Holland v Scotland match was later voted the best of the 1978 tournament.

Like Scotland the Dutch won only one of their group games in Argentina and there were tales of unrest among their squad during the first phase.

There until the final, Vila looks back on Scotland's World Cup exit, 'Most folk seemed pretty encouraged by that result. We were pretty upbeat by that time because at least we went out beating one of the favourites for the tournament.'

At the press conference Ally tried to justify the improved performance, 'We've had such an anti-press that we all got together and just said "stuff the lot of them", and set out there to play as we know we can.'

The next day the party flew to Buenos Aires where they had a one-night stay before catching the flight home.

On the way back Derek Johnstone, who like the still-injured McQueen hadn't played one minute of football during the three matches, walked the length of the plane to tell Ally he no longer wished to be considered for international duty as long as he was the manager before returning to his seat. The last straw for the striker had been Ally's decision to introduce Joe Harper as a substitute during the Iran game while he remained on the bench.

During the 22-hour journey the manager had been asked by radio if he and the players would meet with the press in London. The request was declined with an instruction that no media facilities were to be granted.

Changing flights at Gatwick, Ally shook hands with all the English-based players and thanked them. Some of the Anglos were then collared by reporters and skipper Rioch spoke of 'bitter disappointment'.

After boarding the connecting flight to Glasgow, Ally had no idea what sort of reception to expect. The date was 15 June, exactly three weeks and a lifetime since thousands had cheered the squad off from Hampden Park and Prestwick.

The 1974 team had returned unbeaten to a heroes' welcome from 6,000 cheering fans but there was little likelihood of a repeat in 1978.

Yet there were a surprising number of supporters waiting with the numbers this time counted in hundreds rather than thousands. In his autobiography the manager comments, 'The size of the crowd there in the rain at Glasgow Airport frankly astonished me...there with little show of hostility or trouble.'

A photograph in the *Herald* shows the manager signing autographs for a crowd of fans while the *Daily Record* pictured a supporter clutching a banner reading 'There's Always 1982'. The *Scottish Daily Express*'s Jack Webster reported of several hundred supporters at the airport who apparently 'chanted words of comfort', one of whom displayed a placard reading 'Ally Must Stay'.

Fourteen-year-old Gillian Miller was unhappy that the squad were kept away from the supporters and was quoted in the *Herald* as saying, 'I was at Hampden to see them off and this is chaos by comparison. But we have done our best to welcome them back.'

Bobby Clark's memory supports the manager's version, 'I can't remember any hostility at the airport. I think the final result against Holland helped our frustrated support but certainly I never saw any hostility.'

Faye was there to meet Ally and a friend drove them back to Ayr after he had bid the rest of the squad goodbye. 'The reception he got wasn't bad at all,' she recalls, although she does remember being led to a separate room for the reunion, 'because they thought he was going to get lynched!'

Avoiding waiting press men in Corsehill Place, Ally was glad to be back among those he loved and who had faith in him. It was only then that he was able to sift through all the newspapers and video recordings that had been kept for him and confirm what he suspected, that his one-time journalistic friends had stuck the knife in. If Ally ever came close to swearing in his life it was probably then.

There was a bit of a backlash in Ayr, son Andy remembers, but Ally accepted it as part of the job and there was no physical abuse. Andy's sister Gail, then 14, has bad memories from those days, 'It took a lot out of all of us at the time. We couldn't even go to school because we had the press camped at our front door. One of them was offering Andrew money for a story during the World Cup. We just stayed off school because it just got so bad.

'People were really horrible and you found out who your true friends were. Constantly people were being horrible and nasty. Some didn't want to know you after the World Cup and that hurt has never ever left me. For a long long time I never told my mum and dad about what had been going on and how cruel people were.

'Strangers could be really nasty if they found out and when I first started my work people never knew who my dad was, I just didn't say anything.'

Andy was able to deal with it and remembers a particular incident from the time, 'I was walking across Belmont Academy playing fields one day when this guy came up to me and said my father was nothing but a f*****g b*****d. I just quipped, "Well unlike you at least I know who my father is", and walked away.'

Scotland's 1978 World Cup campaign has been and continues to be analysed and re-analysed. Some conclusions are universal such as had the finals come 12 months earlier or been played in Europe the team would have performed better. There is no question that players such as Rioch and Masson had peaked long before Argentina and were not playing regularly in the run-up to the tournament.

One of Ally's most admirable and dearly-held characteristics was loyalty. The 1978 World Cup unquestionably showed him to be guilty of over-loyalty by keeping faith with the men who had shone in the qualification campaign.

Off the field lessons would be learned regarding planning and organisation. The selected accommodation and bonus payments scandal had taken their toll on team morale yet the secretary and manager had personally viewed and chosen the Sierras as their preferred option.

And despite the age and form of the team the squad showed in the final match they were capable of playing quality football.

Today Joe Harper is adamant that the blame did not lie solely with the manager. 'Ally MacLeod did not let Scotland down one iota,' he insists. 'It was the players in the team that let Scotland down. We had a really good team as we showed when we beat Holland. The team were a lot better than they showed.'

Bobby Clark believes that the manager's overconfidence may have had an adverse effect on the performance of the players in the opening two matches, 'He built up tremendous belief among the fans and this possibly became a weight round the team's neck.'

The performance and result against Holland, who went all the way to the final before losing to the host nation in extra time, was probably enough to keep Ally in a job in the immediate aftermath of the tournament.

Jock Vila reflects on the experience, 'If we'd played to the same sort of level that we'd played in 1977 I'm still convinced we could have went very far in the tournament. Badly prepared? That was more the SFA's fault than Ally's. His biggest mistake was maybe loyalty to the players but you can't blame him for doing that.

'We've never done better at a World Cup since. Why are the rest of them not looked on as disasters? I don't class it as a disaster. I always look back on it with fond memories. I don't think "I wish I'd never went" or anything like that. I was glad I went to that one. I still think it's one of the better places I've been to on my travels.

'I would say I've never seen a Scotland team that played as exciting as it was under Ally MacLeod in his first few games. That was a brand of football that I wanted to go and watch rather than a lot of the stuff I've seen since. I still think that the best game I've seen Scotland play was Czechoslovakia at Hampden in 1977.

'The excitement of those games at Wembley and Anfield…I don't think we've reached those levels of excitement since.'

Vila still follows Scotland everywhere and insists that had it not been for Ally he is unlikely to have ever taken an interest in the national team.

20

Retention and Resignation

THREE weeks after returning home Ally had an appointment to keep at Park Gardens as the SFA's World Cup inquest began with the manager's position first on the agenda.

He was interviewed by the six men who made up the international committee plus chairman Tom Lauchlan. After some intense questioning Ally retired to his office before eventually being asked to return to the boardroom. He was then informed that a vote had been taken with regard to his position and that he was still in a job. Ally then departed for Easterhouse Boys Club to present some trophies after refusing to make any comment to reporters.

Following a four and a half hour wait, secretary Ernie Walker broke the news to the waiting press men, 'I can tell you that Mr MacLeod continues to be the manager. It would be fair to say there was a motion to remove him, but it was defeated.'

Although pleased to still be in a job, Ally knew that things would not be the same as before without the full support of the committee. The vote had produced a 3-3 stalemate with only chairman Lauchlan's casting vote saving him from the axe. Faye remembers that it irked her husband that one of those who had voted against him had not even been on the board during the World Cup and, in his opinion, did not know the full story. He was later angered when the results of the vote were leaked to the press. But for the time being Ally was still the international manager.

Now that the manager's position had been clarified the SFA's inquiry would concentrate on other matters such as Willie Johnston, the behaviour of the players and the choice of accommodation.

When Walker's report became public early in September much of the blame was put on the players with their demands for meetings over bonuses highlighted, and a stricter disciplinary code recommended. Some of the media reporting was called into question with little blame attached to the association themselves. There was a defence of the choice of the Sierras Hotel which 'was perfectly adequate for our purpose' according to the secretary who stressed it was superior to most others used by competing teams. 'It was a dirty and harrowing experience for everyone involved,' was one of Walker's conclusions.

Lessons were learned from Argentina, one of which was that no Scotland manager had to deal with the matter of players' finances.

Scotland were due to start their fixtures in a tough European Championship qualifying group in Austria on 20 September. Perhaps reacting to the criticism of his World Cup preparations, the manager travelled to Oslo at the end of August to watch the group's opening match between Norway and Austria.

One of the most ludicrous criticisms aimed at Ally post-Argentina had come from Ian Archer who had previously called for the manager's resignation. The journalist then criticised him for returning home with the players instead of remaining in Argentina to spy on Austria when Ally couldn't be sure if he would be in a job come September.

On the day of the squad announcement, 11 September, journalists were surprised to find assistant secretary Peter Donald read out the names of the 18 players in Park Gardens. The press were told that the manager had left the building and would not be available to take any questions.

Reflecting on how he had held court in the press club and always taken calls from reporters Ally had come to the conclusion he had been too cooperative in the past. He knew that relations between himself and the press had been damaged irrevocably and that they could never enjoy an easy relationship in the future.

Eleven of the Argentina squad were out, some like Willie Johnston and Lou Macari for obvious reasons. Others such as Rioch were injured while Jardine and Burns were dropped. There were surprise call-ups for Roy Aitken and Tony Fitzpatrick and a recall for Andy Gray.

The omission of Derek Johnstone, still at Rangers but playing in his favoured centre-half position, was questioned by some tabloids. Arriving at Park Gardens the following morning, Ally found the *Evening Times*'s Chick Young waiting. Chick, who had not attended the World Cup, was one of the few reporters Ally now felt he could trust. He told the journalist Johnstone had ruled himself out due to his positional change and added that he was now satisfied with Gray's fitness.

He chose not to divulge that Johnstone had no desire to play for him just as he never told Gray that third-party intervention had prevented his going to the World Cup. He took the flak for these and other decisions as he considered it a part of the job.

As the players rested in the afternoon ahead of the game in Vienna, Ally chose to leave the hotel and go for a walk. On his way out he found members of the press meeting with SFA officials but declined to join them. Earlier he had refused an invitation for a television interview. This was in complete contrast to his earlier dealings with the media.

Ally chose to play Gray and Joe Jordan up front and made Archie Gemmill captain. Gemmill's international career had now come full circle under Ally having been replaced as skipper in one of the manager's first acts. Gray told Jim Reynolds of the *Glasgow Herald* he was 'shocked and delighted' to be back in the team. He admitted to Reynolds he had been very bitter when not selected for the final World Cup squad but added that he bore no grudges against the manager.

Around 2,000 Scottish supporters were in the 70,000 crowd inside the Prater Stadium. Scotland acquitted themselves well before losing a soft goal after 27 minutes. The players then lost heart and were three down with 25 minutes remaining and facing a heavy defeat.

But a substitution by the manager changed things around, introducing Arthur Graham for Jordan. Scotland fought back with headed goals from McQueen and Gray to pull it back to 3-2 with still over 20 minutes left.

Before the end the ball boys who ringed the pitch were withdrawn and crucial seconds were wasted as the ball went out of play. An athletics track circled the field allowing the ball to travel far from the pitch. This forced Ally into action, and he could be seen charging from the bench to return the ball to the players.

Right at the death the comeback was almost complete but Hartford fired wide from right in front of goal when he seemed sure to at least hit the target. It had been that close to 3-3 but Ally was almost back to his old self in the uncomfortable company of the press.

'I thought we played tremendously well – it must have been one of Scotland's greatest ever displays in Europe,' he said. 'With just a little bit of luck in the closing stages we could even have saved the game.' He was credited in the press for the fightback and the introduction of Graham, a move which almost paid dividends.

A mere two days after the Austria match Ally bumped into Ayr United vice-chairman John Ferguson in a corridor at Park Gardens. Ferguson had been attending a committee meeting and told Ally they would be looking for a new manager as Alex Stuart's resignation was imminent.

Sure enough Stuart left that very Friday and after an official approach from Ayr on the Tuesday Ally decided to accept the offer. Knowing that he no longer had the full support of the international committee coupled with an uneasy relationship with the press, along with the fact he still lived in Ayr, eased his decision.

Had Ally remained as Scotland manager he may have found himself in a similar situation to that of Sir Alf Ramsey and Don Revie when orchestrated witch hunts by sections of the media had resulted in them leaving the England job. In Graham McColl's book *'78 How a Nation Lost the World Cup* Ernie Walker states that Ally would eventually have been sacked so his decision to leave was perhaps the correct one.

Chick Young noticed a change not only in his dealings with the press but in Ally himself, 'I felt Ally had changed after Argentina. I remember meeting him after the World Cup one lunchtime outside Park Gardens and he poured his heart out. He was a different man and I think he felt betrayed by some of the big name journalists at the time.

'Everything changed in 1978, the goalposts moved. I was a young journalist at the time of Argentina. A lot of respected senior journalists at the time went along with Ally and what Ally said before Argentina and he said then they turned on him.'

Parallels can be drawn between Ally's first season at Aberdeen and his tenure as Scotland boss. A fantastic start followed by a decline, then an improvement. Aberdeen of course followed that first season with a successful one. Whether the same would have happened had Ally remained in charge of the national side we shall never know.

The predictable names of Jock Stein and Jock Wallace were tipped to take over the Scotland job with Jim McLean and Alex Ferguson also mentioned. Willie Ormond immediately ruled himself out of a return, indicating he had not enjoyed the experience.

Curiously Ally's last match as Scotland manager had ended in the same way as his first, with Asa Hartford missing a good chance in the last minute. Would he have stayed had the score in Vienna finished 3-3? Possibly not.

Overall Ally's record as Scotland manager reads 17 games, seven wins, five defeats and five draws, with 26 goals scored and 21 conceded. It compares favourably with Alex Ferguson's Scotland record during 1985/86 of three wins, four draws and three defeats in ten matches which included the 1986 World Cup.

Once again Ally, as he always did, refused the offer of a contract at Ayr although he did ask the chairman Myles Callaghan about a pension but was told the club did not participate in such a scheme.

Ayr had been relegated from the Premier League the previous season and were sitting fourth-bottom in the First Division at the time with a home match against Arbroath due the day after Ally's return.

Some 2,453 supporters turned up at Somerset that Wednesday night, a fraction of the 70,000 crowd in the Prater Stadium exactly a week earlier. The *Glasgow Herald* match report included the following, 'Ally MacLeod last night returned to Somerset Park and found that he is still a hero. He was given a standing ovation when he led the teams out…and his name was continually chanted by one of the biggest Ayr crowds of the season.'

Alex Stuart had made Jim McSherry, whom Ally had signed at the bank during his previous spell at the club, team captain.

'I was going round geeing up the players before the match,' McSherry remembers of the dressing room before the Arbroath game. 'Ally gave a team talk and then just threw the ball to Davie Wells and told him to take the team out. Big Davie was embarrassed and just looked at me and I just said "let's go". We won easily but there was no point in me going in to see Ally after the game as I knew what he was like from his previous time.'

It is unclear if Ally was aware of McSherry's position or if this was his way of letting the players know he was the boss.

On the pitch it was the perfect start as Ayr won 3-0 and had the supporters singing 'We're going to win the league'.

Ally didn't take long to settle back into his old routine. One of the first things he noticed was that the dugouts had been switched around so he made sure the home bench was back where it had been during his previous ten years at the club. He also changed the training nights back to Tuesday and Thursday rather than the now-established Monday and Wednesday evenings.

He told the *Ayrshire Post*, 'It was nice to get such a big welcome and to get a good result. It will soon pass around the town that the team played well. The gates will double.'

Revealing he had received at least 2,000 letters from all over Britain – including one from England manager Ron Greenwood – wishing him well at Ayr, Ally also told the newspaper that Asa Hartford and Bruce Rioch had telephoned him to say 'good luck'.

'Even if Scotland had won the World Cup I am convinced I would still have made the same decision to come back to Ayr where it really all began for me,' he added. In his next match on the Saturday Ayr defeated St Johnstone 1-0 in front of 3,239 at Somerset.

During Ally's absence from the club scene the League Cup had again been restructured with two-legged ties from the start now replacing the qualifying groups all the way to the final.

Ayr won at Falkirk in the first leg of the third round before drawing at home. Skipper Wells has cause to remember the trip to Brockville. He had been delayed on his way to catch the team bus due to the fire brigade holding up the traffic but knowing they would be stopping for a meal he changed direction. 'The boss said nothing when I caught the bus up at the Fenwick Hotel but when I opened my wage packet later that week I had been fined with a note enclosed telling me not to be late again,' he reflects.

Wells remembers the manager fining numerous players for lateness or dropping them for misbehaviour and recalls Ally dispensing the 'hairdryer' treatment when required, 'You just sat there with your head bowed and didn't look up. I'm sure that was who Alex Ferguson learnt it from.'

'Players never got into his office,' Jim McSherry recalls. 'You'd go in to see him but he'd always be saying he was going to see the chairman or had a meeting. By the time you knew what had happened any gripe or question you had was dealt with in the way he wanted.'

The good run was extended when Montrose and Clydebank were also beaten in the league before Ayr drew with Queen of the South on 28 October.

Three days earlier Scotland had defeated Norway 3-2 in Glasgow in Jock Stein's first match in charge before a huge crowd of 65,372, proving that the public had not deserted the national side after Argentina. The importance of the performance and result against Holland cannot be underestimated when looking at the aftermath of Argentina and the adage 'you are only as good as your last game' springs to mind.

Around this time Ally started working on his autobiography with John Mann of the *Scottish Daily Express* who was a regular visitor to Ally's pub in Kilmarnock during the exercise. Ally's early life and career were covered briefly with inevitably the main focus of *The Ally MacLeod Story* on his time as Scotland manager. When the book was published in 1979 Ally's suggestion for a cover picture of him standing with an assortment of knives in his back was, not surprisingly, deemed unacceptable.

It was like going back in time five years as the good times continued for Ayr with a 2-1 win in the derby at Kilmarnock. The old MacLeod magic was working again with his instant brand of success. Ayr had, in the space of five weeks, climbed eight places in the First Division table from fourth-bottom to third-top, winning six and drawing one of seven league matches.

That first week in November Ally received a letter from his old club Blackburn Rovers asking him to consider the vacant manager's position. There had already been an initial approach but the correspondence laid out the generous terms should Ally be tempted to return to east Lancashire. A salary of £17,500 was coupled with a further bonus of £1,000 should the club remain in the Second Division at the end of that season, rising to £1,500 if they were in the top half of the table. A number of other incentives were included plus the promise of a new blue T-registration Ford Granada car.

The letter from the club chairman contained the following, 'I would dearly love to welcome you back to Ewood Park after all these years because I feel certain you will not only lift the team, you will lift the town and I think you will even lift the board.'

In his autobiography Ally says, 'It was with regret that I turned it down…I felt I owed Ayr more than a couple of weeks.' Had the offer come later the response may very well have been different but the letter does illustrate that there were those who clearly felt Ally still had plenty to offer the game after Argentina.

Not long afterwards Premier League club Motherwell also made an approach for Ally's services but, like the Blackburn offer, it too was politely rejected. Again his principles of loyalty had swayed the decision to remain with Ayr.

Ally's old club Aberdeen came to Somerset Park on Wednesday 8 November for the first leg of the League Cup quarter-final and what a cracker the 6,367 crowd were treated to. Six goals, five bookings, one player sent off – Aberdeen's Steve Archibald – and one carried off.

Ayr led 3-2 before Joe Harper's late equaliser which was considered by most reporters to be a yard offside. Included in those five names in referee Brian McGinlay's book was Ally who was cautioned for protesting about the equaliser.

'It was a superb match. The crowd got great value,' said Dons boss Alex Ferguson, who still fancied his side for the second leg.

A 3-0 home win against Raith Rovers on the Saturday meant that since his return Ayr were unbeaten in 12 games.

Aberdeen won the second leg 3-1 before Ayr lost their first league game since Ally's return at Dumbarton. Ally blamed Jim McSherry for one of the goals in the 2-0 defeat and took him off before the end. The player vividly recalls that day, 'I was taking a long bath hearing him ranting and raving in the dressing room. I thought I had escaped but the next minute he was through the door with "and as for you…" and he went mental at me. He didn't suffer fools and his word was law.'

A win against Clyde followed by a home loss to Stirling Albion left the Honest Men third in the table on 9 December. They were just three points behind leaders Dundee but with a game less played and looking good for promotion.

Early that month Ally opened a letter in his office addressed to The Manager of Ayr United and was shocked at the contents. The correspondence related to a pension scheme for his predecessor Alex Stuart, something that had been denied to him when accepting the job.

After digesting the contents of the letter Ally felt he had been let down and decided he could no longer work for a board that he did not trust.

Unlike Blackburn, Motherwell came back at the right time and on 12 December Ally was announced as the new Motherwell manager and rumoured to be one of the highest-paid in the Premier League on around £15,000. His brief but successful return to Ayr had lasted all of 77 days and his decision not to sign a contract had eased the move. In 15 league and League Cup matches Ayr had lost only three, drawn three and won nine, climbed eight places in the table and seen an increase of over 500 in home attendances.

A number of names had been linked with the Fir Park vacancy since Roger Hynd's departure early in November and Partick Thistle boss Bertie Auld had been interviewed. Hynd had only been in charge for ten months but the club were struggling and pressure from the supporters had forced his resignation. In the meantime Hynd's assistant, and Ally's in Argentina, John Hagart, had been in temporary charge.

When he addressed the assembled media at Fir Park, Ally was as enthusiastic as ever, 'I am an ambitious man and Motherwell are an ambitious club. It has always been my ambition to win the Premier League and I know that Motherwell are capable of doing that.'

In a more realistic tone he did not promise to keep the club in the top league, 'It may be too late to save Motherwell from relegation, but it is a good long-term bet that they can get back to the top.'

Motherwell were anchored at the very foot of the table with eight points and, with still two awarded for a win, seven points from the sanctuary of eighth place. The new manager set a target of 33 points for survival.

There was a backlash in Ayr. The *Ayrshire Post* reported that fans had telephoned in their droves hitting out at the former manager. A letter appeared in the newspaper from James Baillie which included, 'After his welcome return to Ayr then leaving so soon, Ally MacLeod must be feeling quite pleased with himself. Who does he think he is?'

A. Parker of Prestwick felt strongly enough to write to the *Evening Times*'s 'Goalpost' page to say, 'I consider Ally MacLeod should have shown more loyalty to Ayr United. After all they picked him up when he was down.'

Under the headline 'Fury as Ally Quits', vice-chairman John Ferguson, whose chance meeting with Ally had been instrumental in his return, told the local newspaper, 'I can understand the fans' anger. The directors are shattered. For a man to walk out on us twice in such a short time is really hard to take.'

Offering the right of reply, the same journal's Mike Wilson asked Ally if he felt he had betrayed Ayr considering that they had offered him the post when he was in danger of losing the Scotland job. 'That's one-sided,' was his defensive response, adding that Ayr had been in danger of relegation and that he had pulled them up the table leaving them in a healthy position. 'Ayr don't need Ally MacLeod any more,' he concluded.

At no point did he hint at the real reason for the move or mention he had turned down a better offer from Blackburn Rovers.

But accusations of betrayal must have hurt given that loyalty was one of the things Ally prized above most others. The people of Ayr had after all taken him to their hearts and only five years earlier made him their Citizen of the Year. Had the supporters known the full facts would they have been more sympathetic? Possibly, but fans who would never dream of changing their allegiance are notoriously bitter when a popular figure suddenly leaves for another team. Equally most fans require little encouragement to criticise club directors if they have a grievance so there may have been a degree of sympathy.

The MacLeods chose to remain in the town and eldest son Andy has no recollections of a public backlash but says if there had been criticism his father would have accepted it as part of the job just as he had done after the World Cup.

21

The Fir Park Experience

A LATE Willie Pettigrew goal salvaged a point when Motherwell hosted Morton on 16 December in Ally's first game in charge. 'They played with enthusiasm for the last 20 minutes…I want that for 90 minutes,' the new manager told the press.

His first piece of business in the transfer market was to sell unsettled Peter Marinello to Fulham for £40,000 and use some of the proceeds to lure one of his old Pittodrie players, Joe Smith, to Fir Park.

'We can't expect to get out of our difficult position overnight,' Ally told the *Motherwell Times and Advertiser*, 'but I think by the time March comes along we will have pulled ourselves up among the other teams.'

Midfielder Ian Clinging doubts that Ally would have been fully aware of the task he had taken on. There was a lot of disharmony among the players who, with the exception of two higher earners, were all on a basic wage which could only be supplemented by win bonuses. The squad had held a stormy meeting at the start of the season with the club's directors which Ian describes as 'a big blow-up' and many of the players wanted to leave.

Smith started the next match, a home game with second-placed Partick on 23 December. The Thistle game followed an almost identical pattern to the previous match with a late Peter Millar penalty securing another 1-1 result.

A bad winter meant the Steelmen did not play again for another four weeks when Willie Ormond's second-bottom Hearts went to Fir Park in January 1979. The Edinburgh side had a five-point advantage meaning defeat would leave Motherwell stranded at the bottom. Hearts scored first then Ally's men turned it around to lead 3-1 before a late Derek O'Connor goal made the final score 3-2 and Motherwell had their first home league win of the season. 'It's good to get a win under our belts and there are signs of things falling into place,' the manager told the press afterwards.

There had already been an improvement with Motherwell now unbeaten in three with home attendance figures consistent at just above 5,000.

Due to further postponements the next fixture was also at home, against third-bottom Hibernian. This gave 'Well an opportunity to reduce the five-point gap between the sides and drag Ally's old club into the relegation dogfight.

But Motherwell capitulated as Hibs strolled to a 3-0 win with the other Ally McLeod, who had previously starred for St Mirren, in fine form. Coincidentally, both men had played for St Mirren and Hibs.

'This was a crucial one for us, but we never played at all,' the manager conceded in the press room. 'We will still fight on, but we have to be realistic and face the fact we are likely to be relegated.'

A 3-1 Scottish Cup exit at Ibrox was no disgrace but the Hibs defeat had left Motherwell seven points from safety in the league and convinced the manager that the squad at his disposal was not adequate for his ambitions at the club.

Ally's first away match in the league saw his side go down at St Mirren to the only goal of the match after which Paisley boss Jim Clunie accused the visitors of killing the game with offside tactics.

Ally defended his game plan and blamed the surface, 'We had no choice on a pitch like Love Street. My players couldn't turn properly so I told them just to keep running in the same direction.'

At the end of February Ally placed 12 players on the transfer list and gave free transfers to a further two. This meant exactly 50 per cent of the playing staff of 28 were available to leave as the rebuilding process began.

Clinging explains, 'A lot of the players wanted away, I know that for a fact although he seemed quite happy to let a lot of the players go.'

A couple of those players had already sounded out other clubs and Ally had no option but to field youngsters in the team. 'He brought in youths because he had to. He had no money when he took over,' says Clinging.

Clinging and veteran Joe Wark were the only two of Hynd's regulars who Ally had retained and Clinging is under no illusions as to the reason for his retention, 'It was a total turnaround of players. Joe was there because he was a legend so he could never let him go and he obviously kept me because he knew he could get money for me. At the time it was really unusual because teams could last for four or five years but Motherwell just went into transition.'

Around this time Ally had agreed a deal with Jock Wallace to sell Clinging to Leicester to help finance other moves but the midfielder, who grew up a Motherwell fan, would have none of it in spite of the manager's insistence, 'You need to go, I've got other deals coming through!'

The side Ally had taken over was, Clinging believes, not suited to the new manager, 'It was very physical right through the team which wasn't his idea. He loved wingers. He never signed anybody that was a real defender. Even if he was a defender it was always somebody that could score goals and it was always players that could play football he signed throughout all his teams.'

For the match at Partick Motherwell started with two 17-year-olds in John Donnelly and Stewart Rafferty, plus three aged 18. The game concluded without a goal but a really disastrous sequence followed as the gap between Motherwell and the rest of the Premier League increased.

Successive heavy home defeats to Dundee United and St Mirren (4-0 and 3-0) were followed by the loss of six goals at Morton, all within the space of a week. There were signs of improvement with the youngsters credited for their efforts in a 2-1 reverse at Celtic Park on 17 March where Donnelly scored past Pat Bonner, who was making his debut in the home goal.

On the Monday Ally met with around 100 representatives of every branch of the Motherwell Supporters' Club to outline his plans for the way ahead. He asked for a period of 18 months to two years to get the club back as a force in the Premier League, warning that there would likely be further heavy defeats along the way.

He received the backing of the supporters but even they must have been shocked at the margin of defeat in their next match where the final score was Aberdeen 8 Motherwell 0. The result was the highest score recorded in the three years of the Premier League. The club had now lost 34 goals in 12 matches and for once the MacLeod magic wand was just not working.

Defending his youth policy, Ally told the *Herald*'s Jim Reynolds, 'It's not the boys who are letting the club down. Experienced players have not been pulling their weight and I have told them that.' He emphasised that he had the backing of both the board and the fans in his rebuilding process.

Willie Sheridan, president of the Motherwell Supporters' Club, told the *Evening Times*, 'We will stand by Ally because obviously we have the right man for the job. Ally asked for 18 months to two years and I am sure the majority of fans will be willing to grant him that time.'

The margins of defeat decreased as the side lost only 2-1 at Dundee United then by the odd goal in seven in a thriller at home to Celtic after leading at one point.

Defeat at Tynecastle confirmed the inevitability of relegation ahead of a double date with Rangers.

Motherwell lost 3-0 at Ibrox on Tuesday 10 April, but the manager sounded more like his old self in the press room, 'I honestly believe we are going places…I know we might well shock Rangers on Saturday.'

John Greig's side were second in the table and in search of vital league points when they went to Fir Park. In the match programme Ally confidently predicted that a team was 'due to suffer' from Motherwell before too long.

The visitors, with Davie Cooper in top form, dominated the first half without scoring. Then there was a sensation on 59 minutes when Ian Clinging belted in a 20-yarder to put the underdogs ahead. The win was secured when John Donnelly headed home eight minutes later to upset the form book although the manager was surprisingly low key after the match.

'The result speaks for itself,' he told the reporters present. Reflecting his programme prediction, he added, 'We've deserved a break for the past four or five weeks. It was no surprise to me.'

Another point was won at home from Aberdeen before 'Well lost out to Hibs again by conceding four goals. 'It's no use beating Rangers then falling away at another side the following week,' a frustrated Ally told the *Motherwell Times and Advertiser*.

A 3-3 home draw with Morton was followed by revenge for Rangers in the final game. A rearranged Fir Park fixture saw the Ibrox men win by the odd goal in three and there had been definite signs of improvement in the last few matches.

Hugh Taylor praised Motherwell's performance in the *Evening Times* and predicted good times ahead, 'They may be down but the future looks distinctly appealing. If their display last night is anything to go on, Fir Park will be the scene of the greatest First Division enthusiasm next season.'

The day after that final game, Gregor Stevens, not Clinging, was sold to Leicester City for £150,000 and during the same week Ally signed Ayr United goalkeeper Hugh Sproat. Along with Brian McLaughlin and Joe Smith, Sproat was one of the few players Ally spent money on during his time at Fir Park with most signings joining on free transfers or exchange deals.

Motherwell finished bottom with 17 points from their 36 league matches and were demoted along with Hearts. They had totalled just half the manager's target of 33 points and now had games against Ayr United to look forward to. Under Willie McLean the Somerset club had failed to capitalise on Ally's good run and had missed out on promotion, finishing fourth in the First Division.

Just as he had suspected, Ally had been unable to save Motherwell from the drop although the club still registered a net profit of £30,959 for the term. With an encouraging finish plus the backing of both the board and fans the manager aimed for a quick return to the Premier League. This time it would be Ally's team and he would be doing it his way.

But events in that summer of 1979 were to put football and everything else into a whole new perspective as far as the MacLeod family was concerned.

Ally, Faye, Gail and David took their annual overseas family holiday, this time to Ibiza for ten days. Around halfway through their stay Ally felt ill in the hotel room and was sick in the bathroom before returning to bed, telling Faye he had brought up a lot of Coca-Cola. 'He kept saying the bed was on a slope,' says Faye. When she visited the bathroom she found it covered in blood and a local doctor was called who diagnosed Ally with sunstroke.

With no signs of improvement a second opinion was sought and this time Ally was referred to the local hospital. But, being Ally, he refused to be admitted and Faye recalls she had to take a ferry journey to collect the prescribed medicine which had to be taken at various times of the day and night. Just a few days earlier he had been playing table tennis.

Gail has bad memories of the holiday, 'I honestly thought he was going to die, it was horrific. I kept saying they're not letting me in the room because he's dead.'

As they prepared to board the flight home to Glasgow Ally almost didn't get on in case he was carrying some contagious disease.

'He was kind of yellow-looking,' is how Faye remembers him. Fearful of contamination, the other passengers were required to give contact details to immigration and Ally was only allowed into the country on the condition he informed them as soon as possible of any diagnosis. Coincidentally the MacLeods had met Ally's good friend Davie MacParland, now in charge of Hamilton, and his wife before boarding. 'I'd never been so glad to see them,' Faye remembers.

Ally refused the offer of a wheelchair at the airport and aided by the MacParlands he and Faye met up with family friends Cyril and Sylvia Cohen who drove them home to Ayr. Far from having sunstroke, Ally was found to have suffered from a perforated duodenal ulcer brought on by the stress of Argentina 12 months earlier. Had the ulcer not been treated it could have proved fatal and he had lost almost six pints of blood in Ibiza. 'It was the fact that he was just such a fit man he survived,' Faye remembers.

Doctor Bob Patterson, another family friend and the club doctor at Ayr United, dealt with the problem before advising their patient to rest. Ally had lost 14 pounds in weight in the 12 months since the World Cup.

Against the doctors' recommendation Ally was determined to be back at Fir Park for pre-season training. In the edition dated 6 July the *Motherwell Times and Advertiser* reported, 'Ally MacLeod returned from his holiday at the weekend but a virus has kept him away from Fir Park.'

That same week John Hagart left Motherwell to take up the manager's position at Falkirk, leaving Ally without an assistant, but he was indeed back for the start of pre-season training on 16 July. 'He was so ill he should never have been back at work,' Faye says today.

Ally was too proud to give anyone at the club a hint at just how seriously ill he had been during the close-season and tried to carry on as normal.

After announcing the overhaul of the scouting system in line with the club's youth policy, the manager outlined his vision for the season ahead in the *Advertiser*, 'I think we will hold our own and be in a challenging position by the end of the year. I left a secure position with Ayr United and would not come to Motherwell unless I thought I would succeed.'

No sooner had Willie Pettigrew, one of the high earners, played and scored in the Lanarkshire Cup, than was transferred to Dundee United. Motherwell finished third in the tournament after getting the better of Albion Rovers before losing 4-3 to Airdrie.

Ally brought another of his former players to the club when he signed defender Chic McLelland from Aberdeen.

Ian Clinging recalls that the former players Ally had brought in from Ayr and Aberdeen observed a completely different man who now criticised players in a way he would not have done before. In the past a defeat would be dismissed with the focus turning to the next match but he was now seen to 'change drastically' when things were not going well.

Due to 14 clubs making up the First Division the schedule was curious with teams competing against each other three times but it did not start well for Motherwell. They drew their first two matches before losing to Stirling Albion then went out of the League Cup on a 4-3 aggregate to Queen's Park.

They then lost at Dunfermline, Hamilton and Raith and sat joint bottom of the table with Ayr on just three points in mid-September.

During this bad run the Motherwell chairman Bill Samuel and some of the directors had formed the opinion that the manager was not putting everything into the job, unaware of the ordeal Ally had endured in Ibiza. Today Ian Clinging confirms that the players had been given no indication Ally had been in poor health.

Against the odds Motherwell got their first victory of the season – at home to leaders Hearts. The 4-2 result started a run of four victories which saw the Steelmen climb the table. Late in the return game in Edinburgh on 24 November Motherwell trailed by a goal and were pushing for an equaliser when goalkeeper Sproat moved to the halfway line, leaving his goal unattended.

The manager later revealed to the *Advertiser* he had sanctioned Sproat's actions, 'We had nothing to lose at that time and there was always the possibility of grabbing another goal.' The match report conceded, 'it almost paid off – the Hearts woodwork was shaken twice in the dying minutes'.

Ally showed he was still a master at overstating his side's achievements during the press conference, 'This was our best performance of the season. The fact we forced more than 30 corners indicates the kind of pressure we had, but we came away empty-handed.'

At the end of November, Ally appointed a new assistant following a chance conversation between ex-Celtic player Davie Hay and Ally's friend Davie MacParland. Ally had been seeking a replacement for Hagart and when MacParland advised of Hay's desire to get back into the game a meeting was arranged.

'I'd been coaching the Chelsea youth team so it wasn't as if I didn't have any experience,' says Hay. 'I think we just clicked during that first meeting and I will be forever grateful to Ally for helping me in my infancy in management. I learnt a lot from him.'

Ally gave an insight into their working relationship to the *Evening Times*, 'It's most useful to have someone to talk things over with. After training he and I can exchange ideas. There is a contrast in personality…Davie is the quiet type and I'm an extrovert and so we counterbalance each other.'

Hay's recollections are not too dissimilar, 'He gave me responsibility to take the training and we would talk about things. He would ask advice although obviously he made the decision.'

At this point Hay considers the team spirit to have been good and remembers Ally as a 'bubbly character'.

Ally and Hay formed a good partnership and when some months later the chairman approached the manager with a view to releasing his assistant for financial reasons, Ally would have nothing to do with it in another display of loyalty. Hay was completely unaware of this, 'There was never any indication of that and he never mentioned it to me.'

Clinging remembers one occasion shortly after Hay's appointment in the dressing room following a defeat. The manager was addressing the players with

Hay standing behind him next to the treatment table which housed a number of hot drinks. 'Davie had a cup of tea in his hand and was looking immaculate in his suit,' Clinging recalls. 'Ally was ranting and raving and stuck out an arm which sent cups of tea from the table all over Davie's suit.' The players immediately burst out laughing and after a few seconds the manager saw the funny side of the incident too.

In December Ally told the local newspaper he was pleased with the progress the side had been making, 'We have come a long way in the last couple of months. If we don't get promotion in April I would think we won't be far away.'

Training under Ally was more routine at Motherwell than it had been pre-Argentina and Hay remembers a concentration on passing and shooting with nothing unusual. Clinging recalls that the losing players in a practice match were sent for a 12-minute run as punishment.

At the turn of the year Motherwell sat in mid-table on 21 points but in a tight league were far from safe, only two ahead of second-bottom Dunfermline. Paradoxically promotion was still a possibility with second-placed Hearts seven points better off.

The Steelmen fell to Second Division side Queen of the South in the first round proper of the Scottish Cup but the setback was a rare defeat as they went on a terrific league run, losing only three times between January and the end of the season.

The manager's reaction to a home defeat by St Johnstone illustrated the level of consistency he demanded. He was quoted in the *Motherwell Times and Advertiser*, 'This is the first time since I came here that I have been annoyed with the players...if they don't improve they can be replaced.'

Motherwell also lost at Dumbarton, which rendered any possibility of promotion mathematically impossible, and at Airdrie. The biggest victory of the season had been a 5-0 rout at Somerset Park with another highlight the overcoming of a two-goal deficit to triumph 3-2 over Clydebank.

The team finished 1979/80 with a 1-1 draw at home to Dunfermline and would have won but for an 89th-minute equaliser. Their final league placing was sixth with 43 points from 39 games played.

The manager was now 14 months into the 18- to 24-month period he had allowed himself to turn things around. After a poor start things had improved greatly and the gap between Motherwell and champions Hearts had been nine points.

That summer the MacLeods spent their traditional June holiday not in Ibiza, but the United States as the manager recharged his batteries for the challenge a new season always provided.

The pre-season signs were promising as 'Well defeated Airdrie 2-1 to lift the Lanarkshire Cup at the start of August then saw off Coventry City by the same scoreline in a challenge match.

But the club could hardly have got off to a worse start in their push for promotion. Ayr 5 Motherwell 0 was the opening day's result, an exact reversal of the match in February. 'It was a disaster but these things happen,' a philosophical Ally was quoted in the *Motherwell Times*. Motherwell then won their first home match, 3-0, against Falkirk the following Saturday.

A 6-1 aggregate win over Stenhousemuir in the League Cup set up a meeting with Dundee United, the holders. Motherwell won the first match 2-1 and were unlucky to lose the second game. The Tannadice tie also ended 2-1 for the home side after 90 minutes and a Clinging goal gave 'Well the advantage just two minutes into extra time. But United scored twice to go through on a 5-4 aggregate and went on to retain the trophy having been given the fright of their lives.

On the first day of November 1980 leaders Hibs went to Fir Park and attracted a crowd of 3,855. Highlights of the match were screened on *Sportscene* whose viewers watched a 2-0 home win. The visiting fans taunted Ally throughout with a chant of 'Argentina! Argentina!' This activity was by no means restricted to the supporters of Hibernian nor indeed Ally. Alan Rough in the Partick Thistle goal was subjected to similar banter from opposing fans should their team be awarded a free kick in a similar position to that Peru had scored from.

By mid-December Ally's team had acquired 22 points from 21 games and were sixth in the table. Although still in with a chance of one of the promotion places this was not the form the manager was looking for and following defeat at Stirling Albion on 13 December he accused certain players of 'just strolling about'. He warned action would be taken if there was not an improvement in attitude and just days later he transfer-listed his first signing, Joe Smith, along with Gordon Soutar.

A 3-2 home win over Ayr on 10 January 1981 began a remarkable run of 16 league matches in which Motherwell lost only once before the end of the season. That defeat at Dunfermline on 28 March ended any hopes of promotion and the club finished fifth with 49 points, but just three behind promoted Dundee who went up with champions Hibs.

In the Scottish Cup 'Well had required two matches to dispose of Second Division Stenhousemuir before a win against Dumbarton saw them into the quarter-finals. They took 3,000 supporters to Dundee United, the scene of their League Cup battle, although the tie turned out to be less of a contest as United scored early and ran out easy 6-1 winners.

Davie Hay's most abiding memory of that day on Tayside concerned the two managers. United were 4-1 ahead in the second period when Jim McLean was at the side of the pitch tearing into his players for easing off.

Ally turned to Hay in the dugout and uttered, 'I don't understand this game sometimes. If we score a goal I'll be out there cheering and they're winning and he doesn't seem too happy!' McLean later reduced each player's bonus by £20 for failing to entertain the crowd as they had done in the first half.

During the close-season Alfie Conn, one of the few players to turn out for both Old Firm clubs, and an 18-year-old by the name of Brian McClair were added to the squad, fitting in with Ally's attacking strategy.

Midfielder Albert Kidd was sold to newly-promoted Dundee for £80,000 at the end of July, days after his wife had given birth to a son. Kidd's contract had just expired and given the change in his domestic circumstances it was an opportunity for the player to return to his home town as well as stepping up to the Premier League.

At all of the clubs he managed Ally was always conscious of keeping the supporters on board and often the departure of a popular player was accompanied by the accusation he no longer wanted to play for the club. Ally's spin on the Kidd transfer in Motherwell's first match programme of the season read, 'Losing Kidd wasn't perhaps the best thing for us, but the player refused to play for Motherwell fans and had to go.'

Following the incredible run towards the end of the previous term Motherwell had every right to feel confident approaching the 1981/82 season. The League Cup schedule was altered, reverting back to the once-popular qualifying groups. Motherwell found themselves in a section with two Premier Division sides, Partick Thistle and their now regular cup opponents Dundee United, along with Ayr. Only the group winners would play any further part in the competition.

Ally welcomed the change and wrote in the match programme for the Ayr game, 'The return of sections in the League Cup is a good thing from our point of view because in the past we have been slow to start the season. This year we have the opportunity to play six games in the League Cup before the real issue gets under way…promotion to the Premier League.'

Motherwell lost the first match at Partick, 2-0, then went down 3-2 in a thriller at home to Ayr which all but killed off any qualifying hopes. Ally played four forwards and two wingers against his old club but lost to a goal scored four minutes from time.

Pledging to continue with all-out attack, Ally told the *Evening Times*, 'We'll keep plugging away at this style in the belief that we'll win more games this way.'

Ian Clinging, recovering from a leg break at the time, was just back in training and noticed a change in the manager if results were going against him, 'He was not as relaxed as he was previously when he was always smiling. He was totally different and was doubting himself, Ally was definitely a wee bit worse for wear after his Scotland episode.'

His assistant agrees. 'I picked up on how to deal with players as he was a highly experienced manager at the time bit I think on reflection…' Davie Hay hesitates before continuing, 'I think Argentina unfairly left a scar there. We never discussed that funnily enough but I think that did take its toll on him.'

Tactics were still the main talking point after Dundee United took both points at Fir Park. Ally considered it 'a tragedy' that his more attacking 4-2-4 system had lost out to the visitors' 4-4-2 formation. United manager Jim McLean responded to what he considered accusations of defensive football with, in the *Evening Times*, 'No wonder Motherwell are struggling when their manager shows such tactical unawareness.'

The accusation was not a new one for a manager who always viewed attack as the best form of defence.

Clinging considers Ally's approach was not considered naive for the time, 'In those days it was just motivating the team with most managers and you didn't have a lot of coaching. The pre-match team talks were just getting people up for the game and Ally knew how to get under the skin of people. In the 1970s or early 80s there really was very little of "you're doing this" at corners, or "you're doing that". It was more in the 80s when that came in with chalkboards and things like that.'

After losing at Ayr then at home to Partick on 22 August some supporters had had enough and demonstrated against Ally following the match.

'There were only 12 fans involved and this was an incident blown up out of all proportion,' the manager told the *Evening Times*. Motherwell had now lost all five of their opening games which Ally had openly embraced as preparation for the league season.

Chairman Bill Samuel promised to telephone the manager following a board meeting at Fir Park on the Monday evening should there be any developments that might concern him.

The situation then resembled a game of cat and mouse as Samuel denied a decision had been taken over Ally's position with Ally telling reporters that the chairman had gone back on his word of a promised telephone call.

Samuel insisted that he had called no less than three times, claiming that Ally's phone was out of order. Samuel then advised that when he arrived at Fir Park on the Tuesday Ally had left which prompted him to drive to Ayr only to find he was not at home.

A further special board meeting was arranged for the Wednesday morning, 26 August, where the decision to 'terminate the manager's appointment' was taken. Note the careful choice of words as Ally had been offered but refused a three-year deal upon taking office. Unbeknown to the directors Ally still had the contract signed by the board, but not himself, in his desk at Fir Park. Had it not been for his principles he could have easily added his signature and claimed compensation for breach of terms.

Samuel then travelled to Corsehill Place with the news where Ally was given the option of resigning but refused to do so.

'This is no way to do business – to sack a manager only two or three weeks into the season,' Ally told reporters. 'They asked me to resign but I felt I have nothing to regret. I can have no regards for people who take action like this after a run of five games.' Ally added that he would definitely be staying in football.

Davie Hay was given temporary control of the team and Motherwell picked up their only League Cup point at Dundee United that same evening. Following a promising start to the league campaign Hay was appointed manager and he rewarded the club by winning promotion and the championship.

Generously Hay gives full credit to Ally for assembling the side, 'The team I had together was the team I had worked with with Ally. The only one I think

I brought in was Tommy O'Hara and it was a really good squad of players who were pretty much Ally signings.'

'He did have a really good team,' reflects Ian Clinging, 'because Davie Hay took over and never changed the team at all really and he won the league by 12 or 15 points. We would have won it if Ally had stayed it was just the fact he didn't get that long. It was unfortunate because there was such a quick turnaround from Ally going.'

Ally's overall Motherwell record was 78 matches played, 35 won, 22 drawn and 21 lost.

Although the team which won the First Division had been assembled by Ally the fans' reaction to the League Cup results had influenced the directors and in fairness to the board he had been granted the two years he had requested back in March 1979 to achieve promotion.

Motherwell supporter Geoff Nicholson reflects on Ally's departure, 'I went into 1981/82 full of confidence. We had ended the last year with only one defeat in 16 games but again we had a slow start in the League Cup group and that was enough to see Ally out and Davie Hay in and we strolled the league. Would Ally's team have won the league? Possibly but maybe not so convincingly. He had spent a few years building that team and maybe deserved the chance to see the job through.'

Fellow fan Graham Barnstaple had been delighted with Ally's appointment in 1978 but lost faith with the way the season had started, 'I remember driving home from the League Cup defeat at Ayr absolutely furious at the nature of the defeat and the level of progress we had made in over two years with Ally in charge. I drove home like a maniac ranting at my then girlfriend, now my wife of over 30 years, about how I had run out of patience with MacLeod and how he had made no progress and despite supporting him for that time my patience had snapped.

'The next day I wrote a letter to the board at Motherwell Football Club detailing my exasperations as a fan and asking for the manager's position to be considered. I was a bit shocked that days after the letter must have arrived at Fir Park he was sacked and replaced by David Hay.'

Returning the loyalty Ally had shown him, Hay took his coaching staff to the Old Tudor Inn after clinching the championship, 'We felt we wanted to celebrate with him so we took a trip down there and I think he appreciated that. I hadn't forgotten that if it hadn't been for Ally I wouldn't have been there.'

It would of course be wrong not to credit Hay for winning promotion in what was, after all, his first managerial position.

Later in his managerial career Ally's influence stood Hay in good stead when in charge of Celtic. 'Always be wary if a game is tight about taking your striker off even if he's not having a good game,' was one piece of wisdom Ally had imparted.

'It was the 1985 Scottish Cup Final against Dundee United and we were getting beat with 15 minutes to go,' Hay recalls. Having been runners-up to Aberdeen in the league that year the pressure was on to deliver a trophy and he gambled on his substitutions. 'I ended up taking off Paul McStay and Tommy

Burns, which was a big decision as they were well liked by the fans, and kept Frank McGarvey on. It was in the back of my mind this thing that Ally had said about not dispensing with your striker and lo and behold did Frank not score the winner!'

With the former manager still in possession of the club car, the chairman sent groundsman Andy Russell to Ayr by train to collect the Porsche. Russell and Ally had got on well but when Russell called Ally told him he could not have the keys. Russell then caught the next train back to Motherwell with the message that if the chairman wanted the car he had to collect it himself.

22

Life with the Diamonds

W
ITH no football job on the horizon Ally at least had his pub in Kilmarnock to keep him occupied. He would entertain the customers with his football stories, often embellishing them as he went on. 'Never let the truth get in the way of a good story,' he had often told son Andy. Had the after-dinner speaking circuit been more established then, Ally could undoubtedly have made a fortune recounting tales from his career.

With a smile Andy remembers his father telephoning him at 2am advising that the pub alarm had gone off and that he would have to drive to Kilmarnock to sort it out. After moaning, Andy got dressed and made for the car only to find a note on the windscreen with the message 'April Fool'. Ally had originally planned to leave the note on the pub window but Faye had talked him out of it, saving Andy a 30-mile round trip.

Away from the game Ally was able to fully recover from the stress of Argentina which had so nearly cost him his life. He had also found his time at Motherwell a frustrating experience. 'For a long time he lost something without a shadow of a doubt,' Gail reflects of her father.

'It eventually came back, and his enthusiasm, but I think it took a long time. He did eventually get his bounce back but I think it took a lot out of him – more than what people knew – and he was more wary and a bit more careful.'

He and Faye decided to open another licensed premises in 1983, a lounge bar at 48 Newmarket Street in Ayr which he called simply 'Ally's'. There was a coffee shop upstairs which Faye ran herself and Andy was soon working full-time in the family business with his father working between the two pubs.

The two bars were completely different with the Old Tudor in Kilmarnock more of a traditional working man's pub whereas Ally's catered for a younger crowd and held discos at the weekend. It also had a bit of a football theme and many visitors to the town would pop in, hopeful of catching the landlord on duty. Tuesday was always football night and Andy recalls happy times when a lot of his father's football contacts would come in and reminisce for hours about days gone by. Visiting supporters would pop in too and Andy recalls that the Rangers bus used to leave from the bar every week.

But Ally would return to the game he loved more than two years after being dismissed from Fir Park. The approach came from a club which had twice tried to sign him in his playing days – Airdrieonians. Following a home defeat to Meadowbank Thistle at the end of 1983 Bill Munro had had his contract terminated with the club sitting fourth from bottom of the First Division.

It was the Airdrie board who approached Ally on 29 December, the same day Munro was dismissed. They also spoke with Willie Ormond and Benny Rooney but Ally was their preferred candidate. Ally asked for time to think it over and at a meeting 24 hours later accepted the manager's job on a part-time basis which still enabled him to run the bars.

Those closest to Ally recall that the break from football had benefitted him and he was back to his old bubbly self by this time. He still felt he had something to prove in the game as he had never been able to successfully shake off the spectre of Argentina and was now ready to return to the dugout.

George Peat was the Airdrie secretary and a club director who recalls being warned about Ally, 'When we appointed him he was like a breath of fresh air at the club. A number of people said "boy would we have a hard time working with this man as he was so money-orientated" and "he'll drive you nuts".

'However I can swear blind that was never the case. He never asked for a penny for players or expenses. He signed six or seven and never spent a penny – the only player who had played senior was John Sludden and he didn't cost anything. He also signed Hughes, Docherty, Scott, Templeton and Lindsay all from the juniors.'

Ally was in charge for the match at Brechin the very next day, the last of the year. It started well when George Anderson headed Airdrie into a second-minute lead but the home side fought back for a 3-1 victory.

The new manager took training for the first time on Monday 2 January 1984, and was in good form when he spoke to the *Airdrie and Coatbridge Advertiser*, 'Obviously my first priority is to get the team out of trouble and away from the relegation zone. When I accepted the post, believe it or not, I didn't know Airdrie were third from bottom. I had to look twice at the league table.'

He was taking charge of a club in a similar position to that both Aberdeen and Motherwell had been when he had started there, albeit in a lower division.

Ally's first home match took place at Broomfield the following day with a Willie McGuire goal two minutes from time clinching the points against Hamilton and prompting the manager to exit the dugout and jump for joy. It was Airdrie's first victory in six matches and the *Airdrie and Coatbridge Advertiser* commented, 'For the first time in many weeks an Airdrie manager was cheered all the way to and from the dug-out.' Already he seemed to have won over the locals.

As in his Somerset Park days Ally chose Tuesday and Thursday as the training nights and Peat recalls he was spending many more hours at Broomfield than the job description required, 'Ally was part-time Tuesdays and Thursdays. It was Ally, myself and the scouts as it was the scouts' nights. Very little was talked about scouting or players as Ally regaled us with story after story as it got busier and busier – it got packed. We all went down to listen to Ally. Training was supposed to finish at 8pm and we ended up getting out about midnight then Ally still had to get home to Ayr.'

Another McGuire goal sealed another home win, this time against Raith Rovers on 7 January. The two points earned saw the Diamonds climb to sixth from bottom as they moved away from the danger zone.

Next up was a trip to Kilmarnock and Ally showed he had lost none of his sense of humour when speaking to the *Advertiser*, 'I expect a big crowd on Saturday to jeer me on, including some of the people I have barred from my pub.'

Kilmarnock won 4-1, one of only two Scottish games which beat the weather that afternoon, the other the Second Division meeting of East Fife and Albion Rovers. 'Look I'm only back in the game for three weeks and I've already attracted the day's largest crowd,' Ally quipped.

Airdrie led 2-0 at Dumbarton in their next game but lost 4-2, prompting a frustrated reaction from the manager when talking tactics with the local newspaper, 'The defence went back to playing the way they played before I arrived at Broomfield with a spare man at the back and the full-backs going into the centre of defence. I don't want that and I told them so. I like my full-backs to get into attacking positions and the defence to play square.'

During those early days at Broomfield there were hints of a bitter streak emerging in Ally's character when a dispute with the club's second-longest-serving player and captain, Norrie Anderson, became public. As we have seen Ally liked to appoint his own captain when starting a new job and had always had a stubborn streak, but it may be that the experience of Argentina had made him less tolerant of those who crossed him. Following what the *Advertiser* called a 'bitter row' between the two Anderson was replaced as captain by McGuire and promptly asked for a transfer.

'Norrie and I didn't see eye to eye and I feel that a change of captain would be good for the team,' Ally told the newspaper. 'Norrie didn't want to play for the team so has been left out of any future first team plans.'

Anderson was then told he would not be considered for the reserve team either as the row dragged on. Ally was quoted in the local newspaper's 23 March edition as saying, 'I don't want to know him. I am only interested in players who want to play for the club and Anderson certainly isn't one.'

Again, as with Albert Kidd's departure from Motherwell, Ally was playing clever while trying to get the fans onside in case they were sympathetic to the player. Anderson claimed that the manager had not spoken to him since the initial row and said, 'When I walk into the dressing room he walks out.' 'It's a load of baloney,' was Ally's response in the following week's edition, insisting, 'I sat and chatted with him for half an hour last week.' Anderson never played for the club again. But Ally had clearly retained that wicked sense of humour as recalled by George Peat, 'I remember Jimmy Ferguson, the chairman, said to Ally, "I would like to see Airdrie win something before I go", and Ally turned round to him and said, "By the looks of things you haven't given me much time"!'

After a 1-0 victory over promotion hopefuls Partick Thistle, Airdrie had progressed to ninth place in the table, leading to the manager claiming his men were the best side in the division at that time.

Just one point collected from the final three matches may have gone some way to changing Ally's assessment as the Diamonds finished fifth from bottom on 36 points from 39 matches, but just one ahead of relegated Raith Rovers who went down along with Alloa.

The season did finish with two pieces of silverware. The first team won the Lanarkshire Cup on penalties after sharing six goals with Hamilton Accies, and the reserves won the Second XI Cup by beating Rangers at Ibrox in the semi-final then Dundee 5-0 on aggregate in the final. Ally was later fined £50 for ungentlemanly conduct during the Rangers game.

Peat remembers being in the dressing room prior to one of the finals, 'The team was run by Billy Reid who had won a reserve league medal at Motherwell. He was taking the team talk, emphasising the importance of winning the cup final and was showing the boys the medal he had won and saying how important it was to have a medal. "See that medal, it's a wonderful thing. That's what you'll get and you'll have for the rest of your life."

'Just at this point Ally walked in and Billy said, "Boss, I'm just explaining how wonderful it is to have this medal, isn't it boss?" and Ally just said, "I don't know Billy, I never played in the reserves"!'

Conveniently the manager had forgotten about the 1952/53 season at Third Lanark, but then again, never let the truth get in the way of a good story!

Anderson was offered new terms but was one of seven players to refuse to re-sign and was eventually traded with Ayr United as winger Gerry Christie came to Broomfield.

Airdrie defeated Blackpool in a pre-season match in August 1984 before losing the Lanarkshire Cup they had held for less than three months to Motherwell.

Four points were taken from the first two league matches which instilled confidence before Alex Ferguson's Premier League champions came to Broomfield for a second round League Cup tie on 22 August. Again the tournament had been restructured with the early rounds decided on a one-off knockout basis similar to the Scottish Cup.

Peat remembers the evening of the match, 'The night of the Aberdeen game I was in the office with Ally watching Aberdeen warming up. He said, "Look, Miller and McLeish are out there practising heading the ball...They'll not head a ball all night!" Ally played two up front. He thought the centre-halves were the worst distributors of the ball so he just let the centre-halves run with the ball.'

A mix-up in the Dons' defence saw Dave McCabe give the underdogs a sensational second-minute lead. Billy Stark brought Aberdeen level before a John Flood header put the Diamonds ahead for the second time and another headed goal from Tommy Yule just after half-time put the game beyond the Dons. The only threat to the result then came from off the park as Peat recalls, 'We were

3-1 up and the floodlight stanchions were sparking. We hoped they would hold out as we were playing them off the park.'

The manager was jubilant when speaking to John Quinn of the *Evening Times* the next morning, 'My young boys were magnificent last night. They played their hearts out for me and for the club. Everyone in the town should be proud of them,' he beamed. The 3-1 result against Aberdeen, the best team in Scotland at the time, ranks among the best achieved in Ally's career as a club manager.

The reward for beating Aberdeen was another home tie – against Celtic, managed by Ally's old assistant at Motherwell, Davie Hay. But Celtic proved too strong and led by three goals at the break before finishing 4-0 winners.

In recognition of the club's good start in the league as well as the cup shock Ally won the Scottish Brewers Personality of the Month award for August and was presented with a cheque for £250, a cask of beer and a special replica firkin.

The team continued to do well in the First Division and a home win over Falkirk on 22 September saw Airdrie move into first place in the league. The following week they were still there after winning 5-0 at Kilmarnock, a result which prompted the resignation of Killie manager Jim Clunie shortly after the final whistle. The defeat left the Rugby Park side second-bottom of the league and their fans had called for Clunie's head during the game.

Ally demonstrated he was still the master of overstatement, telling the *Airdrie and Coatbridge Advertiser*, 'This was probably the best ever performance by any team under me. It was a magical performance – magic is the one word to describe it.' When asked to comment on reports linking him with the Kilmarnock manager's post Ally's response was, 'After Argentina I just take what I read in the papers with a pinch of salt.'

He was at it again following a 2-0 win over Motherwell the following week which attracted 3,786 to Broomfield for an eagerly awaited top-of-the-table clash. 'Potentially they are the best club team I have ever managed,' he told the *Advertiser*.

For entertainment value the following match with Clyde was one of the best of the season with seven goals, two dismissals, and eight bookings. Clyde led 3-1 at the break but the Diamonds came storming back to win 4-3.

These results formed part of a run of six straight victories and Ally seemed to have the old magic back again which seemed to surprise even himself as he told the *Advertiser* in November, 'I didn't expect to be at the top of the league at this stage. When I took over ten months ago my aim was to build a team for the future at Broomfield...Instead everything clicked into place.'

With Airdrie still in first place the year ended with a 5-0 home win over Meadowbank Thistle. Ally told the *Advertiser* that one year after taking over at Broomfield he had the 'makings of the best side the club has ever seen'.

The first two matches of 1985 ended in defeat for Airdrie but they were then unbeaten in their next six, a run punctuated by Scottish Cup elimination at the hands of Falkirk.

Revenge came in a league match which saw Falkirk lose by the odd goal in three at Broomfield of which Ally, in the way only he could, told the *Airdrie and Coatbridge Advertiser*, 'We could have been seven, eight or nine up by the interval.'

The manager continued to have occasional run-ins with the game's officials as George Peat recalls, 'One night at Airdrie we were watching the reserves against Rangers and Ally was sitting on the old pavilion balcony. He was shouting when Bill Moulds, the linesman, was giving loads of offsides. Moulds kept looking up to see who was shouting and Ally said it was me! Jim McGilvray was the ref and after the game they were walking up the old stairs when Ally banged into them and they both went falling down like a pack of cards! He got off with it as they both had the same spelling mistake in their reports.'

The unbeaten league run came to an end after another top-of-the-table clash at Motherwell which attracted 4,483 to Fir Park on 23 March. Airdrie never recovered from the Fir Park defeat and won just one of their remaining nine matches, losing six.

One of those losses was at home to Meadowbank who turned a two-goal deficit into a 3-2 lead. The Diamonds then levelled to make it 3-3 with two minutes to play only for the Edinburgh side to score twice more. While it would be inaccurate to describe this match as a typical Ally game it did demonstrate that his policy of gambling on conceding goals by concentrating on attack had not altered over the years and no one could complain about the entertainment value.

A 5-1 defeat at Ayr caused Ally to uncharacteristically question himself as he told the press afterwards, 'The manager has to take the blame in a situation like this and I blame myself.'

Airdrie finished fifth in the league table with 42 points from 39 games, six behind Clydebank who went up with champions Motherwell.

Of her husband's days at Airdrie, Faye remembers his frustration over the crowds, 'What used to annoy him when he was travelling up to Airdrie was the number of fans he would pass with Rangers and Celtic caps on not going to support their local team. That used to rankle with him.'

The 1985/86 campaign got off to a slow start with two draws and the two defeats from the opening four league fixtures. During those opening weeks Airdrie went out of the Skol-sponsored League Cup by losing at St Johnstone.

Ally was friendly with ex-Partick and Third Lanark player Joe McInnes, who he had played with for the Scottish Command side during his army days some 30 years earlier. McInnes was at this time managing Shettleston Juniors in Glasgow's East End.

Acting on a tip-off from two of his scouts, Ally went along to watch Shettleston winger Gerry Docherty. But it was the club's other winger who impressed him more, 22-year-old Henry Templeton. Club secretary George Peat was less keen, 'In all the time we were at Airdrie I never did have an argument with Ally. The only time we disagreed was over Henry Templeton. He said one night he was going to sign this player from Shettleston, go and to have a look at him so I went along with another director. The second time we saw him we thought he got into good positions but didn't score. But Ally disagreed and still signed him.'

Templeton went against Joe McInnes's advice to only drink cola when he arrived at Broomfield for signing talks.

He recalls, 'I went into the boardroom and Ally says, "Would you like a drink?" So I said "I'll have a lager please" and he just burst out laughing!' Ally responded, 'That's the way, don't try to be what you're not.'

The winger soon thrived under the manager's attacking ethos, 'He used to say to me just do what you are good at, just get the ball and go at them.' Templeton looks back on the threatened consequences of not carrying out those instructions, 'If I see you in our own half you're off! You'd cause us more problems than anything else,' Ally warned.

Templeton proved Ally's judgement correct by scoring seven times before Christmas.

Following a draw at East Fife on the last Saturday of September Airdrie sat at the very bottom of the league. With eight matches played they had amassed four points from four draws but a home win against Clyde saw the Diamonds jump five places in the space of 90 minutes.

The Clyde manager that day, Craig Brown, remembers the match. The referee was Gerry Evans whom Brown felt had denied his side a penalty a few weeks earlier. 'That's one I owe you!' he told the manager. When Evans went into the visitors' dressing room at Airdrie, Brown was quick to remind him of the debt. Jokingly he asked, 'When do you want the penalty?' to which Craig replied that midway through the second half would do.

'We're getting a penalty,' he said to Ally, 'Gerry Evans owes us one!' 'You'd better no!' was Ally's response. Brown takes up the story, 'Airdrie were winning three nothing and there was an injury and the game was stopped. Ally shouts over to me, "Oh Craig, see if you want a penalty you'd better get somebody up into our penalty box"!'

The improved form continued with a 4-1 home win over Ayr and Airdrie sat in ninth place in the table. At this point speculation mounted that Ally was set to return to Somerset Park for the third time. Ayr were going through a bad spell with two wins from 11 matches and under-pressure boss George Caldwell had quit his post on 21 October, leaving former player and now coach Davie Wells in temporary charge. The following Saturday Ayr fans were heard to chant Ally's name during the match at Hamilton.

Initially Ally refused to comment on the situation but after a meeting with chairman Andrew Charters, his appointment was confirmed on the evening of Friday 1 November. The move appeared to come out of the blue. 'I have been happy with Airdrie but for personal reasons have decided to take the chance of returning to Ayr,' he was quoted in the *Glasgow Herald*.

The personal reasons were that the Airdrie job made it more difficult running his two bars whereas living and working in Ayr would be more convenient from a travelling point of view. As far as the football was concerned there was little to choose between the teams at that time with Airdrie sitting on ten points, just two ahead of Ayr in the First Division.

23

Home Again

AYR United vice-chairman George Smith and Dr Robert Patterson, who had helped Ally recover after his ulcer scare in Ibiza, were instrumental in his move back to Somerset Park.

Smith had worked with the club's two previous managers, Willie McLean and the recently-departed Georgie Caldwell. 'Ally was different from them,' Smith recalls. 'He was so easy to work with and understood both the board and playing side's views.'

Ally was back in the dugout one day after the appointment when Partick visited Somerset Park. The crowd of 2,083 was more than twice the previous home attendance against East Fife and second only to the derby match with Kilmarnock that season.

'Ally is back! Ally is back!' the fans chanted with the return of the messiah promising good times ahead. The supporters had clearly forgiven the events of his previous short spell at the club although Ally would have been able to gauge public opinion when working behind his bar in the town.

The *Evening Times* report on the match contained the following, 'Ally MacLeod received a rapturous reception on his return to Ayr and inspired by his return Ayr immediately took the game to Thistle.' But there was no fairytale start this time as the Jags went home with both points following a 3-1 victory.

Just as in his previous spells Ally rearranged the training nights for Tuesdays and Thursdays which allowed him to watch the reserves on a Monday evening. 'I approach the game differently from most managers – I am attack-minded,' he informed the *Ayrshire Post*, confirming that his philosophy of the game had not changed in his absence.

Seven days later Ayr lost 3-1 at home again, this time to Alloa. 'Just give me a month and let's see the difference. We have got to get back to the stage where every team is frightened to come to Somerset Park,' the manager told the local newspaper.

A 4-1 defeat at Brechin left Ayr joint bottom in the league with Morton on 19 November, and when the Dumbarton match was snowed off on the last day of the month there was no likelihood of Ally giving the players the Saturday off.

Instead he took them to the beach where they were put through a tough training exercise on the sand dunes for a couple of hours.

A home win over fellow strugglers Montrose stopped the run of defeats but bottom club Morton then won 3-0 at Somerset. 'Unbelievably bad,' was Ally's opinion of the team's performance when speaking to the *Post*, adding, 'It's the worst Ayr performance at home in my time as a manager. I am not sure if all the players have the right attitude. In many other jobs they would have been sacked for their second-half performance.'

Worse was to come when the club he had walked out on, Airdrie, scored all of the game's four goals inside the first 45 minutes of the next home match.

With Ayr now isolated at the foot of the First Division, Ally's return had not had anything like the effect the board had envisaged.

Two points gained at East Fife started a revival and confidence soared as Ayr were unbeaten in their next eight games and rose to fourth from bottom of the table at the beginning of March.

In the Scottish Cup Stenhousemuir were beaten 1-0 before Ayr lost by the same scoreline at Hibernian in mid-February, but only to an injury-time Eddie May goal. The match at Easter Road was played on a Sunday due to the Scotland v England rugby international at Murrayfield the previous day. The draw had been made on the Saturday and both clubs knew that a home tie against Celtic awaited the victors so May's late goal was a real sickener. A similar crowd for a replay and the prospect of a full house for the visit of Celtic would have been a welcome financial boost for the club.

In a bid to stay in the First Division Ally negotiated a loan deal for John Sludden from his former club Airdrie, from February until the end of the season, and the signing was soon among the goals by netting at Dumbarton.

After taking both points at Falkirk on 19 March Ayr were fifth but failed to win again in their remaining eight league matches, losing six of them as they descended to second-bottom of the table. A home defeat to Falkirk on the penultimate Saturday of the season all but relegated Ally's team. Only victory at Kilmarnock and a home defeat for Montrose by Dumbarton plus an eight-goal swing on the last day of the season could save Ayr.

Ally told the *Ayrshire Post*, 'Funny things can happen in football. It would be wrong to give in but we must be realistic – it doesn't look on.'

Ayr took the game to Kilmarnock and might have won had a Lex Grant shot not come back off a post with the teams locked at 2-2. But it was the home side who got the winner and Montrose held on for a goalless draw to consign Ayr to the drop along with Alloa. The club finished with 31 points but the late collapse had proved damaging as the Honest Men now prepared for life in the Second Division, Scottish football's third tier.

That evening Ally took the microphone at the Ayr United Supporters' Association Player of the Year Dance and addressed those present, 'Ayr have been down before. Keep the heads up. Good times are around the corner. If we grit our teeth we can get out of it.'

Good times were indeed not far away as the following Tuesday Ayr returned to Rugby Park and left with the Ayrshire Cup after a 2-1 triumph.

During the 1985/86 season attendances at Somerset Park had dropped by a figure of 2,431 to a total of 28,852. Seven players were given free transfers and a further four made available for sale as the manager planned ahead.

In the close-season Rod Stewart, a close friend of director Dr Bob Paterson, was linked to making an investment in Ayr United. Discussions had taken place at the Scotland v Australia World Cup play-off match the previous November and the fact Ally was with the club had tempted the singer. But after consideration he felt the timing was not right as he lived in the United States at that point.

There were changes off the field that year for the MacLeods as the decision was made to sell the bar in Newmarket Street and concentrate on the Old Tudor Inn in Kilmarnock which was still doing well. With the loss of the coffee shop Faye sometimes helped out in the Old Tudor.

Before long the MacLeods would leave Corsehill Place for a house in the town's Bruce Crescent.

In the new season Ayr won their opening Second Division game at home to Queen's Park but then collapsed at Raith Rovers, losing 5-0.

The thrashing at Kirkcaldy was not the best preparation for the League Cup match at Kilmarnock. After weeks of negotiations Airdrie had agreed to Sludden's £3,000 transfer just hours ahead of the kick-off and in front of 3,853 his free kick gave Ayr an advantage. A Craig Buchanan penalty doubled the lead and Ayr held on to win 2-1, sending the travelling fans home happy. Ayr then lost the following league game at Alloa and the manager responded by calling the players in for extra training on the Sunday.

Brian McLaughlin, who had previously been at both Ayr and Motherwell under Ally, returned to Somerset in September as Ally tried to freshen up his attack.

There were changes at boardroom level within the club that autumn with Andrew Charters retiring after three and a half years and George Smith taking over as chairman. Dr Bob Paterson left to be replaced by Brian Dunn and three new board members were accepted. The changes would later prove significant for the manager.

Inconsistent results in the league saw eight wins, five defeats and five draws between the derby and the turn of the year which left the club sitting in sixth place yet only three points adrift of the second promotion slot in what proved to be a tight, competitive division.

Dundee United had put paid to any further progress in the League Cup while the lower-league status now required entry into the Scottish Cup at the first round stage where non-league Annan Athletic were dismissed at Somerset. Attendances were rising with home games now attracting around 1,100, an increase of a couple of hundred since the start of the season, but this was a fraction of the thousands who had flocked to the ground during Ally's heyday in the 1970s.

Ayr's last game of 1986 saw St Johnstone win by two clear goals at Somerset and drew the following response from the manager, 'We were murder.'

Things improved in the new year and an unbeaten six-game league run from the start of 1987 saw the club climb to the top of the division following a 4-0 win at Stenhousemuir in February. The run had been interrupted by Scottish Cup business, and a last-minute Sludden equaliser at Stranraer sparked 'a mini pitch invasion by fans and a dance up the touchline by Ally MacLeod' as reported by the *Ayrshire Post*. Ayr won the replay but went out to Meadowbank in round three.

By mid-April just four points separated four sides seeking the two promotion places at the top of the table with three matches remaining. Ayr were second behind Meadowbank.

A goalless draw with Raith Rovers followed by a win at Stranraer set up an exciting last-day scenario when a point for Meadowbank and Ayr would see them both promoted. Defeat for Ayr at home to Stirling Albion would open the door for both their opponents and Raith Rovers with goal difference possibly coming into play.

Somerset Park hosted Scotland's fourth-largest crowd that 9 May with a few hundred Stirling fans boosting the total figure to 4,348.

After a disastrous first half Ayr trailed by two goals but were given a lifeline with the award of a penalty kick on 54 minutes. But Kenny Wilson's effort was saved and when the visitors scored again it looked all over.

Ayr rallied and fought back through goals from Ian McAllister and Sludden, leaving 14 minutes remaining for them to snatch the crucial point. But goalkeeper Graham deprived Ayr and at the final whistle Stirling believed they had won promotion until it was confirmed Raith had won at Stranraer, ensuring they went up with Meadowbank.

Ayr, Stirling and Raith had all ended the season on 52 points but the Kirkcaldy side's better goal difference proved crucial.

Around a thousand Ayr fans invaded the pitch and chanted Ally's name and in the press room the manager described the day's events as worse than being relegated 12 months earlier. 'This time we have a team that is good enough for the First Division,' he said.

Speaking at the Ayr United Supporters' Association function that evening the manager addressed the fans in familiar tone, 'I've been through Argentina, through the ups and downs but this is possibly the most disappointing time of all. The phoenix doesn't die – I am quite sure that next year, provided we learn from our mistakes, we can rise again.'

After losing six goals at home to Arsenal in a friendly and sharing four with Reading in another, Ayr kicked off the 1987/88 league season with a 0-0 draw in Perth. The St Johnstone result sparked a remarkable sequence of 13 unbeaten league matches of which no less than 11 were won. In the same period they defeated Arbroath before losing to Dumbarton in the League Cup.

In August Henry Templeton had been the sixth player to follow Ally from Airdrie with a fee of £5,000 securing the signature of the 24-year-old. In

Templeton's case, just as at Broomfield, Ally actually signed the player before speaking to the directors. This was a situation few other clubs would have tolerated.

'I'd actually walked out on Airdrie and was chucking football,' Templeton remembers. 'So when Ally came in it was a no-brainer.'

What could be viewed as the plundering of his previous team's assets did not, according to Airdrie chairman George Peat, cause any disharmony, 'The players followed Ally to Ayr and we had no grudge about that as they were his players.' Airdrie did not lose out over the exodus considering Ally had signed some of the players for nothing as the transfers of Sludden and Templeton alone saw £8,000 heading in the opposite direction.

Another addition to the playing staff was Tommy Walker who joined from another of Ally's former clubs, Aberdeen. Chairman George Smith says of the relationship between board and manager, 'He did let the directors know about team progress and the way it was going but we never interfered in team matters.' Smith does however reveal, 'Not all the board members were keen on him as he had his own way.'

Ally's men took part in the first competitive fixture to be played on a synthetic pitch when the league leaders went to Stirling at the beginning of September to sample Albion's new playing surface. 'We could have scored nine clear goals,' he said after his side managed just the one in a drawn match.

A home win over Queen's Park at the end of the month drew an attendance of 2,805 which was the sixth-largest in Scotland on the day. 'I won't be happy until our crowds regularly hit the 4,000-mark,' Ally told the *Ayrshire Post*.

Ayr now had the best strike rate in Scottish football and Templeton's goal against East Stirling on 24 October was the ninth consecutive match in which the player had scored.

Seven days later a bumper crowd of 5,168 visited Somerset Park for the game against St Johnstone with both clubs unbeaten in the league. But it was Saints who kept their record intact by scoring all three goals with Templeton unable to add to his tally.

Smith attended every away match during that season, a period he now looks back on as 'a golden era'. He recalls a great team spirit with each away game treated like a party, 'travelling with friends'.

With some fondness Smith remembers the trip to Stranraer on the second day of 1988 where the side had won 2-1, 'The team was waiting for Ally to board the bus and he was taking ages so I went to get him and found he had been talking to the Stranraer board. On the way back to the bus Ally whispered in my ear to take his arm and he would pretend to be paralytic. The players were flabbergasted – they thought he was pie-eyed! He wasn't at all and the players had the wind knocked right out of them – it was hilarious!'

Ironically Ally would not wait on anyone if the team were heading to an away match, even club directors. Smith recalls setting off for Berwick without club doctor Brian Dunn as he wasn't there at the appointed time. Dunn did catch up with the party when they stopped off for lunch in Edinburgh on that occasion.

Smith remembers another away match at Meadowbank Thistle when the team bus was stuck in traffic in Edinburgh city centre with time running short, 'Ally got the physio to do Henry Templeton's pre-match fitness test in Princes Street. After running round the block Ally told him he was fit.'

Templeton's own memory of the day is that the coach had actually broken down and the manager was fretting that they would be short of time at the stadium. 'All the boys in the team were noising Ally up,' he says, and he was eventually told to get stripped. 'I ran round the block and the physio ran with me with his suit on!'

Smith reminisces further about that promotion season, 'We would stop at our house on the way home and all have a drink. It was one long enjoyable season with a great family feel to it.'

In the Scottish Cup Ayr overcame Montrose and Queen's Park, both away from home, before another away tie required a trip to Premier League side Dunfermline in round three.

The club subsidised a fleet of 19 coaches and five double-deckers to take supporters to Fife at just £2 per head and an away support numbering 1,100 took advantage of the offer.

STV did a special feature on Ally for *Scotsport* which included some footage shot inside the Ayr dressing room ahead of the game.

A match Ayr were considered unlucky not to have won ended 1-1. In the *Glasgow Herald*, Ian Paul marvelled at Ally's performance in the post-match press briefing, 'If there is an example of man's unquenchable spirit in football, he is it. Ally MacLeod, battered, bloodied and bruised after a decade of traumas that would have doused the fire of the most rabid revolutionary, looks little different, sounds much the same, and talks just as much.'

The Pars won the replay 2-0 but perhaps the most impressive statistic about the match was not the result but the huge attendance of 11,712 on a Wednesday evening which surpassed even the impressive figure of 8,484 who had watched the game in Fife.

Early in March, Ally issued a triple challenge to his players. The priority was to win the Second Division title but he also had his eye on Forfar's record points haul for the division of 63 and targeted 100 goals by the end of the season. At the time Ayr had eight games to play with 51 points secured and 85 goals scored.

Promotion was sealed with the luxury of six games to spare on the last Saturday in March with a 2-2 result at Stirling, the very team who had denied them the previous year. The Honest Men had surrendered the lead twice but a point was enough to guarantee a place in the First Division. The celebrating Ayr fans invaded the plastic pitch at the final whistle.

The *Ayrshire Post* had access to the dressing room and reported that the players had burst into a chorus of 'Super Ally' as the champagne flowed.

'I have only a few years left in football but I want back in the Premier League to have another go at the big boys,' the Super one told the newspaper's reporter. Typically he drew parallels with his team's style of play and that of the Dutch international side which had recently impressed in a 2-2 game at Wembley – quipping that he could not recall the Dutch skipper's name 'but I don't know if he would make our team!'

Although he may have been jesting when comparing his players Ally did attempt to emulate the Dutch style with his part-timers.

One of Ally's old Motherwell players, Ian Clinging, remembers being surprised at the tactics during a visit to Somerset after he had moved to Morton, 'They were trying to play it with passing out from the goalie through the defenders kind of thing. That was the first time I had seen a Scottish team playing like that. In those days when the goalkeeper got the ball it was just a big kick up the park.'

Later that evening the manager, directors and many of the players joined members of the Ayr United Travel Club in their base at the Ayr Labour Club to continue the celebrations. Even at this time of triumph Ally still saw the value of strengthening the links between the board and supporters.

As if the day had not been eventful enough Ally was called from his bed at 4am on the Sunday and drove to Kilmarnock to find a fire alert at his pub was no more than a false alarm. His eldest son might just have found some amusement in that.

A national newspaper had offered a crate of champagne for the first team in the country to score 100 goals. On the ninth day of April Ayr hosted Stranraer requiring three goals to reach the target with the only threat coming from Rangers. The Ibrox side would have to score six times against Morton before Ally's men had hit three to secure the champagne. Ayr won 3-1 to claim the prize while the Glasgow team lost 3-2 in Greenock.

Dunfermline's record of 91 league goals in the Second Division was surpassed with another 3-1 win at Alloa seven days later, and the championship was secured in the final home match against East Stirling. The point gained in the goalless game was enough to ensure they could not be caught with their goal difference far superior to second-placed St Johnstone. Ayr had been at the top of the table since taking up residence at the end of August.

They then stuttered to the finishing line, losing both of their last two matches – at Stenhousemuir and Brechin.

The goals for column totalled 95 in the league plus nine in the cups. On three occasions Ayr had netted six times and twice scored five with Sludden scoring 30 times for the second season running. The champions finished with 61 points, the same total as also-promoted St Johnstone, but had a goal difference better by 12 and were regularly entertaining home crowds around the 3,000-mark.

Just to top a remarkable season the Ayrshire Cup was added to the trophy cabinet after Kilmarnock – who had three players sent off in the match – surrendered to a 2-0 defeat at Rugby Park.

Ally was presented with a crystal trophy and a £50 cheque, his reward for the March Manager of the Month award from sponsors Tartan Special. Following the dismissal of Alex Smith he was linked with the St Mirren job and was alongside Archie MacPherson to give his analysis during BBC Scotland's live transmission of the Scottish Cup Final between Celtic and Dundee United.

After the nadir of the World Cup he was suddenly in demand again and things seemed to be going well for Ally MacLeod.

24

Somerset Sunset

AYR had been the best-supported club outside the Premier Division in the 1987/88 season – watched by a total of 55,503 in their home league matches, 2,378 in the Skol Cup and 11,712 for that midweek Scottish Cup replay. Sponsorship deals were agreed with Bukta and Centrum and the new season could not come quickly enough with a feel-good factor once again engulfing the town. 'Financially the club was in great health under Ally's stewardship,' says chairman George Smith. 'In all the years that he was there when I was chairman they turned a profit. Crowds got bigger so revenue swelled. With Ally there it was easier to get sponsorship and increase commercial revenues. He always sold the game to the fans.'

At the beginning of March the manager had been unhappy about what he considered another distraction just as his players were preparing themselves for the final promotion push. The board had rejected an offer from businessman David Murray of Murray International Holdings to invest £700,000 in the club for a controlling interest. Suspicion surrounded his motives which would see control of the club effectively passed to one person.

Ally told the *Ayrshire Post*, 'I want things left alone. We have an ambitious board of directors who have never turned down a request I have made. Why should the shareholders change something when it is going well?'

The manager was also said to be annoyed at comments made by Murray referring to 'bargain basement players' and was unhappy about 'the boat being rocked at such a time in the season'.

The board wrote to all shareholders expressing the opinion that the business-man was 'looking for too much too soon and for so little a price' and considered that the share price on offer was 'grossly inadequate'.

The shareholders rejected Murray's approach in May with only four out of 47 voting in favour of his proposal.

Ally did something that summer that he had always avoided in 22 years of football management – he actually signed a contract. Increased speculation linking him to both St Mirren and Dundee had alerted the board, given the circumstances of his previous two departures from Somerset Park.

Speaking to the local newspaper Ally gave his reasons for agreeing to the three-year deal, 'I want people to know I am happy where I am. I left the club once before for ambition and the second time when a problem turned up. But now I am back to build a side.'

Henry Templeton reflects on the terrific team spirit which Ally encouraged at Ayr, 'Every week we all went out together. Ally got on with everybody.' He also has cause to remember some of the more unusual training sessions including playing head tennis in the Carrick Hills with the manager doubling as a net between two piles of cow dung which the players more often than not came into contact with. Ally seemed to revert to his old methods in the familiar surroundings as Templeton noticed the training became more eventful at Ayr than it had been under him at Broomfield.

Ayr lost four goals at home to both Rangers (in front of over 10,000) and Leicester City in pre-season matches before the championship flag was unfurled prior to the opening First Division match with Clydebank on 13 August 1988. Some 3,151 supporters saw Ayr get off to a winning start with a 3-2 victory.

Asked about his side's Premier League prospects by the *Ayrshire Post* the manager was confident, 'Yes I think we can make it. The way we played on Saturday was how we would play in the Premier League – pure football.'

The League Cup first round draw could not have been more difficult with a trip to Celtic Park in the club's centenary year. Ahead of the kick-off Celtic manager Billy McNeill entered the away dressing room and handed Ally his starting line-up. The team read: Rough, Morris, Rogan, Whyte, McCarthy, Grant, Miller, McStay, McAvennie, Walker, Burns, with McGhee and Stark listed as the substitutes. Alan Rough was making his debut for Celtic that evening.

Conscious that he had the attention of his players, most of whom had never played against Celtic, Ally sensed an opportunity to boost their confidence. He took the sheet of paper which he then crushed into a ball, telling Billy there was little point in him reading it as none of his players would get into the Ayr team.

The Celtic manager was apparently less than impressed at Ally's actions although it had the desired effect of relaxing the Ayr players, if only for a short time. 'Don't worry about them,' he said while tossing the paper into a bin. 'Ally had us thinking we were going to win,' says Templeton.

The players were out on the pitch when the referee Mr McGilvray, apparently acting on a complaint from Celtic, told Ally his players would have to change as both teams were wearing white socks. Back in the dressing room Templeton remembers the manager telling the team to take their time getting changed even when the referee kept entering. 'My boys are getting changed!' he shouted before repeating to the players, 'Let them wait.'

Ayr's change strip happened to be blue. 'You want to have heard them when we went back out!' laughs Templeton today.

The match eventually started nine minutes late and Ayr were praised for their attacking play. They halved a two-goal deficit just after the break but ultimately went out 4-1. Ian Paul's *Glasgow Herald* match report contained the following,

'They certainly did not let the manager down last night as they went out of the Skol Cup to a Celtic team which had to play very well indeed to tame them.'

Ally spoke about the change of kit the next day. 'What can you say?' he asked *Evening Times* journalist Alan Davidson. 'It's just as well I took along a blue change strip. I didn't want to use it because it could have been looked on as inflammatory and there's no point in upsetting people. It all affected our preparations.'

The Honest Men then won their second league match at Meadowbank Thistle before going down at Kilmarnock. They then defeated Forfar, lost to Falkirk and drew with Partick before overcoming their bogey team St Johnstone. Then followed a bad stretch of 11 winless matches before they got the better of Morton in mid-December.

Derby revenge came with a 4-1 win over Kilmarnock on 3 January 1989, a result which lifted Ayr to ninth in the table.

Two heavy defeats followed, 4-1 at home to Airdrie and 5-1 at Clydebank. 'I was disgusted to be in charge of a side that gave a performance like that,' Ally told the press at Kilbowie, unable to defend the players in what he considered 'the lowest point in my managerial career'.

Ally was still capable of dispensing the hairdryer treatment to his players after such a performance and although he considered himself one of the boss's favourites, Templeton did not escape. 'He used to throw things at me!' he laughs.

Ally watched Scottish Cup opponents Hearts draw 0-0 at home to Motherwell and told the local newspaper in his typical style, 'I saw nothing to frighten us.' Hearts won 4-1 in Edinburgh and the cup exit was followed by an up-and-down sequence of results until the end of the season. This loss of form during the latter stages of the season was not unusual for one of Ally's teams as their part-time status took its toll.

With both sides level on points and just two clear of relegation danger, a 3-2 home win against Meadowbank in February resulted in a confession from the manager to the *Ayrshire Post*, 'For the first time as Ayr manager I wasn't out to entertain. I was after two points – no messing. I flooded the midfield with battlers although I still left three men up.'

Ayr won the third derby 2-1 but slipped into relegation territory as the weeks wore on until a 3-1 home win over Airdrie guaranteed another season in the First Division in the penultimate game.

There was still time for a classic Ally quote before the season concluded following Morton's one-goal win at Somerset on the last day. 'The most disappointing game in all my years as Ayr boss,' he told the journalists in the press room.

Ayr's final placing was fourth from bottom with 35 points, just one ahead of Kilmarnock who were relegated due to an inferior goal difference to Clyde. Those derby results had, after all, proved to be about more than local pride. The average attendance at Somerset Park had been 2,632 and Ayr had succeeded in establishing First Division status. The next step for Ally was to plot the team's return to the Premier League.

Having avoided the drop back to the Second Division, the Ayr United board announced ambitious plans for full-time football at the club to be phased in over three seasons.

Ayr failed to win any of their first five league matches in 1989/90 and departed the League Cup to Hamilton during the same spell. Following a 1-0 victory at Falkirk the club were then unbeaten in four before losing to both Airdrie and Raith Rovers.

Five new players were added to the staff and approaches from Kilmarnock for John Sludden. who had rejected a new two-year deal, were initially rejected. In December Sludden was sold to Killie with Ally explaining, 'No club likes to sell to their local rivals but to make it clear he wasn't happy and I wasn't happy with the situation.'

On the park things improved and just two defeats in their next 11 matches saw Ayr in the relative safety of seventh place in the league table as 1990 began.

The first match of the new decade saw Hamilton put four goals past Ayr without reply although the team rallied and collected three points from their next two games. A Somerset crowd of 7,869 contributed welcome gate receipts of £20,700 for the goalless Scottish Cup tie with St Mirren. Saints won the rematch 2-1.

Ayr lost seven, won three and drew four of their remaining 14 fixtures which included another heavy defeat – 6-0 at Airdrie in February. It was the club's worst loss in 17 years, since the 8-1 Hibernian result in December 1972. Discontent spread among the supporters and there was talk of a half-time walk-out in the home match with Forfar.

The final league placing was tenth. Although the club finished one position further up the table than the previous season, points-wise there had been no improvement and the haul of 35 was identical to the 1988/89 tally. There had also been a slight fall in attendances with the average home gate for the season down to 2,492.

Ally was invited to appear on BBC Scotland's World Cup panel that summer where he offered his views as Scotland yet again exited the tournament after the first phase.

In a bid to improve their promotion prospects Ally signed striker Ally Graham from Albion Rovers and St Johnstone midfielder Sammy Johnston in time for the new campaign.

Ayr took part in a small piece of Scottish football history when their League Cup second round tie at Celtic Park on 22 August 1990 was shown live by satellite company BSB. This was the first occasion apart from the final when a League Cup match had been televised live. At the time around 140,000 Scottish homes had access to BSB with the UK figure close to 400,000.

Unfortunately Ayr failed to impress the viewers and found themselves three behind after 40 minutes, eventually losing 4-0.

Their First Division campaign got under way three days later when the points were shared with Forfar at Somerset. After another two draws the Honest Men recorded their first victory at Brechin. Four defeats in the next five matches led up to the first derby of the season at Rugby Park in October where 9,802 paying customers watched Kilmarnock score three times to Ayr's solitary reply.

That month did see some success for Ayr in a tournament organised to celebrate the Scottish Football League's centenary season. The Centenary Cup, also known as the B&Q Centenary Cup after sponsorship was agreed, was contested by First and Second Division clubs.

Ayr put out Brechin at home in round one then survived a trip to Second Division Montrose who put up a real fight. With the sides deadlocked at 1-1 the match entered extra time when Ayr went behind only for Ally Graham to equalise at the end of the first period. Templeton then got the winner with the match just two minutes from a penalty shoot-out. 'We were a bit lucky and didn't play well,' Ally graciously conceded to the press.

Queen of the South were well beaten 4-1 at Somerset in the quarter-final to set up a home semi against Second Division Clyde. A comfortable 2-0 win put Ayr into the final against First Division Dundee at neutral Fir Park.

Ayr were said to have 6,000 supporters in the crowd of 11,506 who watched an exciting match. McAllister gave Ayr an early lead which was cancelled out just after the restart through a Billy Dodds penalty. The same player then headed his side into the lead but a deflected shot from David Smyth forced extra time.

With penalty kicks looming Dodds completed his hat-trick from the edge of the box and the cup went north to Tayside along with the £100,000 prize money. Ally was in good form after the match, telling the press, 'Now we will have to go for the Scottish Cup as consolation.'

Ayr bounced back to defeat Clyde 4-1 in the league but failed to win any of their next seven games. A 3-0 defeat at Raith Rovers on 8 December 1990 saw them slump to fourth-bottom with 14 points acquired from 17 matches.

The Ayr fans at Kirkcaldy had had enough and turned their frustration on the manager. Ally had got wind even before the match that a demonstration was planned against him but still left complimentary tickets for some supporters at the reception although the briefs went unclaimed.

'People who pay their money are entitled to do what they want,' was his response in the press room when asked about the fans' discontent.

With his contract due to expire at the end of that season it was indicated to Ally in the wake of the Rovers result that he would not then be offered new terms by the board. The club were prepared to consider another position at Somerset Park for him, perhaps in public relations or coaching youngsters in the new season.

But with his pride getting the better of him, as it had done throughout his career, Ally decided to leave Ayr on Thursday 13 December rather than hang on until the end of the season. His last match in the Somerset Park dugout was a testimonial for Ian McAllister two days earlier, when Celtic had beaten Ayr 2-1. Davie Wells was put in temporary charge of the first team just as he had been following George Caldwell's departure.

Unhappy at recent boardroom developments, George Smith had already stepped down as chairman. 'I got the feeling the board wasn't happy we had made a commitment to go full-time and some of the board members wanted a change. They wanted a scapegoat. I personally didn't want that so I wouldn't be party to his sacking and resigned.'

It was the new chairman, Sandy Loudon, who informed Ally of the contract decision which led to his immediate departure.

Looking back now Smith considers the problems started four seasons earlier when the club missed out on promotion on the very last day. 'I believe that if the team had been promoted at the end of the 1986/87 season when a missed penalty cost them, that team would have romped the First Division. There wouldn't have been a team that would have touched us and we would have been in the Premier League. Some things went wrong after that and there was sniping behind the scenes.'

The directors were hopeful that Willie Miller would take up the vacant post but after consideration he turned it down. They then looked to Brian McLaughlin, who had assumed a coaching role at the club once his playing days had ended, but he failed to appear for the interview.

Eventually George Burley was appointed as player-manager and Ayr went on to finish third-bottom in the table that season, five points above relegation. Burley was dismissed two years later after a series of bad results, vindicating Smith's view, 'I didn't feel that George Burley was the right person to replace Ally and I think in the long term I was proved right as the team never really progressed.'

Now 59 years of age, Ally refused to rule out a future in football and told the *Ayrshire Post*, 'I'll take some time off then wait and see what happens.' One unnamed Second Division club had already been linked with a move for him.

25

A Dumfries Swansong

QUEEN of the South had finished third from bottom of the Second Division in 1990/91 and player-manager Frank McGarvey had been relieved of his duties in March, just nine months into a two-year contract. McGarvey then became involved in a dispute with the club and claimed £30,000 for loss of wages and damage to his reputation. In the meantime he was still tied to Queens on a playing contract which prevented him from signing for anyone else.

In his autobiography *Totally Frank* he later described his time in Dumfries as 'a horrible experience' and revealed he had been warned not to take the job. McGarvey had been the club's fourth manager in five years.

It was against this background that Ally was invited to take over at Palmerston Park. The move had been rumoured as Ally had been spotted in Dumfries and indeed at the ground on more than one occasion leading up to the approach.

Appointed on Thursday 27 June 1991, Ally told Carlos Alba of the *Dumfries and Galloway Standard*, 'I have told the Queens directors I will come here for at least two years – and at the end of those two years Queens will be in the First Division.' Expressing a desire to deliver attractive football, Ally chose not to work with a contract.

Willie Harkness had been the club chairman since 1967 and had previously held the post of president of the SFA at the time of the 1978 World Cup in Argentina.

Harkness was quoted in the *Standard* as saying, 'I think he will lift the club. There is no such thing as defeat in Ally's book.'

When questioned about his relationship with the chairman Ally's coded response was that relations between them had 'always been cordial', adding, 'I worked with him when I was the Scotland manager and found him okay. I have my own way of doing things and no one will influence me.'

Alan Roxburgh had been a Queens fan since 1969 and recalls the revolving door of managers, 'Some of those that got the job would only put up with it for so long. We all assumed they had their hands tied as it always seemed like Harkness was pulling the strings and he was known for picking the team.'

Already it looked as though the seeds had been sown for an uneasy working relationship.

After pre-season training commenced on 6 July the new manager bemoaned the fact some players would still be on holiday three weeks later. 'This won't happen next year!' he assured the *Standard*.

Holidays were a further irritant to Ally when he tried to secure the services of Henry Templeton once again. Templeton was now with Clydebank and Ally found he could not enter into negotiations until the Bankies' chairman returned from his vacation.

In Ally's first match Queens defeated Southern Counties side Maxweltown High School 3-1 on 13 July but tougher opposition lay in wait for the weekend of 27–28 July.

The Willie Harkness Borders Cup was a four-team pre-season tournament played at Palmerston over the two days. Queens defeated Carlisle United with a late goal on the Saturday in one of the semi-finals before taking care of Stranraer in the Sunday final with a 2-1 win.

In conversation with Carlos Alba the manager remarked he had heard some departing fans saying that the side were sure to win the league now. 'I have never promised that I have a magic wand and will refuse to talk about titles,' he said in concerned language before harking back to his darkest days. 'It reminded me of when I was Scotland manager and I said that only one British team could win the World Cup. The next day the papers had me as saying Scotland will win it.'

There was little time to polish the silverware before a benefit game for Cancer Research at Raydale Park on the last day of the month. Queens lost eight goals to Northern League side Gretna, scoring just once themselves. The game had actually been goalless until the 53rd minute when, as Ally put it, Queens 'threw the sponge in'. He continued in the *Dumfries and Galloway Standard*, 'We have now seen the two sides of Queen of the South. At the weekend they played very well…but here they could have lost 30.'

A win over Premier Division and Scottish Cup holders Motherwell was followed by defeat to Hamilton before the serious business of league football began.

'The warm-up games have been a useful indicator and I now know the best team available,' Ally told the *Standard*.

First up for the Doonhamers was a trip to Cowdenbeath where the crowd totalled just 340. It was a dream start as Jimmy McGuire scored the only goal after 75 minutes to secure a deserved two points. But Queens were brought back to earth four days later as they crashed out of the League Cup, beaten 4-0 at home by Albion Rovers. They then only picked up one point in their next four matches, ironically in a 1-1 draw at Albion Rovers.

The manager considered his players 'a wee bit unlucky' to lose at home to Alloa. With the teams level on a goal each Queens were fully committed to winning the match. 'We got caught out by two late goals when we were going for the winner,' Ally told the *Standard*. 'I have never been one to look for a draw,' he added in justification of his attacking strategy.

Andy Thomson scored both goals in a 2-1 home victory over Stenhousemuir to end the bad run. Ally had paid Stirling Albion £10,000 for striker Willie Waters in August in a bid to freshen up the attack and he finally succeeded in bringing Templeton to Palmerston in September for £20,000. The player had no hesitation in rejoining Ally. 'I went right away,' he recalls, and he was soon among the goals to reward the manager's faith.

Queens' first away win was convincing enough as they defeated Queen's Park 4-1 at the end of September to occupy the third-bottom spot in the table with seven points. 'They are not as bad a team as a lot of people think,' Ally told the *Standard*. 'My job is to give them the confidence to chase victories.' He added that he had set a target of being in the top four by the end of the year.

Two victories followed. Thomson scored three times in a 5-1 home win in front of 560 against East Stirling and Queens then came away from the long trip to Arbroath with a 3-2 result.

After the success of the Centenary Cup the previous year it was decided to continue the tournament, now known as the Challenge Cup, and again Ally enjoyed a good run with his Queens team involved in some exciting matches.

After sharing six goals with Stirling Albion at Palmerston, Queens won the penalty contest 6-5 during which goalkeeper Alan Davidson saved no less than four kicks and scored one himself.

A trip to Montrose saw another thrilling match again end 3-3 after 90 minutes. Stevie King had grabbed all of the home side's goals but Jimmy McGuire went one better with four on the night as the Doonhamers scored four more times during the extension to run out 7-4 winners. For the second time Ally had guided a side to the semi-final.

The draw meant a return to Somerset Park for the manager who conceded he would have preferred to have met Ayr in the final.

Queens took 17 coaches on the 78-mile journey to Ayr on 5 November with their support numbering around 1,500 in a crowd of 4,254. The *Glasgow Herald* reported, 'MacLeod received an ambiguous welcome on his return to Somerset Park,' but he was soon smiling as Thomson scored twice and Queens looked good for the final.

Ally Graham, one of Ally's last signings at Somerset, pulled Ayr back into the match just ahead of the break before a double from substitute Mike Smith overturned the Doonhamers' advantage. Smith had looked in an offside position for the winner ten minutes from time but the goal stood and Ayr went on to lose the final for the second year running, this time to Hamilton.

'I was very unhappy at some of the decisions. Smith was at least five yards offside for the final goal and I thought Ally Graham should have been sent off,' a clearly frustrated Ally told the press after the match.

Henry Templeton's memory of the night suggests that Ally's enthusiasm may have contributed to the defeat, 'I always remember Ally was angry with the linesman while they were attacking. The linesman couldn't keep up with the play because he was shouting and bawling at him and they scored, but it was miles offside.'

'Unbelievably offside,' is how supporter Alan Roxburgh remembers the winning goal today. 'How anybody got away with that I just don't know. It was absolutely scandalous, not even close!'

Continuing his good form, Templeton was named the Second Division Player of the Month for October. Striker Andy Thomson had already hit 18 goals and had been watched by Aberdeen, Dundee United and Falkirk with Liverpool also said to have been alerted to his talents.

The league form had suffered during the cup run and after losing seven goals at Brechin, Queens went a further three matches without a win. A 3-1 result at Stenhousemuir inspired a run of six unbeaten matches which saw only one point dropped.

In November a 3-0 home lead over Cowdenbeath was squandered as the game ended all square, exposing the risk of the manager's attack and entertain policy. He told the *Standard*, 'The players tried to make up for the 7-1 defeat at Brechin. Even when we were 3-0 up we tried to get more goals.'

Accepting that this strategy had on this occasion cost the club a point, Ally explained it had been a straightforward choice between negative or attacking football and that he had chosen the latter.

As with the Alloa match in September the manager here is acknowledging that his attacking philosophy sometimes backfired. One of Ally's critics' main accusations of his career in management is that he was tactically naive but these comments demonstrate he was acutely aware that his game plan had an element of risk but that it was a gamble he was prepared to take. In short he did know what he was doing although some may have considered his strategy rather outdated.

Later that season Ally was linked with a coaching role in Saudi Arabia but chose to remain focused on the job at Dumfries.

At the end of 1991 Queens had risen to eighth in the table, four places short of the manager's target, with 21 points collected from the same number of matches. The *Dumfries and Galloway Standard* did highlight the goals against column in December, observing that the only clubs in Scotland with a worse defensive record were the bottom teams in the other two divisions, Dunfermline and Forfar.

'We were one of those teams that if we won we won well and if we got beat we got well beat,' says Templeton. 'Ally didn't worry about defence, he just told us to go out and score more goals than them.'

Dismissing accusations of tactical naivety, Templeton defends this policy, 'He knew what he was doing. You've got to put it into context that we were a Second Division team. If it had been in the Premier he would have been a bit more tactical. In that league you didn't need to be.'

Early in January 1992 the team made the 72-mile trip to Stranraer in the Scottish Cup where they lost 4-1. In the league there was just one victory – against Albion Rovers – in the next 12 outings.

During this bad run there was a welcome distraction for the Queens manager when supporters of his former club Ayr United organised a testimonial dinner to honour his 27-year career in management. The event was held at Glasgow's Hospitality Inn on the evening of Thursday 27 February with attendees paying £30 a head plus VAT for a ticket.

Chick Young, now BBC Scotland's chief football reporter, chaired proceedings and guest speakers for the evening included former players Stan Quinn, Johnny Graham, John Murphy, Alex Ingram and John Sludden. Ally was presented with an oil painting of himself as he relaxed away from the pressures of football management. He was not a big drinker but when socialising would generally partake in a whisky or occasionally Bacardi and Coke.

Wife Faye still laughs at the memory of being awoken overnight in the hotel by banging on the room door in the small hours. Ally, having got up to visit the bathroom, had opened the wrong door and found himself stranded in the corridor.

Around this time the MacLeods decided to sell the Old Tudor Inn in Kilmarnock and retired from the licensed trade although the pub was still doing well.

Just two days after the dinner some home fans in the crowd of 506 called for the chairman's resignation with repeated chants of 'Harkness must go!' as Queens lost at home to Stenhousemuir.

The manager was spared the fans' wrath but a couple of letters appeared in the *Standard* questioning his ability. Signing himself as 'Ex fan (but 'name and address supplied'),' one reader penned the following, 'Surely the time has come for the directors to resign and take Ally MacLeod with them. The Harkness/MacLeod partnership as in Argentina has been a disaster at Palmerston.

'It is clear to everyone that the players are just not interested in playing for the present regime and the latest display against Stenhousemuir was the worst in many years. Talk of promotion has been a load of tripe from the start. I for one will not be going back until a young ambitious manager is appointed.'

An exciting home match with Queen's Park on the first Saturday in April saw the amateurs take a two-goal lead but Queen of the South rallied and fought back to go ahead 4-2 at one point, eventually winning 5-3. The result prompted the following letter from 'Loyal Larry' from Lochfoot in the *Standard* defending the manager, 'Ally MacLeod is the best manager Queens have ever had – his loyalty and faith are unquestioned – witness his refusing a terrific offer from Saudi Arabia, preferring to stay with the Doonhamers and see them through their present bad patch.'

With four weeks of the season remaining Ally was frustrated but philosophical when assessing the small squad he had available with four first-team matches remaining plus no less than 14 reserve league and cup fixtures. 'It's a farcical situation but I knew the constraints when I took the job so we just have to get on with it,' he told the *Standard*.

The lack of players meant some first-team regulars turned out for the reserves and at one point Templeton played five matches in seven days but still managed to score the winner at Celtic Park. But in addition to the registered playing staff,

Queen of the South had one other option should they require his services on the field – his name was Ally MacLeod.

With the squad further reduced through injuries Ally listed himself as a substitute trialist for the reserve game with Stenhousemuir on Sunday 12 April. Yet another injury saw him come on for the last 20 minutes of the 4-0 defeat. 'Just as I went on another player had to go off so I played as left-winger and left-half,' he told the local newspaper.

The following evening he again contributed the last 20 minutes as his side lost 6-2 at Stirling Albion. But his playing days were not quite over yet as just 24 hours later, and with only ten fit players, he answered the call and started against St Mirren reserves in Paisley.

Saints fielded a team almost entirely made up of youths, some of whom were on a work experience scheme, and the average age of their line-up was 20. Again the match went badly and Queens were seven goals in arrears before being awarded a penalty kick. Ally elected to take it himself – and scored.

Even the few St Mirren fans in attendance cheered the goal. 'I reckon I must be the oldest scorer in the league,' he told the *Standard*. So Ally had scored his first goal for Third Lanark reserves direct from a corner at the age of 18 and his last from a penalty kick for St Mirren reserves aged 61. He lasted the full 90 minutes of the match which ended in an 8-1 win for the home team but scoring the penalty was a fitting finale to what would soon be the end of his eccentric life in football.

Henry Templeton's recollection is that the 'trialist' also managed to get his name in the referee's book on the night.

By then managing St Mirren, Davie Hay was astonished to see Ally take to the field against opponents a third of his age and has mixed feelings over the night, 'I actually felt a bit sorry seeing him like that if I'm being honest but such was his enthusiasm he never saw it that way.'

Davie's belief is that Ally should never have been put in the position by any club that he had to play, 'He probably felt it was his duty such was Ally. Considering his age he did alright but I felt it was a wee bit sad watching him.'

Thomson scored all the goals in a 3-0 win for the first team at Arbroath. 'It's all coming together a bit late, but we are looking a much more settled side,' the manager assured *Standard* readers, adding that the Arbroath manager had not been the first to say Queens had been the best side they had faced all season.

If it had been coming together it soon fell apart again as the Doonhamers lost their next two matches, conceding three goals in each to Berwick and Cowdenbeath.

After the game at Berwick the manager's attitude had hardened when speaking to the *Standard*, 'We have to get sorted out which players are ambitious enough to stay at Queen of the South. Many of them have an unprofessional attitude to playing and training and quite frankly we are better off without them.'

The players responded for the last fixture of the campaign, another trip to Stranraer on 2 May, where some revenge was exacted for the Scottish Cup defeat and the season ended on a high with a 3-1 win.

The final points tally from the 39-match schedule was 33 and Queen of the South finished fourth from bottom in the 14-team division, an improvement of one place on the previous term. Andy Thomson had finished the season with 32 goals, just one short of Jimmy Gray's club record set in 1927/28.

A total of 104 goals had been conceded in league and cup matches with 86 of those in the league. This figure ensured that Queens had lost more goals than any other Scottish league club throughout the season. The total number of goals scored by the team in all competitions was 80.

The following Tuesday Ally was preparing to attend a board meeting at Palmerston when he was told it had been postponed for a week. On the Thursday, 7 May, he received a letter in the mail from the club secretary Doreen Alcorn stating that his services were no longer required.

The correspondence advised that the decision had been taken after a run of poor results and highlighted the team's final league placing. It further informed that the club was to be restructured financially which left no place for Ally.

It seems apparent that the board meeting must have taken place as scheduled but that the directors were not prepared to inform their outgoing manager in person.

'I feel very bitter,' Ally confessed to Carlos Alba of the *Dumfries and Galloway Standard*. 'I was given no warning at all.' He told Alba it was too soon to talk about any future plans but was adamant he had no regrets about taking on the job, 'The players are a smashing bunch of lads, but there are problems at the club.' When asked to comment for the newspaper, chairman Willie Harkness was unavailable.

Peter Copeland, chairman of the largest Queens supporters' club, the Emerald Park Doonhamers, was supportive of the outgoing manager and was quoted in the *Standard*'s front page article, 'What can you expect in ten months? It's not as if he was given a lot of money.'

The club had now gone through five managers in six years and the following week a letter offering more support for the deposed manager from D. Johnston of Georgetown, Dumfries, appeared in the local newspaper, 'May I express my deepest regret for Ally MacLeod for wasting ten months of his time at Queen of the South. I am very angry as are many other fans at the shameful way he was "booted out" of the club and also because he was not given a chance to prove his worth. MacLeod is a good manager who will easily find another workplace but who will manage Queens while Harkness is still in control?'

'A lot of the players were shocked because we had the makings of a good side,' is how Henry Templeton remembers his team-mates' reaction to the news.

True to his principles of loyalty, Ally was back in Dumfries on Wednesday 27 May to honour a commitment he had made while still in office. The occasion was a supporters' function attended by some 200 Queens fans in the Emerald Park Hotel. When taking the microphone Ally had some points of interest for the attendees. He informed them that Willie Harkness had been in contact warning him not to attend the meeting.

Further revelations were that, just like his predecessor, he had been advised against accepting the Queens job by five managers, and that the club secretary interfered in team affairs. He assured the supporters he had tried to strengthen the side but the promised cash for players had not been forthcoming.

Ally was presented with a cut glass bowl and a bunch of flowers as he exited the meeting to what the *Dumfries and Galloway Standard* recorded as 'tumultuous applause'. 'It's the first time I've been sacked by a club and cheered out by the fans,' he whispered to Carlos Alba, who summed up the evening's events when closing the article with 'Ally MacLeod is still larger than life'.

The supporters' protests continued into the following season as the gulf between them and the board, two entities of any club he had been at Ally had always tried to unite, widened. 'Why don't these fans shut up and let us get on with it?' Harkness was quoted in the *Herald* on 14 September.

That same month the chairman said that the club could not afford to appoint a manager, which was at least consistent with one of the reasons given for Ally's dismissal in the secretary's letter.

'Willie Harkness started picking the team and it just went right downhill,' Templeton recalls of life after Ally, citing as an example being dropped for a match against Forfar days after scoring a hat-trick at Berwick.

26

A Commercial Opportunity

IT would be wrong to gloss over the fact that Ally was dismissed from three out of his last four management positions. At both Ayr and Motherwell he was losing the support of the fans, a difficult situation for any board although there would likely have been a position for him in another capacity had he seen out his contract at Somerset Park. With Motherwell he had lost just one of his last 16 league matches and the team he had assembled did achieve promotion following his departure although five successive League Cup defeats had heaped pressure on him. He does appear to have been unfortunate at Queen of the South where finance was the overriding factor as demonstrated when the chairman later revealed the club could not afford to hire a replacement, although Queens did have a habit of dispensing with managers.

Ally's preference of working without a contract made his dismissals relatively uncomplicated but it had also aided his choices to leave Ayr (twice), Aberdeen and Airdrie as well as the national job.

It looked as though full time had been called on Ally's career in football but an unexpected offer came out of the blue from one of his previous employers 12 months after he left Palmerston.

Airdrieonians had recently parted company with their commercial manager and George Peat, now club chairman, sounded out Ally. 'I was instrumental in bringing him back to Airdrie as a commercial manager as I felt he was the type of man who could bring in revenues,' Peat reveals.

On 8 June 1993 and now aged 62, Ally took up the position at Broomfield and spoke of his enthusiasm for the job with Alex Dowdalls of the *Airdrie and Coatbridge Advertiser*, 'I enjoyed my time as manager of Airdrie but this job will be completely different. Having been a manager for so many years I totally appreciate the commercial side and I will be doing the best I can for Alex to bring in the cash for the club.'

Ally was referring to football manager Alex MacDonald and he made a point of stating that he would not be involved in the playing side of the club. He also referred to his eight years of experience as a salesman before going into football management.

Ally had one other commitment to fulfil at another of his former clubs the following month when a testimonial match had been arranged for him between Ayr United and Blackburn Rovers. Rovers were then managed by Kenny Dalglish and the club's chairman Jack Walker had been only too happy to help. Walker had been a supporter of Rovers during Ally's playing days at Ewood and had always been grateful to Ally for giving him complimentary tickets.

Alex Ferguson sent a personal donation to the testimonial fund as well as some Manchester United souvenirs to be raffled or auctioned on the night. Among the tributes in the lead-up to the event, Johnny Graham told the *Ayrshire Post*, 'What an experience it was to play under him. There was never a dull moment with Ally the supreme motivator.'

The souvenir programme for the match featured on its cover the very photograph Ally had earmarked for his autobiography. The image of him standing with arms upraised against the background of a saltire did not however include the assortment of knives protruding from his back.

The game took place on Wednesday 28 July and was preceded by a gala match at 6.45pm involving many of Ally's former Ayr players. Chick Young, who had hosted the testimonial dinner the previous year, ran a team of ex-players and celebrities who played under the banner of Dukla Pumpherston. Dukla provided the opposition to the 'Ayr United Supercrocks' team with STV's Glen Michael commentating on the match for the 5,121 spectators paying tribute inside Somerset Park.

The Supercrocks team lined up as follows: Hugh Sproat, Davie Wells, Joe Filippi, Stan Quinn, Alex McAnespie, Dougie Mitchell, Quinton Young, Johnny Graham, Alex Ingram, Gerry Philips and Bobby Rough. The substitutes were George (Dandy) McLean, Davie Paterson and John Murphy.

Dukla fielded the following 11: Ally Hunter, John McCormack, John Blackley, Jackie McNamara, Johnny Hamilton, Jim Baxter, Bobby McCullan, Chick Young, Bobby Russell, Alex MacDonald and Andy Ritchie. Pat Clinton, Gordon Wallace, Davie Armour and Davie McKinnon were their subs.

Chick's Dukla team scored both goals through boxer Clinton and Russell, by now a Morton player. Ally was presented to the crowd before the main event kicked off and existing home video footage shows him looking rather embarrassed, waving briefly to the crowd, in body language not dissimilar to the Argentina send-off at Hampden Park.

The game was played with a competitive edge for a friendly but produced just the one goal when Rovers' Nicky Marker scored from ten yards after 76 minutes.

Despite rumours otherwise, Dalglish did not come on as a substitute but he did speak to the *Ayrshire Post* after the match, 'Everybody keeps going on about the World Cup but Ally had many successes at other times.' Still displaying his sense of humour Ally commented that it had been his 'happiest day since Argentina'.

With no hospitality facilities at the club then, a reception was held after the match at Ayr Racecourse in the Western House. Ally was estimated to have made around £25,000 from the evening.

He settled into the job at Airdrie well and with his profile was able to attract companies to utilise the advertising boards around the pitch and other commercial opportunities such as classifieds in the match programme.

The club were planning to move to a new stadium in 1995 and Broomfield was sold to supermarket group Safeway for redevelopment in 1994. The last match was played at the ground on 7 May that year when a Neale Cooper own goal gave Airdrie victory over Dunfermline. The club then planned to share facilities with Clyde at Broadwood in Cumbernauld for 12 months before moving to their new ground.

During the first week of August 1994 Ally left the post of commercial manager, denying rumours there had been a fall-out with the club and stressing he had not been pushed into a decision. There was no facility for him at Broadwood where, for example, Clyde had their own deals in place for pitchside advertising.

Ally explained his move to Alex Dowdall of the *Advertiser*, 'I told chairman George Peat they didn't need a commercial manager during the period they don't have their own ground. Possibly once they get their own ground they may come back to me and that would be no problem.'

He then announced he was entering semi-retirement and admitted he was approaching the end of his shelf life in footballing terms, but felt he still had something to offer on the commercial side.

Peat confirms that the parting was amicable, 'Things were going well until we sold the ground and moved to Broadwood. There was no need for commercial activities there as Clyde had that. Ally had a chat with me one day and he said to me that he was quite happy to walk away as he said there was not enough work to justify keeping him, so that's why Ally decided to leave.'

Airdrie did however have a new commercial manager in place within a matter of weeks as the new season began which was probably just as well when their plans for an all-seater stadium at Raebog were rejected by Strathclyde Regional Council. The club's tenancy at Broadwood was extended to four years before they finally returned to the town and the new Excelsior stadium in 1998, also referred to as New Broomfield.

27
The Final Whistle

WIFE Faye, the person who knew Ally best, insists that, despite the traumas of Argentina after which he 'changed for a wee while', he did eventually revert to his old self with that devilish sense of humour and upbeat nature. Living in Ayr helped and Faye gratefully recalls, 'The locals were very loyal to him.'

Life after football did not mean Ally would sit with his feet up. A keen golfer since his Blackburn days, he was a member of three local golf courses and there would often be requests for public appearances or interviews to keep him occupied.

If Ally did relax his musical tastes veered towards country and western, particularly Tammy Wynette, with Johnny Cash another favourite.

Ally and Faye were both occasional visitors to Somerset Park where the couple had been given seats for life by the club. They had become grandparents in 1988 when Andy's wife Jacquie gave birth to Ryan and three years later added Liam to their family.

'Ally absolutely doted on his grandkids,' says Andy, adding that they all referred to him by his name. On one occasion Ryan's school teacher asked how many of the class had a granddad, to which Ryan held up his hand to inform that he didn't have a granddad but he did have an Ally!

Ally would kick a football around with the boys who, just like his sister Christine had some 60 years earlier, sometimes complained he was kicking it too hard at them. Andy always remembers his father as a great family man first, then a football man.

The MacLeods adopted a stray cat which they christened Henry – after Henry Templeton whom Ally had taken from junior football to three different league clubs.

It was during his time as commercial manager at Airdrie that Ally first began to display signs of Alzheimer's disease. The most common form of dementia, Alzheimer's is incurable and worsens as it progresses, eventually leading to death.

Most commonly diagnosed among over-65s, some of the earliest indicators of the disease are short-term memory loss which later leads to mood swings and loss of long-term memory. It is a gradual process and it was only when looking back at a later stage that Ally's family recognised the early signs had been there.

'It creeps up on you,' says Faye, reflecting on those difficult times. 'It starts off with "You're not listening to me" and "I've told you that".'

Jacquie first began to suspect something was wrong when Ally was doing a spot of decorating in their Troon home where he would forget to paint skirting boards or even which room he was working in.

With his stubborn streak Faye knew he would never agree to visit the family doctor so she arranged for a letter from their GP inviting Ally to attend a Wellmans clinic.

After some coaxing he went along and was referred to the memory clinic where Faye remembers he proved himself good at the maths tests he was set. Scans showed the onset of brain degeneration although his pride would never allow him to admit he was ill. 'I had a job to get him to go to the clinic,' says Faye.

The MacLeod family cannot help but link the condition to his time in the game and all those years of heading a leather ball. The early onset of brain degeneration can be triggered by repetitive head trauma and it was only later that it became known Ally had sustained three documented concussions during his playing career.

At the time Andy was working as the club physio at Kilmarnock. He took his father along for a home game against Rangers and found that Jock Wallace was a guest of the visitors.

'Neither knew the other was going to be there and we all ended up in the physio room chatting for ages. Jock had Parkinson's disease by then and Ally had the onset of Alzheimer's. Funny how the memories came flooding back for both of them.'

Initially the family agreed to keep his condition quiet but when it worsened they decided to go public for two reasons. Firstly Faye noticed that when they were out in Ayr he would fail to recognise people and she didn't want them to think he was ignoring them. Also, with Ally a well-known figure, it seemed a good opportunity to highlight the condition.

'He'd ask me to marry him and I'd show him the wedding album,' Faye remembers. Then she laughs and adds, 'If we had a disagreement he said he'd divorce me! It was hard but you had to start seeing the funny side or you would be crying all the time.'

During this period Craig Brown was manager of the national side and when Scotland were training in Troon he invited Ally to come along one day and was struck by his reaction, 'You would actually have thought you had given him a lottery win he was so delighted.'

Andy started to get telephone calls from his dad asking to be driven to visit his mother and on one occasion the police brought Ally home after finding him trying to walk to Glasgow. 'He always wanted to go home to Glasgow,' remembers daughter Gail.

Another day Faye received a call to the house from the manager of Buchanan Street coach station. A concerned couple had met Ally on the Glasgow bus and rather than abandon him had sought help on arrival. Ally had still been able to remember his telephone number and Faye thanked the manager then asked for her husband to be put on the next bus to Ayr where he was met and taken home.

Looking back on those difficult days Faye explains, 'You start to lose the person you know. He used to have twinkling, sparkling eyes but I noticed that they looked more dead. "What's wrong with you?" I would ask him and he'd say, "I don't know, I feel sad".'

Ayr United reached their first ever major cup final shortly after Ally's condition had become known and his family had no hesitation in taking him to Hampden Park. The occasion was the final of the League Cup against Rangers on 17 March 2002.

They travelled to the game on one of the supporters' coaches and at Hampden Ally signed autographs for ages outside the ground. Now aware of the condition, many of those signature hunters asked permission first. As the family made their way to their seats the Ayr fans stood up to a man to applaud Ally in what was a moving moment. It was a reminder that even in troubled times the people of the town were still behind him.

Ayr were one minute from going in level at half-time when Rangers broke the deadlock. Three further goals gave the Glasgow side a 4-0 win and the trophy but the Ayr fans on his coach felt as though they had been in the company of royalty that day.

On 23 July The following year representatives of the Tartan Army Message Board made a special presentation to Ally at the Scottish Football Museum inside Hampden Park. He was given an engraved decanter to mark his contribution to Scottish football 25 years after leaving the Scotland job. The crystal decanter is still on display in the MacLeod household alongside the bowl he received from the Emerald Park Doonhamers 11 years earlier.

In BBC Scotland's *Footballers' Lives* documentary broadcast that year Ally demonstrated that in spite of his condition he could still recite the names of the Third Lanark team he had played in half a century earlier and he still knew all of his family.

Chick Young was a member of the production team for the documentary. He says, 'I dealt with him for *Footballers' Lives* and Ally was suffering from Alzheimer's. When we talked about Blackburn the old sparkle came back to his eyes but my everlasting memory would be his love of the game. My abiding memory will be of sitting late in the evening listening to him talking about the game he loved in that small manager's office at Somerset Park.'

By this time he and Faye had six grandchildren with Andy's third boy Sean having arrived in 1997, the year before Gail gave birth to her son Jordan, named after Joe. Their brother David provided the only granddaughter, Megan, plus another boy, Jamie.

Then in his early 70s Ally could still be seen kicking a ball about with the children in the garden at Bruce Crescent. Gail remembers how watching the children playing football reignited her father's passion, 'You could see his football brain working and the sparkle in his eyes because that's what he had lost.'

On the morning of the first day of February in 2004, a Sunday, Ally was sitting in his favourite armchair as Faye left the room to fetch his breakfast. When she re-entered the sitting room she could see that he was no longer in the chair which was directly opposite the door.

'Where are you?' she asked in a voice weak with worry. Ally had moved no further than the couch opposite where Faye normally sat. 'I just sat down beside him and that was it – he was away.'

Looking back, Faye considers the passing could have been more traumatic when she speaks of a cousin who lost her husband to a similar illness in a care home. 'It was sudden, it was drastic, but I was spared a lot,' she acknowledges.

Ally passed away peacefully with the woman he had shared so much with over the last 50 years. He was just 25 days short of his 73rd birthday.

The funeral was arranged for the following Friday at Saint Columba's Church in Ayr. With many standing, around 900 mourners were piped into the church for the ceremony including many from the world of football. Among the bigger names were Sir Alex Ferguson, Davie Hay, Alex McLeish, Alan Rough and the players of Ayr United past and present. His old Blackburn team-mates Dave Whelan, Bryan Douglas, Ronnie Clayton and Harry Leyland flew up in a helicopter and landed at Ayr Racecourse.

Faye read a moving poem dedicated to her late husband about the life of a footballer's wife while Alex Ingram and son Andy gave readings. Andy brought the house down when he related the tale of the American businessman whom Ally had misled into thinking he had paddled in the waters of Loch Lomond. Leading the service, the Reverend Fraser Aitken paid tribute to a family man.

The mourners then moved on to Masonhill Crematorium on the outskirts of the town under police escort. Faye smiles as she remembers how the people of Ayr lined the streets for Ally's final journey.

She has two vivid images of the drive to the crematorium. One was of two women 'trying to throw flowers at the hearse' and the other when they passed by the site of Dobbies Garden Centre, which was just being built at the time. 'All the workmen were standing when we drove past with their hard hats off and their heads bowed,' she reflects.

There was laughter inside the crematorium too which was fitting for someone who himself had possessed such a great sense of humour. Just as the coffin began to be lowered the sounds of Julie Covington's 'Don't Cry For Me Argentina' filled the room. Ally had always liked the song and his family had continually told him they would have it played at his funeral.

A reception was held at the town's Abbotsford Hotel that evening although Faye recalls some guests did not attend due to the fact they thought it would be full.

The following day all six Scottish Cup matches held a minute's silence ahead of their kick-offs as did the two Sunday ties.

Scotland played an international in Cardiff on 18 February and the Welsh FA agreed to their Scottish counterparts' request for a minute's silence. In each case the silence was respected impeccably. The tribute in the Millennium Stadium was immediately followed by the several thousand Scottish supporters launching into a prearranged rendition of Andy Cameron's 'Ally's Tartan Army'. I can't help thinking that he would have been proud.

Postscript
Blackburn Revisited

TEN years to the day after his father's passing Andy decided to take his mother for a nostalgic visit to Blackburn. Rovers were playing at home that Saturday, 1 February 2014, with Blackpool visiting Ewood Park.

Before the match they visited Livesey Branch Road where Faye and Ally had spent their first years of married life. Faye remembered happy days when they walked the poodles in the lane between the fields and recalled the time when her husband claimed to have taken refuge in a tree when two horses came running towards him.

Completely rebuilt, the stadium was unrecognisable from the 1960s but Faye particularly liked the fact one end of the ground housed the Bryan Douglas Stand and the other the Ronnie Clayton Stand. This was particularly appropriate she feels as they were 'two local lads'. Local lads indeed but they had gone out of their way not only to make the MacLeods welcome but also others from outside the town like Derek Dougan, Roy Vernon and Mick McGrath.

Since leaving Blackburn in 1961, Ally and Faye had always kept in touch with Bryan and Joyce Douglas and were godparents to the couple's oldest son, Graham. Over the years they had visited each other on both sides of the border.

Faye and Andy were welcomed into the Clayton and Douglas Room by Bryan and Ronnie's widow Val before the game, the first time they had all met since the funeral exactly ten years earlier.

Not to be outdone by his former team-mates, Ally had his own suite at Somerset Park where the area had been renamed the Ally MacLeod Suite in February 2011. Each of the five hospitality boxes are named after players from Ally's time at the club – Cutty Young, Stan Quinn, John Murphy, Davie Stewart and Henry Templeton.

Word got around as to the identity of the guests at Ewood and Andy was surprised by, 'The number of people who came over to talk to us who had really fond memories of Ally.'

Long-gone days were recounted with Ally's antics still providing much laughter for his friends and family after all those years. Glasses were raised to the man himself and it was perhaps fitting that Blackburn won the match 2-0.

Ally MacLeod touched so many lives during his time but his family will always remember him for the way he made people laugh. It was a tribute to the man that there was much joy and laughter among those closest to him ten years after his passing that day in Blackburn, a man who gave so much more to the game of football than just a few days in Argentina.